Texas Success Initiative (TSI)

Email: info@smarteditionmedia.com

Library of Congress Cataloging-in-Publication Data
Smart Edition Media.
TSI: Full Study Guide and Test Strategies for the Texas Success Initiative Assessment/Smart Edition Media.
ISBN: 978-1-949147-71-1, 2nd edition

1. Texas Success Initiative
2. Study Guides
3. TSI
4. College Preparation
5. Careers

Disclaimer:

The opinions expressed in this publication are the sole works of Smart Edition Media and were created independently from the College Board or other testing affiliates. Between the time of publication and printing, specific standards as well as testing formats and website information may change that are not included in part or in whole within this product. Smart Edition Media develops sample test questions, and they reflect similar content as on real tests; however, they are not former tests. Smart Edition Media assembles content that aligns with exam standards but makes no claims nor guarantees candidates a passing score.

Printed in the United States of America

TSI: Full Study Guide and Test Strategies for the Texas Success Initiative Assessment/Smart Edition Media.

ISBN: 978-1-949147-71-1 (Paperback)
    978-1-949147-72-8 (Ebook)

Print and Ebook Composition by Book Genesis, Inc. (info@bookgenesis.com)

HOW TO ACCESS THE ONLINE RESOURCES

To access your online resources, follow these instructions:

1. Go to www.smarteditionmedia.com.
2. Select Sign In in the website navigation at the top of the page .
3. Select your book.
4. Follow the instructions on the login page for locating the password in your book (the password is case sensitive, so be sure to include any capital letters at the beginning of the password).

  Practice tests

 Flashcards

 Videos

  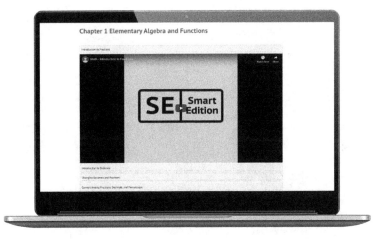

TABLE OF CONTENTS

Introduction vii
How to Use This Book x

Section I Mathematics 1
Chapter 1 Elementary Algebra and Functions 3
   Practice Quiz 1 22
   Practice Quiz 2 26
Chapter 2 Intermediate Algebra and Functions 30
   Practice Quiz 1 45
   Practice Quiz 2 48
Chapter 3 Geometry and Measurement 51
   Practice Quiz 1 66
   Practice Quiz 2 69
Chapter 4 Data Analysis, Statistics, and Probability 73
   Practice Quiz 1 89
   Practice Quiz 2 92

Section II Reading 95
Chapter 5 Literary Analysis 97
   Practice Quiz 1 109
   Practice Quiz 2 112
Chapter 6 Making Inferences & Evaluating an Argument 115
   Practice Quiz 1 127
   Practice Quiz 2 130
Chapter 7 The Author's Use of Language 132
   Practice Quiz 1 143
   Practice Quiz 2 146

Section III Writing 149
Chapter 8 The Mechanics of Writing 151
   Practice Quiz 1 160
   Practice Quiz 2 162
Chapter 9 Parts of Speech 164
   Practice Quiz 1 178
   Practice Quiz 2 181
Chapter 10 Sentence Structure & Logic 184
   Practice Quiz 1 196
   Practice Quiz 2 199

Section IV The Essay 203
Chapter 11 Essay Writing 205

Section V Full-Length Practice Exams 215

TSI Practice Exam 1 217
  Section I. Math 217
  Section II. Reading 220
  Section III. Writing 228
  Answer Explanations 231

INTRODUCTION

Texas Success Initiative Assessment (TSI) Overview

The Texas Success Initiative Assessment (TSI) is a standardized exam that is administered by state colleges and universities in Texas as part of an overall assessment of qualifications to assess an individual's preparedness for postsecondary education. The assessment must be taken by all degree-seeking Texas college students prior to enrollment in the first semester, and it is accepted by all Texas public colleges and universities.

The TSI helps determine how prepared a student is for college-level courses and assists in determining the appropriate level of course work for each student prior to enrollment. Students who do not perform well on a section of the TSI will be required to take a remedial course in that subject area prior to enrollment. Students may be able to retest and aim for a better score. Receiving a satisfactory score on the exam will determine your readiness for college and reduce time and money spent on remedial coursework.

The test is composed of computer adaptive, multiple choice questions in three subject areas: math, reading, and writing. In addition, there is an essay writing section. The level of difficulty for each question is determined by how previous questions have been answered. The school in which a student will be enrolling will administer the test. It is important to contact your school prior to taking the test to learn specific information about registering to take the test.

About This Book

This book provides you with an accurate and complete representation of the Texas Success Initiative Assessment (TSI) and includes all four sections found on the exam: Math, Reading, Writing, and Essay Writing.

The reviews in this book are designed to provide the information and strategies you need to do well on all four sections of the exam. The full-length practice test in the book is based on the TSI and contain questions similar to those you can expect to encounter on the official test. A detailed answer key follows each practice quiz and test. These answer keys provide explanations designed to help you completely understand the test material. Each explanation references the book chapter to allow you to go back to that section for additional review, if necessary.

Online Sample Tests

The purchase of this book grants you access to two additional full-length practice tests online. You can locate these exams on the Smart Edition Media website.

Go to the URL: **https://smarteditionmedia.com/pages/tsi-online-practice-test** and follow the password/login instructions.

TSI BASICS

- Test dates:

  - Dates will vary. Contact the school that you will be attending for test dates and times.

- How to register for the TSI:

  - Check with your school for registration and payment information.
  - Registration may be restricted to enrolled students only, check with the school if you need special arrangements or accommodations.

- Price:

  - Approximately $29,
  - Fees may be waived; inquire to see if you are eligible to have the fee waived.

- How long is the test?

  - There is are three subject sections, each with approximately 20 questions.
  - There is an essay writing section.
  - There is no set time limit per section; though a maximum of 5 hours is permitted to complete the exam.

- What subjects are on the test?

  - Reading, Writing, Math, Essay Writing

- How many questions are on the test?

  - Each section test contains 20 questions; there is one essay writing prompt.

- Where do I take the test?

  - At the college where you will be enrolled

- Do I need to take the test?:

  - Most students will be required to take the TSI, your school will likely contact you. If not, be sure to contact them about taking the test.
  - Some students may be exempt from portions of or the entire test, check with your school to determine this eligibility.

- What is the Pre-Assessment Activity (PAA)?:

  - A mandatory assignment needed prior to taking the TSI exam
  - You will need to present a certificate of completion when checking in to take the TSI

- What do I need to do prior to taking the test?:

  - Mandatory Pre-Assessment Activity (PAA)
  - Arrive at least 15 minutes early to the test, late arrivals will not be allowed into the test.

- What to bring/not bring to the test?

  - Bring:

    - Valid Photo ID.
    - Receipt of payment for the test, or proof of waived fee.
    - Certificate of completion (print out) of the pre-assessment activity (PAA)

  - Do Not Bring

    - Calculator, one will be provided to you.

HOW TO USE THIS BOOK

Studies show that most people begin preparing for college-entry exams approximately 8 weeks before their test date. If you are scheduled to take your test in sooner than 8 weeks, do not despair! Smart Edition Media has designed this study guide to be flexible to allow you to concentrate on areas where you need the most support.

Whether you have 8 weeks to study – or much less than that – we urge you to take one of the online practice tests to determine areas of strength and weakness, if you have not done so already. These tests can be found in your online resources.

Once you have completed a practice test, use this information to help you create a study plan that suits your individual study habits and time frame. If you are short on time, look at your diagnostic test results to determine which subject matter could use the most attention and focus the majority of your efforts on those areas. While this study guide is organized to follow the order of the actual test, you are not required to complete the book from beginning to end, in that exact order.

HOW THIS BOOK IS ORGANIZED

Take a look at the Table of Contents. Notice that each **Section** in the study guide corresponds to a subtest of the exam. These sections are broken into **Chapters** that identify the major content categories of the exam.

Each chapter is further divided into individual **Lessons** that address the specific content and objectives required to pass the exam. Some lessons contain embedded example questions to assess your comprehension of the content "in the moment." All lessons contain a bulleted list called "**Let's Review.**" Use this list to refresh your memory before taking a practice quiz, test, or the actual exam. A **Practice Quiz**, designed to check your progress as you move through the content, follows each chapter.

Whether you plan on working through the study guide from cover to cover, or selecting specific sections to review, each chapter of this book can be completed in one sitting. If you must end your study session before finishing a chapter, try to complete your current lesson in order to maximize comprehension and retention of the material.

STUDY STRATEGIES AND TIPS

MAKE STUDY SESSIONS A PRIORITY.

- Use a calendar to schedule your study sessions. Set aside a dedicated amount of time each day/week for studying. While it may seem difficult to manage, given your other responsibilities, remember that in order to reach your goals, it is crucial to dedicate the time now to prepare for this test. A satisfactory score on your exam is the key to unlocking a multitude of opportunities for your future success.

- Do you work? Have children? Other obligations? Be sure to take these into account when creating your schedule. Work around them to ensure that your scheduled study sessions can be free of distractions.

TIPS FOR FINDING TIME TO STUDY.
- Wake up 1-2 hours before your family for some quiet time
- Study 1-2 hours before bedtime and after everything has quieted down
- Utilize weekends for longer study periods
- Hire a babysitter to watch children

TAKE PRACTICE TESTS

- Smart Edition Media offers practice tests, both online and in print. Take as many as you can to help be prepared. This will eliminate any surprises you may encounter during the exam.

KNOW YOUR LEARNING STYLE

- Identify your strengths and weaknesses as a student. All students are different and everyone has a different learning style. Do not compare yourself to others.
- Howard Gardner, a developmental psychologist at Harvard University, has studied the ways in which people learn new information. He has identified seven distinct intelligences. According to his theory:

  "we are all able to know the world through language, logical-mathematical analysis, spatial representation, musical thinking, the use of the body to solve problems or to make things, an understanding of other individuals, and an understanding of ourselves. Where individuals differ is in the strength of these intelligences - the so-called profile of intelligences -and in the ways in which such intelligences are invoked and combined to carry out different tasks, solve diverse problems, and progress in various domains."

- Knowing your learning style can help you to tailor your studying efforts to suit your natural strengths.
- What ways help you learn best? Videos? Reading textbooks? Find the best way for you to study and learn/review the material

WHAT IS YOUR LEARNING STYLE?

- **Visual-Spatial** – Do you like to draw, do jigsaw puzzles, read maps, daydream? Creating drawings, graphic organizers, or watching videos might be useful for you.
- **Bodily-kinesthetic** – Do you like movement, making things, physical activity? Do you communicate well through body language, or like to be taught through physical activity? Hands-on learning, acting out, role playing are tools you might try.
- **Musical** – Do you show sensitivity to rhythm and sound? If you love music, and are also sensitive to sounds in your environments, it might be beneficial to study with music in the background. You can turn lessons into lyricsor speak rhythmically to aid in content retention.
- **Interpersonal** – Do you have many friends, empathy for others, street smarts, and interact well with others? You might learn best in a group setting. Form a study group with other students who are preparing for the same exam. Technology makes it easy to connect, if you are unable to meet in person, teleconferencing or video chats are useful tools to aid interpersonal learners in connecting with others.
- **Intrapersonal** – Do you prefer to work alone rather than in a group? Are you in tune with your inner feelings, follow your intuition and possess a strong will, confidence and opinions? Independent study and introspection will be ideal for you. Reading books, using creative materials, keeping a diary of your progress will be helpful. Intrapersonal learners are the most independent of the learners.
- **Linguistic** – Do you use words effectively, have highly developed auditory skills and often think in words? Do you like reading, playing word games, making up poetry or stories? Learning tools such as computers, games, multimedia will be beneficial to your studies.
- **Logical-Mathematical** – Do you think conceptually, abstractly, and are able to see and explore patterns and relationships? Try exploring subject matter through logic games, experiments and puzzles.

CREATE THE OPTIMAL STUDY ENVIRONMENT

- Some people enjoy listening to soft background music when they study. (Instrumental music is a good choice.) Others need to have a silent space in order to concentrate. Which do you prefer? Either way, it is best to create an environment that is free of distractions for your study sessions.
- Have study guide – Will travel! Leave your house: Daily routines and chores can be distractions. Check out your local library, a coffee shop, or other quiet space to remove yourself from distractions and daunting household tasks will compete for your attention.
- Create a Technology Free Zone. Silence the ringer on your cell phone and place it out of reach to prevent surfing the Web, social media interactions, and email/texting exchanges. Turn off the television, radio, or other devices while you study.
- Are you comfy? Find a comfortable, but not *too* comfortable, place to study. Sit at a desk or table in a straight, upright chair. Avoid sitting on the couch, a bed, or in front of the TV. Wear clothing that is not binding and restricting.
- Keep your area organized. Have all the materials you need available and ready: Smart Edition study guide, computer, notebook, pen, calculator, and pencil/eraser. Use a desk lamp or overhead light that provides ample lighting to prevent eye-strain and fatigue.

HEALTHY BODY, HEALTHY MIND

- Consider these words of wisdom from Buddha, "To keep the body in good health is a duty – otherwise we shall not be able to keep our mind strong and clear."

> **KEYS TO CREATING A HEALTHY BODY AND MIND:**
> - Drink water – Stay hydrated! Limit drinks with excessive sugar or caffeine.
> - Eat natural foods – Make smart food choices and avoid greasy, fatty, sugary foods.
> - Think positively – You can do this! Do not doubt yourself, and trust in the process.
> - Exercise daily – If you have a workout routine, stick to it! If you are more sedentary, now is a great time to begin! Try yoga or a low-impact sport. Simply walking at a brisk pace will help to get your heart rate going.
> - Sleep well – Getting a good night's sleep is important, but too few of us actually make it a priority. Aim to get eight hours of uninterrupted sleep in order to maximize your mental focus, memory, learning, and physical wellbeing.

FINAL THOUGHTS

- Remember to relax and take breaks during study sessions.
- Review the testing material. Go over topics you already know for a refresher.
- Focus more time on less familiar subjects.

EXAM PREPARATION

In addition to studying for your upcoming exam, it is important to keep in mind that you need to prepare your mind and body as well. When preparing to take an exam as a whole, not just studying, taking practice exams, and reviewing math rules, it is critical to prepare your body in order to be mentally and physically ready. Often, your success rate will be much higher when you are *fully* ready.

Here are some tips to keep in mind when preparing for your exam:

SEVERAL WEEKS/DAYS BEFORE THE EXAM

- Get a full night of sleep, approximately 8 hours
- Turn off electronics before bed
- Exercise regularly
- Eat a healthy balanced diet, include fruits and vegetable
- Drink water

THE NIGHT BEFORE

- Eat a good dinner
- Pack materials/bag, healthy snacks, and water

- Gather materials needed for test: your ID and receipt of test. You do not want to be scrambling the morning of the exam. If you are unsure of what to bring with you, check with your testing center or test administrator.
- Map the location of test center, identify how you will be getting there (driving, public transportation, uber, etc.), when you need to leave, and parking options.
- Lay your clothes out. Wear comfortable clothes and shoes, do not wear items that are too hot/cold
- Allow minimum of ~8 hours of sleep
- Avoid coffee and alcohol
- Do not take any medications or drugs to help you sleep
- Set alarm

THE DAY OF THE EXAM

- Wake up early, allow ample time to do all the things you need to do and for travel
- Eat a healthy, well-rounded breakfast
- Drink water
- Leave early and arrive early, leave time for any traffic or any other unforeseeable circumstances
- Arrive early and check in for exam. This will give you enough time to relax, take off coat, and become comfortable with your surroundings.

Take a deep breath, get ready, go! You got this!

SECTION I
MATHEMATICS

Math: 20 questions, untimed

Areas assessed: Elementary Algebra and Functions; Intermediate Algebra and Functions; Geometry and Measurement; and Data Analysis, Statistics, and Probability

MATH TIPS

- Read the questions thoroughly and slowly. Reread if necessary. The order/value they are expecting may be different that you are anticipating.
- Brush up on decimals, ratios, fractions, PEMDAS, percentages.
- Know addition, subtraction, multiplication, division problems.
- Be sure to know how to add, subtract, multiply, and divide fractions.
- Brush up on common math rules. i.e. when adding a fraction, they must have same common denominator.
- You will be able to use a calculator. It will be provided by the testing center.

CHAPTER 1 ELEMENTARY ALGEBRA AND FUNCTIONS

DECIMALS AND FRACTIONS

This lesson introduces the basics of decimals and fractions. It also demonstrates changing decimals to fractions, changing fractions to decimals, and converting between fractions, decimals, and percentages.

Introduction to Fractions

A fraction represents part of a whole number. The top number of a fraction is the **numerator**, and the bottom number of a fraction is the **denominator**. The numerator is smaller than the denominator for a **proper fraction**. The numerator is larger than the denominator for an **improper fraction**.

Proper Fractions	Improper Fractions
$\frac{2}{5}$	$\frac{5}{2}$
$\frac{7}{12}$	$\frac{12}{7}$
$\frac{19}{20}$	$\frac{20}{19}$

An improper fraction can be changed to a **mixed number**. A mixed number is a whole number and a proper fraction. To write an improper fraction as a mixed number, divide the denominator into the numerator. The result is the whole number. The remainder is the numerator of the proper fraction, and the value of the denominator does not change. For example, $\frac{5}{2}$ is $2\frac{1}{2}$ because 2 goes into 5 twice with a remainder of 1. To write an improper fraction as a mixed number, multiply the whole number by the denominator and add the result to the numerator. The results become the new numerator. For example, $2\frac{1}{2}$ is $\frac{5}{2}$ because 2 times 2 plus 1 is 5 for the new numerator.

KEEP IN MIND

When comparing fractions, the denominators of the fractions must be the same.

When comparing fractions, the denominators must be the same. Then, look at the numerator to determine which fraction is larger. If the fractions have different denominators, then a **least common denominator** must be found. This number is the smallest number that can be divided evenly into the denominators of all fractions being compared.

To determine the largest fraction from the group $\frac{1}{3}, \frac{3}{5}, \frac{2}{3}, \frac{2}{5}$, the first step is to find a common denominator. In this case, the least common denominator is 15 because 3 times 5 and 5 times 3 is 15. The second step is to convert the fractions to a denominator of 15. The fractions with a denominator of 3 have the numerator and denominator multiplied by 5, and the fractions with a denominator of 5 have the numerator and denominator multiplied by 3, as shown below:

$$\frac{1}{3} \times \frac{5}{5} = \frac{5}{15}, \ \frac{3}{5} \times \frac{3}{3} = \frac{9}{15}, \ \frac{2}{3} \times \frac{5}{5} = \frac{10}{15}, \ \frac{2}{5} \times \frac{3}{3} = \frac{6}{15}$$

Now, the numerators can be compared. The largest fraction is $\frac{2}{3}$ because it has a numerator of 10 after finding the common denominator.

Examples

1. **Which fraction is the least?**

   A. $\frac{3}{5}$
   B. $\frac{3}{4}$
   C. $\frac{1}{5}$
   D. $\frac{1}{4}$

   The correct answer is **C**. The correct solution is $\frac{1}{5}$ because it has the smallest numerator compared to the other fractions with the same denominator. The fractions with a common denominator of 20 are $\frac{3}{5} = \frac{12}{20}, \frac{3}{4} = \frac{15}{20}, \frac{1}{5} = \frac{4}{20}, \frac{1}{4} = \frac{5}{20}$.

2. **Which fraction is the greatest?**

   A. $\frac{5}{6}$
   B. $\frac{1}{2}$
   C. $\frac{2}{3}$
   D. $\frac{1}{6}$

   The correct answer is **A**. The correct solution is $\frac{5}{6}$ because it has the largest numerator compared to the other fractions with the same denominator. The fractions with a common denominator of 6 are $\frac{5}{6} = \frac{5}{6}, \frac{1}{2} = \frac{3}{6}, \frac{2}{3} = \frac{4}{6}, \frac{1}{6} = \frac{1}{6}$.

Introduction to Decimals

A **decimal** is a number that expresses part of a whole. Decimals show a portion of a number after a decimal point. Each number to the left and right of the decimal point has a specific place value. Identify the place values for 645.3207.

> **KEEP IN MIND**
> When comparing decimals, compare the place value where the numbers are different.

When comparing decimals, compare the numbers in the same place value. For example, determine the greatest decimal from the group 0.4, 0.41, 0.39, and 0.37. In these numbers, there is a value to the right of the decimal point. Comparing the tenths places, the numbers with 4 tenths (0.4 and 0.41) are greater than the numbers with three tenths (0.39 and 0.37).

Then, compare the hundredths in the 4 tenths numbers. The value of 0.41 is greater because there is a 1 in the hundredths place versus a 0 in the hundredths place.

0.4

0.41

0.39

0.37

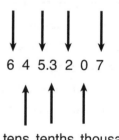

6 4 5.3 2 0 7

tens tenths thousandths

0.4

0.41

Here is another example: determine the least decimal of the group 5.23, 5.32, 5.13, and 5.31. In this group, the ones value is 5 for all numbers. Then, comparing the tenths values, 5.13 is the smallest number because it is the only value with 1 tenth.

Examples

1. **Which decimal is the greatest?**

   A. 0.07   B. 0.007   C. 0.7   D. 0.0007

   The correct answer is **C.** The solution is 0.7 because it has the largest place value in the tenths.

2. **Which decimal is the least?**

   A. 0.0413   B. 0.0713   C. 0.0513   D. 0.0613

   The correct answer is **A.** The correct solution is 0.0413 because it has the smallest place value in the hundredths place.

5.23

↓

5.32

↓

5.13

↓

5.31

Changing Decimals and Fractions

Three steps change a decimal to a fraction.

> **STEP BY STEP**
>
> **Step 1.** Write the decimal divided by 1 with the decimal as the numerator and 1 as the denominator.
>
> **Step 2.** Multiply the numerator and denominator by 10 for every number after the decimal point. (For example, if there is 1 decimal place, multiply by 10. If there are 2 decimal places, multiply by 100).
>
> **Step 3.** Reduce the fraction completely.

To change the decimal 0.37 to a fraction, start by writing the decimal as a fraction with a denominator of one, $\frac{0.37}{1}$. Because there are two decimal places, multiply the numerator and denominator by 100, $\frac{0.37 \times 100}{1 \times 100} = \frac{37}{100}$. The fraction does not reduce, so $\frac{37}{100}$ is 0.37 in fraction form.

Similarly, to change the decimal 2.4 to a fraction start by writing the decimal as a fraction with a denominator of one, $\frac{0.4}{1}$, and ignore the whole number. Because there is one decimal place, multiply the numerator and denominator by 10, $\frac{0.4 \times 10}{1 \times 10} = \frac{4}{10}$. The fraction does reduce: $2\frac{4}{10} = 2\frac{2}{5}$ is 2.4 in fraction form.

The decimal $0.\overline{3}$ as a fraction is $\frac{0.\overline{3}}{1}$. In the case of a repeating decimal, let $n = 0.\overline{3}$ *and* $10n = 3.\overline{3}$. Then, $10n - n = 3.\overline{3} - 0.\overline{3}$, resulting in $9n = 3$ and solution of $n = \frac{3}{9} = \frac{1}{3}$. The decimal $0.\overline{3}$ is $\frac{1}{3}$ as a fraction.

Examples

1. **Change 0.38 to a fraction. Simplify completely.**

    A. $\frac{3}{10}$ B. $\frac{9}{25}$ C. $\frac{19}{50}$ D. $\frac{2}{5}$

    The correct answer is **C**. The correct solution is $\frac{19}{50}$ because $\frac{0.38}{1} = \frac{38}{100} = \frac{19}{50}$.

2. **Change $1.\overline{1}$ to a fraction. Simplify completely.**

    A. $1\frac{1}{11}$ B. $1\frac{1}{9}$ C. $1\frac{1}{6}$ D. $1\frac{1}{3}$

    The correct answer is **B**. The correct solution is $1\frac{1}{9}$. Let $n = 1.\overline{1}$ and $10n = 11.\overline{1}$. Then, $10n - n = 11.\overline{1} - 1.\overline{1}$, resulting in $9n = 10$ and solution of $n = \frac{10}{9} = 1\frac{1}{9}$.

Two steps change a fraction to a decimal.

> **STEP BY STEP**
>
> **Step 1.** Divide the numerator by the denominator. Add zeros after the decimal point as needed.
>
> **Step 2.** Complete the process when there is no remainder or the decimal is repeating.

To convert $\frac{1}{5}$ to a decimal, rewrite $\frac{1}{5}$ as a long division problem and add zeros after the decimal point, $1.0 \div 5$. Complete the long division and $\frac{1}{5}$ as a decimal is 0.2. The division is complete because there is no remainder.

To convert $\frac{8}{9}$ to a decimal, rewrite $\frac{8}{9}$ as a long division problem and add zeros after the decimal point, $8.00 \div 9$. Complete the long division, and $\frac{8}{9}$ as a decimal is $0.\overline{8}$. The process is complete because the decimal is complete.

To rewrite the mixed number $2\frac{3}{4}$ as a decimal, the fraction needs changed to a decimal. Rewrite $\frac{3}{4}$ as a long division problem and add zeros after the decimal point, $3.00 \div 4$. The whole number is needed for the answer and is not included in the long division. Complete the long division, and $2\frac{3}{4}$ as a decimal is 2.75.

Examples

1. **Change $\frac{9}{10}$ to a decimal. Simplify completely.**

    A. 0.75   B. 0.8   C. 0.85   D. 0.9

    The correct answer is **D**. The correct answer is 0.9 because $\frac{9}{10} = 9.0 \div 10 = 0.9$.

2. **Change $\frac{5}{6}$ to a decimal. Simplify completely.**

    A. 0.73   B. $0.7\overline{6}$ C. $0.8\overline{3}$ D. 0.86

    The correct answer is **C**. The correct answer is $0.8\overline{3}$ because $\frac{5}{6} = 5.000 \div 6 = 0.8\overline{3}$.

Convert among Fractions, Decimals, and Percentages

Fractions, decimals, and percentages can change forms, but they are equivalent values.

There are two ways to change a decimal to a percent. One way is to multiply the decimal by 100 and add a percent sign. 0.24 as a percent is 24%.

Another way is to move the decimal point two places to the right. The decimal 0.635 is 63.5% as a percent when moving the decimal point two places to the right.

Any decimal, including repeating decimals, can change to a percent. $0.\overline{3}$ as a percent is $0.\overline{3} \times 100 = 33.\overline{3}\%$.

Example

Write 0.345 as a percent.

    A. 3.45%   B. 34.5%   C. 345%   D. 3450%

    The correct answer is **B**. The correct answer is 34.5% because 0.345 as a percent is .

There are two ways to change a percent to a decimal. One way is to remove the percent sign and divide the decimal by 100. For example, 73% as a decimal is 0.73.

Another way is to move the decimal point two places to the left. For example, 27.8% is 0.278 as a decimal when moving the decimal point two places to the left.

Any percent, including repeating percents, can change to a decimal. For example, $44.\overline{4}\%$ as a decimal is $44.\overline{4} \div 100 = 0.\overline{4}$.

Example

Write 131% as a decimal.

    A. 0.131   B. 1.31   C. 13.1   D. 131

    The correct answer is **B**. The correct answer is 1.31 because 131% as a decimal is 131 ÷ 100 = 1.31.

Two steps change a fraction to a percent.

> **STEP BY STEP**
> **Step 1.** Divide the numerator and denominator.
> **Step 2.** Multiply by 100 and add a percent sign.

To change the fraction $\frac{3}{5}$ to a decimal, perform long division to get 0.6. Then, multiply 0.6 by 100 and $\frac{3}{5}$ is the same as 60%.

To change the fraction $\frac{7}{8}$ to a decimal, perform long division to get 0.875. Then, multiply 0.875 by 100 and $\frac{7}{8}$ is the same as 87.5%.

Fractions that are repeating decimals can also be converted to a percent. To change the fraction $\frac{2}{3}$ to a decimal, perform long division to get $0.\overline{6}$. Then, multiply $0.\overline{6}$ by 100 and the percent is $66.\overline{6}\%$.

Example

Write $2\frac{1}{8}$ as a percent.

   A. 21.2%   B. 21.25%   C. 212%   D. 212.5%

The correct answer is **D**. The correct answer is 212.5% because $2\frac{1}{8}$ as a percent is 2.125 x 100 = 212.5%.

Two steps change a percent to a fraction.

> **STEP BY STEP**
>
> **Step 1.** Remove the percent sign and write the value as the numerator with a denominator of 100.
>
> **Step 2.** Simplify the fraction.

Remove the percent sign from 45% and write as a fraction with a denominator of 100, $\frac{45}{100}$. The fraction reduces to $\frac{9}{20}$.

Remove the percent sign from 22.8% and write as a fraction with a denominator of 100, $\frac{22.8}{100}$. The fraction reduces to $\frac{228}{1000} = \frac{57}{250}$.

Repeating percentages can change to a fraction. Remove the percent sign from $16.\overline{6}\%$ and write as a fraction with a denominator of 100, $\frac{16.\overline{6}}{100}$. The fraction simplifies to $\frac{0.1\overline{6}}{1} = \frac{1}{6}$.

Example

Write 72% as a fraction.

   A. $\frac{27}{50}$ B. $\frac{7}{10}$ C. $\frac{18}{25}$ D. $\frac{3}{4}$

The correct answer is **C**. The correct answer is $\frac{18}{25}$ because 72% as a fraction is $\frac{72}{100} = \frac{18}{25}$.

Let's Review!

- A fraction is a number with a numerator and a denominator. A fraction can be written as a proper fraction, an improper fraction, or a mixed number. Changing fractions to a common denominator enables you to determine the least or greatest fraction in a group of fractions.
- A decimal is a number that expresses part of a whole. By comparing the same place values, you can find the least or greatest decimal in a group of decimals.
- A number can be written as a fraction, a decimal, and a percent. These are equivalent values. Numbers can be converted between fractions, decimals, and percents by following a series of steps.

MULTIPLICATION AND DIVISION OF FRACTIONS

This lesson introduces how to multiply and divide fractions.

Multiplying a Fraction by a Fraction

The multiplication of fractions does not require changing any denominators like adding and subtracting fractions do. To multiply a fraction by a fraction, multiply the numerators together and multiply the denominators together. For example, $\frac{2}{3} \times \frac{4}{5}$ is $\frac{2 \times 4}{3 \times 5}$, which is $\frac{8}{15}$.

Sometimes, the final solution reduces. For example, $\frac{3}{5} \times \frac{1}{9} = \frac{3 \times 1}{5 \times 9} = \frac{3}{45}$. The fraction $\frac{3}{45}$ reduces to $\frac{1}{15}$.

Simplifying fractions can occur before completing the multiplication. In the previous problem, the numerator of 3 can be simplified with the denominator of 9: $\frac{\cancel{13}}{5} \times \frac{1}{\cancel{39}} = \frac{1}{15}$. This method of simplifying only occurs with the multiplication of fractions.

KEEP IN MIND
The product of multiplying a fraction by a fraction is always less than 1.

Examples

1. **Multiply $\frac{1}{2} \times \frac{3}{4}$.**

   A. $\frac{1}{4}$ B. $\frac{1}{2}$ C. $\frac{3}{8}$ D. $\frac{2}{3}$

   The correct answer is **C**. The correct solution is $\frac{3}{8}$ because $\frac{1}{2} \times \frac{3}{4} = \frac{3}{8}$.

2. **Multiply $\frac{2}{3} \times \frac{5}{6}$.**

   A. $\frac{1}{9}$ B. $\frac{5}{18}$ C. $\frac{5}{9}$ D. $\frac{7}{18}$

   The correct answer is **C**. The correct solution is $\frac{5}{9}$ because $\frac{2}{3} \times \frac{5}{6} = \frac{10}{18} = \frac{5}{9}$.

Multiply a Fraction by a Whole or Mixed Number

Multiplying a fraction by a whole or mixed number is similar to multiplying two fractions. When multiplying by a whole number, change the whole number to a fraction with a denominator of 1. Next, multiply the numerators together and the denominators together. Rewrite the final answer as a mixed number. For example: $\frac{9}{10} \times 3 = \frac{9}{10} \times \frac{3}{1} = \frac{27}{10} = 2\frac{7}{10}$.

When multiplying a fraction by a mixed number or multiplying two mixed numbers, the process is similar.

For example, multiply $\frac{10}{11} \times 3\frac{1}{2}$. Change the mixed number to an improper fraction, $\frac{10}{11} \times \frac{7}{2}$. Multiply the numerators together and multiply

KEEP IN MIND
Always change a mixed number to an improper fraction when multiplying by a mixed number.

the denominators together, $\frac{70}{22}$. Write the improper fraction as a mixed number, $3\frac{4}{22}$. Reduce if necessary, $3\frac{2}{11}$.

This process can also be used when multiplying a whole number by a mixed number or multiplying two mixed numbers.

Examples

1. **Multiply** $4 \times \frac{5}{6}$.

    A. $\frac{5}{24}$ B. $2\frac{3}{4}$ C. $3\frac{1}{3}$ D. $4\frac{5}{6}$

    The correct answer is **C**. The correct solution is $3\frac{1}{3}$ because $\frac{4}{1} \times \frac{5}{6} = \frac{20}{6} = 3\frac{2}{6} = 3\frac{1}{3}$.

2. **Multiply** $1\frac{1}{2} \times 1\frac{1}{6}$.

    A. $1\frac{1}{12}$ B. $1\frac{1}{4}$ C. $1\frac{3}{8}$ D. $1\frac{3}{4}$

    The correct answer is **D**. The correct solution is $1\frac{3}{4}$ because $\frac{3}{2} \times \frac{7}{6} = \frac{21}{12} = 1\frac{9}{12} = 1\frac{3}{4}$.

Dividing a Fraction by a Fraction

Some basic steps apply when dividing a fraction by a fraction. The information from the previous two sections is applicable to dividing fractions.

STEP BY STEP

Step 1. Leave the first fraction alone.

Step 2. Find the reciprocal of the second fraction.

Step 3. Multiply the first fraction by the reciprocal of the second fraction.

Step 4. Rewrite the fraction as a mixed number and reduce the fraction completely.

Divide, $\frac{3}{10} \div \frac{1}{2}$. Find the reciprocal of the second fraction, which is $\frac{2}{1}$.

Now, multiply the fractions, $\frac{3}{10} \times \frac{2}{1} = \frac{6}{10}$. Reduce $\frac{6}{10}$ to $\frac{3}{5}$.

Divide, $\frac{4}{5} \div \frac{3}{8}$. Find the reciprocal of the second fraction, which is $\frac{8}{3}$.

Now, multiply the fractions, $\frac{4}{5} \times \frac{8}{3} = \frac{32}{15}$. Rewrite the fraction as a mixed number, $\frac{32}{15} = 2\frac{2}{15}$.

Examples

1. **Divide** $\frac{1}{2} \div \frac{5}{6}$.

    A. $\frac{5}{12}$ B. $\frac{3}{5}$ C. $\frac{5}{6}$ D. $1\frac{2}{3}$

    The correct answer is **B**. The correct solution is $\frac{3}{5}$ because $\frac{1}{2} \times \frac{6}{5} = \frac{6}{10} = \frac{3}{5}$.

2. **Divide** $\frac{2}{3} \div \frac{3}{5}$.

    A. $\frac{2}{15}$ B. $\frac{2}{5}$ C. $1\frac{1}{15}$ D. $1\frac{1}{9}$

    The correct answer is **D**. The correct solution is $1\frac{1}{9}$ because $\frac{2}{3} \times \frac{5}{3} = \frac{10}{9} = 1\frac{1}{9}$.

Dividing a Fraction and a Whole or Mixed Number

Some basic steps apply when dividing a fraction by a whole number or a mixed number.

> **STEP BY STEP**
>
> **Step 1.** Write any whole number as a fraction with a denominator of 1. Write any mixed numbers as improper fractions.
>
> **Step 2.** Leave the first fraction (improper fraction) alone.
>
> **Step 3.** Find the reciprocal of the second fraction.
>
> **Step 4.** Multiply the first fraction by the reciprocal of the second fraction.
>
> **Step 5.** Rewrite the fraction as a mixed number and reduce the fraction completely.

Divide, $\frac{3}{10} \div 3$. Rewrite the expression as $\frac{3}{10} \div \frac{3}{1}$. Find the reciprocal of the second fraction, which is $\frac{1}{3}$. Multiply the fractions, $\frac{3}{10} \times \frac{1}{3} = \frac{3}{30} = \frac{1}{10}$. Reduce $\frac{3}{30}$ to $\frac{1}{10}$.

Divide, $2\frac{4}{5} \div 1\frac{3}{8}$. Rewrite the expression as $\frac{14}{5} \div \frac{11}{8}$. Find the reciprocal of the second fraction, which is $\frac{8}{11}$.

Multiply the fractions, $\frac{14}{5} \times \frac{8}{11} = \frac{112}{55} = 2\frac{2}{55}$. Reduce $\frac{112}{55}$ to $2\frac{2}{55}$.

Examples

1. **Divide $\frac{2}{3} \div 4$**

   A. $\frac{1}{12}$ B. $\frac{1}{10}$ C. $\frac{1}{8}$ D. $\frac{1}{6}$

   The correct answer is **D**. The correct answer is $\frac{1}{6}$ because $\frac{2}{3} \times \frac{1}{4} = \frac{2}{12} = \frac{1}{6}$.

2. **Divide $1\frac{5}{12} \div 1\frac{1}{2}$.**

   A. $\frac{17}{18}$ B. $1\frac{5}{24}$ C. $1\frac{5}{6}$ D. $2\frac{1}{8}$

   The correct answer is **A**. The correct answer is $\frac{17}{18}$ because $\frac{17}{12} \div \frac{3}{2} = \frac{17}{12} \times \frac{2}{3} = \frac{34}{36} = \frac{17}{18}$.

Let's Review!

- The process to multiply fractions is to multiply the numerators together and multiply the denominators together. When there is a mixed number, change the mixed number to an improper fraction before multiplying.
- The process to divide fractions is to find the reciprocal of the second fraction and multiply the fractions. As with multiplying, change any mixed numbers to improper fractions before dividing.

EQUATIONS WITH ONE VARIABLE

This lesson introduces how to solve linear equations and linear inequalities.

One-Step Linear Equations

A **linear equation** is an equation where two expressions are set equal to each other. The equation is in the form $ax + b = c$, where a is a non-zero constant and b and c are constants. The exponent on a linear equation is always 1, and there is no more than one solution to a linear equation.

There are four properties to help solve a linear equation.

Property	Definition	Example with Numbers	Example with Variables
Addition Property of Equality	Add the same number to both sides of the equation.	$x-3 = 9$ $x-3 + 3 = 9 + 3$ $x = 12$	$x-a = b$ $x-a + a = b + a$ $x = a + b$
Subtraction Property of Equality	Subtract the same number from both sides of the equation.	$x + 3 = 9$ $x + 3-3 = 9-3$ $x = 6$	$x + a = b$ $x + a-a = b-a$ $x = b-a$
Multiplication Property of Equality	Multiply both sides of the equation by the same number.	$\frac{x}{3} = 9$ $\frac{x}{3} \times 3 = 9 \times 3$ $x = 27$	$\frac{x}{a} = b$ $\frac{x}{a} \times a = b \times a$ $x = ab$
Division Property of Equality	Divide both sides of the equation by the same number.	$3x = 9$ $\frac{3x}{3} = \frac{9}{3}$ $x = 3$	$ax = b$ $\frac{ax}{a} = \frac{b}{a}$ $x = \frac{b}{a}$

Example

Solve the equation for the unknown, $\frac{w}{2} = -6$.

   A. −12   B. −8   C. −4   D. −3

The correct answer is **A**. The correct solution is −12 because both sides of the equation are multiplied by 2.

Two-Step Linear Equations

A two-step linear equation is in the form $ax + b = c$, where a is a non-zero constant and b and c are constants. There are two basic steps in solving this equation.

STEP BY STEP

Step 1. Use addition and subtraction properties of an equation to move the variable to one side of the equation and all number terms to the other side of the equation.

Step 2. Use multiplication and division properties of an equation to remove the value in front of the variable.

Examples

1. **Solve the equation for the unknown, $\frac{x}{-2} - 3 = 5$.**

    A. −16   B. −8   C. 8   D. 16

    The correct answer is **A**. The correct solution is −16.

    $\frac{x}{-2} = 8$ Add 3 to both sides of the equation.

    $x = -16$ Multiply both sides of the equation by −2.

2. **Solve the equation for the unknown, $4x + 3 = 8$.**

    A. −2   B. $-\frac{5}{4}$ C. $\frac{5}{4}$ D. 2

    The correct answer is **C**. The correct solution is $\frac{5}{4}$.

    $4x = 5$ Subtract 3 from both sides of the equation.

    $x = \frac{5}{4}$ Divide both sides of the equation by 4.

3. **Solve the equation for the unknown w, $P = 2l + 2w$.**

    A. $2P - 2l = w$ B. $\frac{P - 2l}{2} = w$ C. $2P + 2l = w$ D. $\frac{P + 2l}{2} = w$

    The correct answer is **B**. The correct solution is $\frac{P - 2l}{2} = w$.

    $P - 2l = 2w$ Subtract 2l from both sides of the equation.

    $\frac{P - 2l}{2} = w$ Divide both sides of the equation by 2.

Multi-Step Linear Equations

In these basic examples of linear equations, the solution may be evident, but these properties demonstrate how to use an opposite operation to solve for a variable. Using these properties, there are three steps in solving a complex linear equation.

STEP BY STEP

Step 1. Simplify each side of the equation. This includes removing parentheses, removing fractions, and adding like terms.

Step 2. Use addition and subtraction properties of an equation to move the variable to one side of the equation and all number terms to the other side of the equation.

Step 3. Use multiplication and division properties of an equation to remove the value in front of the variable.

In Step 2, all of the variables may be placed on the left side or the right side of the equation. The examples in this lesson will place all of the variables on the left side of the equation.

When solving for a variable, apply the same steps as above. In this case, the equation is not being solved for a value, but for a specific variable.

Examples

1. Solve the equation for the unknown, $2(4x + 1)-5 = 3-(4x-3)$.

   A. $\frac{1}{4}$ B. $\frac{3}{4}$ C. $\frac{4}{3}$ D. 4

   The correct answer is **B**. The correct solution is $\frac{3}{4}$.

$8x + 2-5 = 3-4x + 3$	Apply the distributive property.
$8x-3 = -4x + 6$	Combine like terms on both sides of the equation.
$12x-3 = 6$	Add 4x to both sides of the equation.
$12x = 9$	Add 3 to both sides of the equation.
$x = \frac{3}{4}$	Divide both sides of the equation by 12.

2. Solve the equation for the unknown, $\frac{2}{3}x + 2 = -\frac{1}{2}x + 2(x + 1)$.

   A. 0   B. 1   C. 2   D. 3

   The correct answer is **A**. The correct solution is 0.

$\frac{2}{3}x + 2 = -\frac{1}{2}x + 2x + 2$	Apply the distributive property.
$4x + 12 = -3x + 12x + 12$	Multiply all terms by the least common denominator of 6 to eliminate the fractions.
$4x + 12 = 9x + 12$	Combine like terms on the right side of the equation.
$-5x = 12$	Subtract 9x from both sides of the equation.
$-5x = 0$	Subtract 12 from both sides of the equation.
$x = 0$	Divide both sides of the equation by -5.

3. Solve the equation for the unknown for x, $y-y_1 = m(x-x_1)$.

   A. $y-y_1 + mx_1$ B. $my-my_1 + mx_1$ C. $\frac{y-y_1 + x_1}{m}$ D. $\frac{y-y_1 + mx_1}{m}$

   The correct answer is **D**. The correct solution is $\frac{y-y_1 + mx_1}{m}$.

$y-y_1 = mx-mx_1$	Apply the distributive property.
$y-y_1 + mx_1 = mx$	Add mx_1 to both sides of the equation.
$\frac{y-y_1 + mx_1}{m} = x$	Divide both sides of the equation by m.

Solving Linear Inequalities

A **linear inequality** is similar to a linear equation, but it contains an inequality sign ($<$, $>$, $\leq$, $\geq$). Many of the steps for solving linear inequalities are the same as for solving linear equations. The major difference is that the solution is an infinite number of values. There are four properties to help solve a linear inequality.

Property	Definition	Example
Addition Property of Inequality	Add the same number to both sides of the inequality.	$x-3 < 9$ $x-3+3 < 9+3$ $x < 12$
Subtraction Property of Inequality	Subtract the same number from both sides of the inequality.	$x+3 > 9$ $x+3-3 > 9-3$ $x > 6$
Multiplication Property of Inequality (when multiplying by a positive number)	Multiply both sides of the inequality by the same number.	$\frac{x}{3} \geq 9$ $\frac{x}{3} \times 3 \geq 9 \times 3$ $x \geq 27$
Division Property of Inequality (when multiplying by a positive number)	Divide both sides of the inequality by the same number.	$3x \leq 9$ $\frac{3x}{3} \leq \frac{9}{3}$ $x \leq 3$
Multiplication Property of Inequality (when multiplying by a negative number)	Multiply both sides of the inequality by the same number.	$\frac{x}{-3} \geq 9$ $\frac{x}{-3} \times -3 \geq 9 \times -3$ $x \leq -27$
Division Property of Inequality (when multiplying by a negative number)	Divide both sides of the inequality by the same number.	$-3x \leq 9$ $\frac{-3x}{-3} \leq \frac{9}{-3}$ $x \geq -3$

Multiplying or dividing both sides of the inequality by a negative number reverses the sign of the inequality.

In these basic examples, the solution may be evident, but these properties demonstrate how to use an opposite operation to solve for a variable. Using these properties, there are three steps in solving a complex linear inequality.

STEP BY STEP

Step 1. Simplify each side of the inequality. This includes removing parentheses, removing fractions, and adding like terms.

Step 2. Use addition and subtraction properties of an inequality to move the variable to one side of the equation and all number terms to the other side of the equation.

Step 3. Use multiplication and division properties of an inequality to remove the value in front of the variable. Reverse the inequality sign if multiplying or dividing by a negative number.

In Step 2, all of the variables may be placed on the left side or the right side of the inequality. The examples in this lesson will place all of the variables on the left side of the inequality.

Examples

1. **Solve the inequality for the unknown, $3(2 + x) < 2(3x-1)$.**

    A. $x < -\frac{8}{3}$
    B. $x > -\frac{8}{3}$
    C. $x < \frac{8}{3}$
    D. $x > \frac{8}{3}$

    The correct answer is **D**. The correct solution is $x > \frac{8}{3}$.

$6 + 3x < 6x-2$	Apply the distributive property.
$6-3x < -2$	Subtract $6x$ from both sides of the inequality.
$-3x < -8$	Subtract 6 from both sides of the inequality.
$x > \frac{8}{3}$	Divide both sides of the inequality by -3.

2. **Solve the inequality for the unknown, $\frac{1}{2}(2x-3) \geq \frac{1}{4}(2x + 1)-2$.**

    A. $x > -7$
    B. $x > -3$
    C. $x \geq -\frac{3}{2}$
    D. $x \geq -\frac{1}{2}$

    The correct answer is **D**. The correct solution is $x \geq -\frac{1}{2}$.

$2(2x-3) \geq 2x + 1-8$	Multiply all terms by the least common denominator of 4 to eliminate the fractions.
$4x-6 \geq 2x + 1-8$	Apply the distributive property.
$4x-6 \geq 2x-7$	Combine like terms on the right side of the inequality.
$2x-6 \geq -7$	Subtract $2x$ from both sides of the inequality.
$2x \geq -1$	Add 6 to both sides of the inequality.
$x \geq -\frac{1}{2}$	Divide both sides of the inequality by 2.

Let's Review!

- A linear equation is an equation with one solution. Using opposite operations solves a linear equation.
- The process to solve a linear equation or inequality is to eliminate fractions and parentheses and combine like terms on the same side of the sign. Then, solve the equation or inequality by using inverse operations.

EQUATIONS WITH TWO VARIABLES

This lesson discusses solving a system of linear equations by substitution, elimination, and graphing, as well as solving a simple system of a linear and a quadratic equation.

Solving a System of Equations by Substitution

A **system of linear equations** is a set of two or more linear equations in the same variables. A solution to the system is an ordered pair that is a solution in all the equations in the system. The ordered pair (1, -2) is a solution for the system of equations $\begin{aligned} 2x + y = 0 \\ -x + 2y = -5 \end{aligned}$ because $\begin{aligned} 2(1) + (-2) = 0 \\ -1 + 2(-2) = -5 \end{aligned}$ makes both equations true.

One way to solve a system of linear equations is by substitution.

> **STEP BY STEP**
>
> **Step 1.** Solve one equation for one of the variables.
>
> **Step 2.** Substitute the expression from Step 1 into the other equation and solve for the other variable.
>
> **Step 3.** Substitute the value from Step 2 into one of the original equations and solve.

All systems of equations can be solved by substitution for any one of the four variables in the problem. The most efficient way of solving is locating the $1x$ or $1y$ in the equations because this eliminates the possibility of having fractions in the equations.

Examples

1. **Solve the system of equations,** $\begin{aligned} x = y + 6 \\ 4x + 5y = 60 \end{aligned}$.

   A. (10, 12)   B. (6, 12)   C. (6, 4)   D. (10, 4)

   The correct answer is **D**. The correct solution is (10, 4).

   The first equation is already solved for x.

$4(y + 6) + 5y = 60$	Substitute $y + 6$ in for x in the first equation.
$4y + 24 + 5y = 60$	Apply the distributive property.
$9y + 24 = 60$	Combine like terms on the left side of the equation.
$9y = 36$	Subtract 24 from both sides of the equation.
$y = 4$	Divide both sides of the equation by 9.
$x = 4 + 6$	Substitute 4 in the first equation for y.
$x = 10$	Simplify using order of operations

2. Solve the system of equations, $\begin{array}{l}3x + 2y = 41 \\ -4x + y = -18\end{array}$.

A. $(5, 13)$ B. $(6, 6)$ C. $(7, 10)$ D. $(10, 7)$

The correct answer is **C**. The correct solution is $(7, 10)$.

$y = 4x{-}18$	Solve the second equation for y by adding $4x$ to both sides of the equation.
$3x + 2(4x{-}18) = 41$	Substitute $4x{-}18$ in for y in the first equation.
$3x + 8x{-}36 = 41$	Apply the distributive property.
$11x{-}36 = 41$	Combine like terms on the left side of the equation.
$11x = 77$	Add 36 to both sides of the equation.
$x = 7$	Divide both sides of the equation by 11.
$-4(7) + y = -18$	Substitute 7 in the second equation for x.
$-28 + y = -18$	Simplify using order of operations.
$y = 10$	Add 28 to both sides of the equation.

Solving a System of Equations by Elimination

Another way to solve a system of linear equations is by elimination.

STEP BY STEP

Step 1. Multiply, if necessary, one or both equations by a constant so at least one pair of like terms has opposite coefficients.

Step 2. Add the equations to eliminate one of the variables.

Step 3. Solve the resulting equation.

Step 4. Substitute the value from Step 3 into one of the original equations and solve for the other variable.

All system of equations can be solved by the elimination method for any one of the four variables in the problem. One way of solving is locating the variables with opposite coefficients and adding the equations. Another approach is multiplying one equation to obtain opposite coefficients for the variables.

Examples

1. Solve the system of equations, $\begin{array}{l}3x + 5y = 28 \\ -4x{-}5y = -34\end{array}$.

A. $(12, 6)$ B. $(6, 12)$ C. $(6, 2)$ D. $(2, 6)$

The correct answer is **C**. The correct solution is $(6, 2)$.

$-x = -6$	Add the equations.
$x = 6$	Divide both sides of the equation by -1.
$3(6) + 5y = 28$	Substitute 6 in the first equation for x.

$18 + 5y = 28$	Simplify using order of operations.
$5y = 10$	Subtract 18 from both sides of the equation.
$y = 2$	Divide both sides of the equation by 5.

2. **Solve the system of equations,** $\begin{array}{c} -5x + 5y = 0 \\ 2x - 3y = -3 \end{array}$.

   A. $(2, 2)$ B. $(3, 3)$ C. $(6, 6)$ D. $(9, 9)$

The correct answer is **B**. The correct solution is $(3, 3)$.

$-10x + 10y = 0$	Multiply all terms in the first equation by 2.
$10x - 15y = -15$	Multiply all terms in the second equation by 5.
$-5y = -15$	Add the equations.
$y = 3$	Divide both sides of the equation by -5.
$2x - 3(3) = -3$	Substitute 3 in the second equation for y.
$2x - 9 = -3$	Simplify using order of operations.
$2x = 6$	Add 9 to both sides of the equation.
$x = 3$	Divide both sides of the equation by 2.

Solving a System of Equations by Graphing

Graphing is a third method of a solving system of equations. The point of intersection is the solution for the graph. This method is a great way to visualize each graph on a coordinate plane.

STEP BY STEP

Step 1. Graph each equation in the coordinate plane.

Step 2. Estimate the point of intersection.

Step 3. Check the point by substituting for x and y in each equation of the original system.

The best approach to graphing is to obtain each line in slope-intercept form. Then, graph the y-intercept and use the slope to find additional points on the line.

Example

Solve the system of equations by graphing, $\begin{matrix} y = 3x-2 \\ y = x-4 \end{matrix}$.

A.

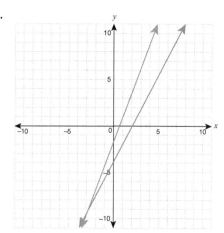

C.

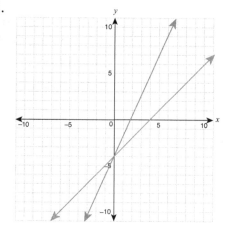

B.

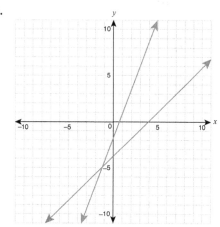

D.

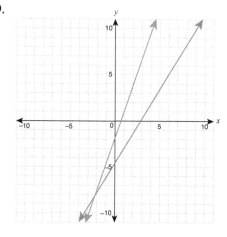

The correct answer is **B.** The correct graph has the two lines intersect at (-1, -5).

Solving a System of a Linear Equation and an Equation of a Circle

There are many other types of systems of equations. One example is the equation of a line $y = mx$ and the equation of a circle $x^2 + y^2 = r^2$ where r is the radius. With this system of equations, there can be two ordered pairs that intersect between the line and the circle. If there is one ordered pair, the line is tangent to the circle.

This system of equations is solved by substituting the expression mx in for y in the equation of a circle. Then, solve the equation for x. The values for x are substituted into the linear equation to find the value for y.

KEEP IN MIND

There will be two solutions in many cases with the system of a linear equation and an equation of a circle.

Example

Solve the system of equations, $\begin{array}{l} y = -3x \\ x^2 + y^2 = 10 \end{array}$.

  A. (1, 3) and (−1, −3)

  B. (1, −3) and (−1, 3)

  C. (−3, 10) and (3, −10)

  D. (3, 10) and (−3, −10)

The correct answer is **B.** The correct solutions are (1, −3) and (−1, 3).

$x^2 + (-3x)^2 = 10$	Substitute −3x in for y in the second equation.
$x^2 + 9x^2 = 10$	Apply the exponent.
$10x^2 = 10$	Combine like terms on the left side of the equation.
$x^2 = 1$	Divide both sides of the equation by 10.
$x = \pm 1$	Apply the square root to both sides of the equation.
$y = -3(1) = -3$	Substitute 1 in the first equation and multiply.
$y = -3(-1) = 3$	Substitute −1 in the first equation and multiply.

Let's Review!

• There are three ways to solve a system of equations: graphing, substitution, and elimination. Using any method will result in the same solution for the system of equations.

• Solving a system of a linear equation and an equation of a circle uses substitution and usually results in two solutions.

CHAPTER 1 ELEMENTARY ALGEBRA AND FUNCTIONS
PRACTICE QUIZ 1

1. Which decimal is the greatest?

   A. 1.7805   C. 1.7085

   B. 1.5807   D. 1.8057

2. Change $0.\overline{63}$ to a fraction. Simplify completely.

   A. $\frac{5}{9}$ C. $\frac{2}{3}$

   B. $\frac{7}{11}$ D. $\frac{5}{6}$

3. Which fraction is the greatest?

   A. $\frac{5}{12}$ C. $\frac{1}{6}$

   B. $\frac{1}{3}$ D. $\frac{1}{4}$

4. Solve the equation for the unknown, $\frac{c}{-4} = -12$.

   A. -16

   B. -8

   C. 3

   D. 48

5. Solve the inequality for the unknown, $3(x + 1) + 2(x + 1) \geq 5(3-x) + 4(x + 2)$.

   A. $x \geq 0$ C. $x \geq 2$

   B. $x \geq 1$ D. $x \geq 3$

6. Solve the equation for P, $A = P + Prt$.

   A. $A(1 + rt) = P$ C. $Art + 1 = P$

   B. $Art = P$ D. $\frac{A}{1 + rt} = P$

7. Solve the system of equations,
   $2y + x = -20$
   $y = -x-12$.

   A. $(4, 8)$ C. $(-4, 8)$

   B. $(4, -8)$ D. $(-4, -8)$

8. Solve the system of equations,
   $-2x + 2y = 28$
   $3x + y = -22$.

   A. $(9, 5)$ C. $(9, -5)$

   B. $(-9, -5)$ D. $(-9, 5)$

9. Solve the system of equations by graphing, $\begin{array}{l}2x + y = 4\\4x + y = 14\end{array}$.

A.
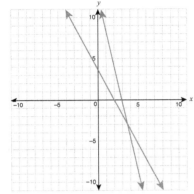

B.
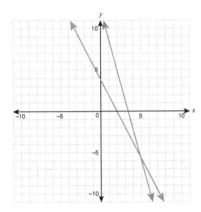

C.
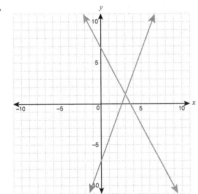

D.
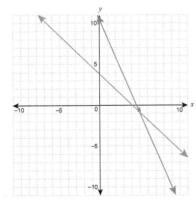

10. Divide $1\frac{2}{3} \div 3\frac{7}{12}$.

   A. $\frac{20}{43}$ C. $3\frac{3}{4}$

   B. $3\frac{7}{18}$ D. $5\frac{35}{36}$

11. Multiply $\frac{6}{7} \times \frac{7}{10}$.

   A. $\frac{1}{17}$ C. $\frac{3}{5}$

   B. $\frac{1}{3}$ D. $\frac{13}{17}$

12. Multiply $3\frac{1}{5} \times \frac{5}{8}$.

   A. 1   C. 3

   B. 2   D. 4

13. Solve $x^3 = 343$.

   A. 6   C. 8

   B. 7   D. 9

14. One online seller has about 6×10^8 online orders, and another online seller has about 5×10^7 online orders. How many times more orders does the first company have?

   A. 12   C. 20

   B. 15   D. 32

15. Simplify $\frac{x^2 y^{-2}}{x^{-3} y^3}$.

   A. $\frac{x^5}{y^5}$ C. $\frac{1}{x^5 y^5}$

   B. $\frac{y^5}{x^5}$ D. $x^5 y^5$

CHAPTER 1 ELEMENTARY ALGEBRA AND FUNCTIONS
PRACTICE QUIZ 1 – ANSWER KEY

1. D. The correct solution is 1.8057 because 1.8075 contains the largest value in the tenths place. **See Lesson: Decimals and Fractions.**

2. B. The correct solution is $\frac{7}{11}$. Let $n = 0.\overline{63}$ and $100n = 63.\overline{63}$ Then, $100n{-}n = 63.\overline{63}{-}0.\overline{63}$ resulting in $99n = 63$ and solution of $n = \frac{63}{99} = \frac{7}{11}$. **See Lesson: Decimals and Fractions.**

3. A. The correct solution is $\frac{5}{12}$ because $\frac{5}{12}$ has the largest numerator when comparing to the other fractions with the same denominator. The fractions with a common denominator of 12 are $\frac{5}{12} = \frac{5}{12}, \frac{1}{3} = \frac{4}{12}, \frac{1}{6} = \frac{2}{12}, \frac{1}{4} = \frac{3}{12}$. **See Lesson: Decimals and Fractions.**

4. D. The correct solution is 48 because both sides of the equation are multiplied by −4. **See Lesson: Equations with One Variable.**

5. D. The correct solution is x $\geq$ 3.

$3x + 3 + 2x + 2 \geq 15{-}5x + 4x + 8$	Apply the distributive property.
$5x + 5 \geq -x + 23$	Combine like terms on both sides of the inequality.
$6x + 5 \geq 23$	Add x to both sides of the inequality.
$6x \geq 18$	Subtract 5 from both sides of the inequality.
$x \geq 3$	Divide both sides of the inequality by 6.

See Lesson: Equations with One Variable.

6. D. The correct solution is $\frac{A}{1 + rt} = P$.

$A{=}P(1{+}rt)$	Factor P from the left side of the equation.
$\frac{A}{1 + rt} = P$	Divide both sides of the equation by 1+rt.

See Lesson: Equations with One Variable.

7. D. The correct solution is (-4, -8).

The second equation is already solved for y.

$2{-}x{-}12{+}x{=}{-}20$	Substitute $-x{-}12$ in for y in the first equation.
$-2x{-}24{+}x{=}{-}20$	Apply the distributive property.
$-x{-}24{=}{-}20$	Combine like terms on the left side of the equation.
$-x{=}4$	Add 24 to both sides of the equation.
$x{=}{-}4$	Divide both sides of the equation by -1.
$y{=}{-}{-}4{-}12$	Substitute -4 in the second equation for x.
$y{=}4{-}12{=}{-}8$	Simplify using order of operations.

See Lesson: Equations with Two Variables.

8. D. The correct solution is (-9, 5).

$-6x-2y=44$	Multiply all terms in the second equation by -2.
$-8x=72$	Add the equations.
$x=-9$	Divide both sides of the equation by -8.
$3-9+y=-22$	Substitute -9 in the second equation for x.
$-27+y=-22$	Simplify using order of operations.
$y=5$	Add 27 to both sides of the equation.

See Lesson: Equations with Two Variables.

9. B. The correct graph has the two lines intersect at (5, -6). **See Lesson: Equations with Two Variables.**

10. A. The correct answer is $\frac{20}{43}$ because $\frac{5}{3} \div \frac{43}{12} = \frac{5}{3} \times \frac{12}{43} = \frac{60}{129} = \frac{20}{43}$. **See Lesson: Multiplication and Division of Fractions.**

11. C. The correct solution is $\frac{3}{5}$ because $\frac{6}{7} \times \frac{7}{10} = \frac{42}{70} = \frac{3}{5}$. **See Lesson: Multiplication and Division of Fractions.**

12. B. The correct solution is 2 because $\frac{16}{5} \times \frac{5}{8} = \frac{80}{40} = 2$. **See Lesson: Multiplication and Division of Fractions.**

13. B. The correct solution is 7 because the cube root of 343 is 7. **See Lesson: Powers, Exponents, Roots, and Radicals.**

14. A. The correct solution is 12 because the first company has about 600,000,000 orders and the second company has about 50,000,000 orders. So, the first company is about 12 times larger. **See Lesson: Powers, Exponents, Roots, and Radicals.**

15. A. The correct solution is $\frac{x^5}{y^5}$ because $\frac{x^2 y^{-2}}{x^{-3} y^3} = x^{2-(-3)} y^{-2-3} = x^5 y^{-5} = \frac{x^5}{y^5}$. **See Lesson: Powers, Exponents, Roots, and Radicals.**

CHAPTER 1 ELEMENTARY ALGEBRA AND FUNCTIONS
PRACTICE QUIZ 2

1. Which decimal is the least?

    A. 2.22   C. 2.002

    B. 2.02   D. 2.2

2. Change 0.375 to a fraction. Simplify completely.

    A. $\frac{3}{8}$ C. $\frac{1}{2}$

    B. $\frac{2}{5}$ D. $\frac{7}{16}$

3. Write $83.\overline{3}\%$ as a decimal.

    A. $8.\overline{3}$ C. $0.08\overline{3}$

    B. $0.8\overline{3}$ D. 0.0083

4. Solve the equation for the unknown, $a-10 = -20$.

    A. −30

    B. −10

    C. 2

    D. 200

5. Solve the inequality for the unknown, $\frac{2}{3}x-4 \leq \frac{4}{5}x + 2$.

    A. $x < -45$ C. $x < 90$

    B. $x > -45$ D. $x > 90$

6. Solve the equation for the unknown, $\frac{1}{2}x + 3 = \frac{1}{4}x-2$.

    A. −20   C. 10

    B. −10   D. 20

7. Solve the system of equations, $\begin{array}{l}-2x + 6y = -6 \\ 4x-5y = 26\end{array}$.

    A. (2, 3)   C. (6, 9)

    B. (3, 6)   D. (9, 2)

8. Solve the system of equations, $\begin{array}{l}x + 2y = 5 \\ -5x + 3y = -25\end{array}$.

    A. (5, 0)   C. (-5, 0)

    B. (0, -5)   D. (0, 5)

9. Solve the system of equations by graphing,

$y = \frac{1}{3}x + 2$
$y = \frac{2}{3}x + 5$.

A.

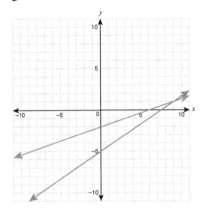

B.

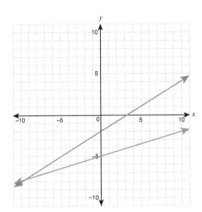

C.

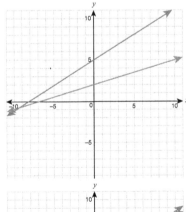

D.

10. Multiply $\frac{4}{5} \times \frac{1}{5}$.

A. $\frac{4}{25}$ C. $\frac{3}{5}$

B. $\frac{2}{5}$ D. $\frac{16}{25}$

11. Multiply $2\frac{1}{2} \times 3\frac{3}{4}$.

A. $5\frac{3}{8}$ C. $7\frac{3}{8}$

B. $6\frac{3}{8}$ D. $9\frac{3}{8}$

12. Divide $\frac{3}{4} \div \frac{1}{2}$.

A. $\frac{1}{4}$ C. $1\frac{1}{5}$

B. $\frac{3}{8}$ D. $1\frac{1}{2}$

13. Simplify $\left(\frac{x^3 y^{-2}}{x^{-2} y^3} \right)^5$.

A. $\frac{1}{x^{25} y^{25}}$ C. $\frac{x^{25}}{y^{25}}$

B. $\frac{y^{25}}{x^{25}}$ D. $x^{25} y^{25}$

14. One athlete had a salary of about 3×10^7 dollars per year and another athlete had a salary of about 2×10^6 dollars per year. How many times larger is the salary of the first athlete?

A. 2   C. 10

B. 5   D. 15

15. Solve $x^3 = -216$.

A. –6

B. –4

C. 4

D. 6

CHAPTER 1 ELEMENTARY ALGEBRA AND FUNCTIONS
PRACTICE QUIZ 2 – ANSWER KEY

1. **C.** The correct solution is 2.002 because 2.002 contains the smallest value in the tenths and the hundredths places. **See Lesson: Decimals and Fractions.**

2. **A.** The correct solution is $\frac{3}{8}$ because $\frac{0.375}{1} = \frac{375}{1000} = \frac{3}{8}$. **See Lesson: Decimals and Fractions.**

3. **B.** The correct answer is $0.8\overline{3}$ because $83.\overline{3}\%$ as a decimal is $0.8\overline{3}$. **See Lesson: Decimals and Fractions.**

4. **B.** The correct solution is -10 because 10 is added to both sides of the equation. **See Lesson: Equations with One Variable.**

5. **B.** The correct solution is $x > -45$.

$10x - 60 \leq 12x + 30$	Multiply all terms by the least common denominator of 15 to eliminate the fractions.
$-2x - 60 \leq 30$	Subtract $12x$ from both sides of the inequality.
$-2x \leq -90$	Add 60 to both sides of the inequality.
$x \geq -45$	Divide both sides of the inequality by -2.

See Lesson: Equations with One Variable.

6. **A.** The correct solution is -20.

$2x + 12 = x - 8$	Multiply all terms by the least common denominator of 4 to eliminate the fractions.
$x + 12 = -8$	Subtract x from both sides of the equation.
$x = -20$	Subtract 12 from both sides of the equation.

See Lesson: Equations with One Variable.

7. **D.** The correct solution is (9, 2).

$-4x + 12y = -12$	Multiply all terms in the first equation by 2.
$7y = 14$	Add the equations.
$y = 2$	Divide both sides of the equation by 7.
$-2x + 6(2) = -6$	Substitute 2 in the first equation for y.
$-2x + 12 = -6$	Simplify using order of operations.
$-2x = -18$	Subtract 12 from both sides of the equation.
$x = 9$	Divide both sides of the equation by -2.

See Lesson: Equations with Two Variables.

8. **A.** The correct solution is (5, 0).

$x = -2y + 5$	Solve the first equation for x by subtracting $2y$ from both sides of the equation.
$-5(-2y + 5) + 3y = -25$	Substitute $-2y + 5$ in for x in the first equation.
$10y - 25 + 3y = -25$	Apply the distributive property.
$13y - 25 = -25$	Combine like terms on the left side of the equation.
$13y = 0$	Add 25 to both sides of the equation.
$y = 0$	Divide both sides of the equation by 13.
$x + 2(0) = 5$	Substitute 0 in the second equation for y.
$x = 5$	Simplify using order of operations.

See Lesson: Equations with Two Variables.

9. **C.** The correct graph has the two lines intersect at (-9, -1). **See Lesson: Equations with Two Variables.**

10. **A.** The correct solution is $\frac{4}{25}$ because $\frac{4}{5} \times \frac{1}{5} = \frac{4}{25}$. **See Lesson: Multiplication and Division of Fractions.**

11. **D.** The correct solution is $9\frac{3}{8}$ because $\frac{5}{2} \times \frac{15}{4} = \frac{75}{8} = 9\frac{3}{8}$. **See Lesson: Multiplication and Division of Fractions.**

12. **D.** The correct solution is $1\frac{1}{2}$ because $\frac{3}{4} \times \frac{2}{1} = \frac{6}{4} = 1\frac{2}{4} = 1\frac{1}{2}$. **See Lesson: Multiplication and Division of Fractions.**

13. **C.** The correct solution is $\frac{x^{25}}{y^{25}}$ because $\left(\frac{x^3 y^{-2}}{x^{-2} y^3}\right)^5 = \left(x^{3-(-2)} y^{-2-3}\right)^5 = \left(x^5 y^{-5}\right)^5 = x^{5\times5} y^{-5\times5} = x^{25} y^{-25} = \frac{x^{25}}{y^{25}}$. **See Lesson: Powers, Exponents, Roots, and Radicals.**

14. **D.** The correct solution is 15 because the first athlete's salary is about \$30,000,000 and the second athlete's salary is about \$2,000,000. So, the first athlete's salary is about 15 times larger. **See Lesson: Powers, Exponents, Roots, and Radicals.**

15. **A.** The correct solution is –6 because the cube root of –216 is –6. **See Lesson: Powers, Exponents, Roots, and Radicals.**

CHAPTER 2 INTERMEDIATE ALGEBRA AND FUNCTIONS

SOLVING QUADRATIC EQUATIONS

This lesson introduces solving quadratic equations by the square root method, completing the square, factoring, and using the quadratic formula.

Solving Quadratic Equations by the Square Root Method

A **quadratic equation** is an equation where the highest variable is squared. The equation is in the form $ax^2 + bx + c = 0$, where a is a non-zero constant and b and c are constants. There are at most two solutions to the equation because the highest variable is squared. There are many methods to solve a quadratic equation.

This section will explore solving a quadratic equation by the square root method. The equation must be in the form of $ax^2 = c$, or there is no x term.

STEP BY STEP

Step 1. Use multiplication and division properties of an equation to remove the value in front of the variable.

Step 2. Apply the square root to both sides of the equation.

Note: The positive and negative square root make the solution true. For the equation $x^2 = 9$, the solutions are –3 and 3 because $3^2 = 9$ and $(-3)^2 = 9$.

Example

Solve the equation by the square root method, $4x^2 = 64$.

A. 4   B. 8   C. ±4   D. ±8

The correct answer is **C**. The correct solution is ±4.

$x^2 = 16$	Divide both sides of the equation by 4.
$x = \pm 4$	Apply the square root to both sides of the equation.

Solving Quadratic Equations by Completing the Square

A quadratic equation in the form $x^2 + bx$ can be solved by a process known as completing the square. The best time to solve by completing the square is when the b term is even.

STEP BY STEP

Step 1. Divide all terms by the coefficient of x^2.

Step 2. Move the number term to the right side of the equation.

Step 3. Complete the square $\left(\frac{b}{2}\right)^2$ and add this value to both sides of the equation.

Step 4. Factor the left side of the equation.

Step 5. Apply the square root to both sides of the equation.

Step 6. Use addition and subtraction properties to move all number terms to the right side of the equation.

Examples

1. **Solve the equation by completing the square, $x^2 - 8x + 12 = 0$.**

   A. –2 and –6   B. 2 and –6   C. –2 and 6   D. 2 and 6

   The correct answer is **D**. The correct solutions are 2 and 6.

$x^2 - 8x = -12$	Subtract 12 from both sides of the equation.
$x^2 - 8x + 16 = -12 + 16$	Complete the square, $\left(-\frac{8}{2}\right)^2 = (-4)^2 = 16$.
	Add 16 to both sides of the equation.
$x^2 - 8x + 16 = 4$	Simplify the right side of the equation.
$(x-4)^2 = 4$	Factor the left side of the equation.
$x - 4 = \pm 2$	Apply the square root to both sides of the equation.
$x = 4 \pm 2$	Add 4 to both sides of the equation.
$x = 4-2 = 2, x = 4 + 2 = 6$	Simplify the right side of the equation.

2. **Solve the equation by completing the square, $x^2 + 6x - 8 = 0$.**

   A. $-3 \pm \sqrt{17}$ B. $3 \pm \sqrt{17}$ C. $-3 \pm \sqrt{8}$ D. $3 \pm \sqrt{8}$

   The correct answer is **A**. The correct solutions are $-3 \pm \sqrt{17}$.

$x^2 + 6x = 8$	Add 8 to both sides of the equation.
$x^2 + 6x + 9 = 8 + 9$	Complete the square, $\left(\frac{6}{2}\right)^2 = 3^2 = 9$. Add 9 to both sides of the equation.
$x^2 + 6x + 9 = 17$	Simplify the right side of the equation.
$(x + 3)^2 = 17$	Factor the left side of the equation.
$x + 3 = \pm\sqrt{17}$	Apply the square root to both sides of the equation.
$x = -3 \pm \sqrt{17}$	Subtract 3 from both sides of the equation.

Solving Quadratic Equations by Factoring

Factoring can only be used when a quadratic equation is factorable; other methods are needed to solve quadratic equations that are not factorable.

> **STEP BY STEP**
>
> **Step 1.** Simplify if needed by clearing any fractions and parentheses.
>
> **Step 2.** Write the equation in standard form, $ax^2 + bx + c = 0$.
>
> **Step 3.** Factor the quadratic equation.
>
> **Step 4.** Set each factor equal to zero.
>
> **Step 5.** Solve the linear equations using inverse operations.

The quadratic equation will have two solutions if the factors are different or one solution if the factors are the same.

Examples

1. **Solve the equation by factoring, $x^2 - 13x + 42 = 0$.**

   A. $-6, -7$ B. $-6, 7$ C. $6, -7$ D. $6, 7$

   The correct answer is **D**. The correct solutions are 6 and 7.

$(x-6)(x-7) = 0$	Factor the equation.
$(x-6) = 0$ or $(x-7) = 0$	Set each factor equal to 0.
$x-6 = 0$	Add 6 to both sides of the equation to solve for the first factor.
$x = 6$	
$x-7 = 0$	Add 7 to both sides of the equation to solve for the second factor.
$x = 7$	

2. **Solve the equation by factoring, $9x^2 + 30x + 25 = 0$.**

   A. $-\frac{5}{3}$ B. $-\frac{3}{5}$ C. $\frac{3}{5}$ D. $\frac{5}{3}$

   The correct answer is **A**. The correct solution is $-\frac{5}{3}$.

$(3x + 5)(3x + 5) = 0$	Factor the equation.
$(3x + 5) = 0$ or $(3x + 5) = 0$	Set each factor equal to 0.
$(3x + 5) = 0$	Set one factor equal to zero since both factors are the same.
$3x + 5 = 0$	Subtract 5 from both sides of the equation and divide both sides of the equation by 3 to solve.
$3x = -5$	
$x = -\frac{5}{3}$	

Solving Quadratic Equations by the Quadratic Formula

Many quadratic equations are not factorable. Another method of solving a quadratic equation is by using the quadratic formula. This method can be used to solve any quadratic equation in the form . Using the coefficients a, b, and c, the quadratic formula is $x = \frac{-b \pm \sqrt{b^2-4ac}}{2a}$. The values are substituted into the formula, and applying the order of operations finds the solution(s) to the equation.

The solution of the quadratic formula in these examples will be exact or estimated to three decimal places. There may be cases where the exact solutions to the quadratic formula are used.

KEEP IN MIND

Watch the negative sign in the formula. Remember that a number squared is always positive.

Examples

1. **Solve the equation by the quadratic formula, $x^2-5x-6 = 0$.**

    A. –6 and –1   B. 6 and –1   C. –6 and 1   D. 6 and 1

    The correct answer is **B**. The correct solutions are 6 and –1.

    $x = \frac{-(-5) \pm \sqrt{(-5)^2-4(1)(-6)}}{2(1)}$ — Substitute 1 for a, –5 for b, and –6 for c.

    $x = \frac{5 \pm \sqrt{25-(-24)}}{2}$ — Apply the exponent and perform the multiplication.

    $x = \frac{5 \pm \sqrt{49}}{2}$ — Perform the subtraction.

    $x = \frac{5 \pm 7}{2}$ — Apply the square root.

    $x = \frac{5+7}{2}$, $x = \frac{5-7}{2}$ — Separate the problem into two expressions.

    $x = \frac{12}{2} = 6$, $x = \frac{-2}{2} = -1$ — Simplify the numerator and divide.

2. **Solve the equation by the quadratic formula, $2x^2 + 4x-5 = 0$.**

    A. –5.74 and –1.74   B. 5.74 and –1.74   C. –5.74 and 1.74   D. 5.74 and 1.74

    The correct answer is **C**. The correct solutions are –5.74 and 1.74.

    $x = \frac{-4 \pm \sqrt{4^2-4(2)(-5)}}{2(2)}$ — Substitute 2 for a, 4 for b, and –5 for c.

    $x = \frac{-4 \pm \sqrt{16-(-40)}}{4}$ — Apply the exponent and perform the multiplication.

    $x = \frac{-4 \pm \sqrt{56}}{4}$ — Perform the subtraction.

    $x = \frac{-4 \pm 7.48}{2}$ — Apply the square root.

    $x = \frac{-4+7.48}{2}$, $x = \frac{-4-7.48}{2}$ — Separate the problem into two expressions.

    $x = \frac{3.48}{2} = 1.74$, $x = \frac{-11.48}{2} = -5.74$ — Simplify the numerator and divide.

Let's Review!

There are four methods to solve a quadratic equation algebraically:

- The square root method is used when there is a squared variable term and a constant term.
- Completing the square is used when there is a squared variable term and an even variable term.
- Factoring is used when the equation can be factored.
- The quadratic formula can be used for any quadratic equation.

POLYNOMIALS

This lesson introduces adding, subtracting, and multiplying polynomials. It also explains polynomial identities that describe numerical expressions.

Adding and Subtracting Polynomials

A **polynomial** is an expression that contains exponents, variables, constants, and operations. The exponents of the variables are only whole numbers, and there is no division by a variable. The operations are addition, subtraction,

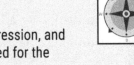

KEEP IN MIND

The solution is an expression, and a value is not calculated for the variable.

multiplication, and division. Constants are terms without a variable. A polynomial of one term is a **monomial**; a polynomial of two terms is a **binomial**; and a polynomial of three terms is a **trinomial**.

To add polynomials, combine like terms and write the solution from the term with the highest exponent to the term with the lowest exponent. To simplify, first rearrange and group like terms. Next, combine like terms.

$(3x^2 + 5x–6) + (4x^3–3x + 4) = 4x^3 + 3x^2 + (5x–3x) + (–6 + 4) = 4x^3 + 3x^2 + 2x–2$

To subtract polynomials, rewrite the second polynomial using an additive inverse. Change the minus sign to a plus sign, and change the sign of every term inside the parentheses. Then, add the polynomials.

$(3x^2 + 5x–6)–(4x^3–3x + 4) = (3x^2 + 5x–6) + (–4x^3 + 3x–4) = –4x^3 + 3x^2 + (5x + 3x) + (–6–4)$
$= –4x^3 + 3x^2 + 8x–10$

Examples

1. **Perform the operation, $(2y^2–5y + 1) + (–3y^2 + 6y + 2)$.**

    A. $y^2 + y + 3$ B. $–y^2–y + 3$ C. $y^2–y + 3$ D. $–y^2 + y + 3$

    The correct answer is **D**. The correct solution is $–y^2 + y + 3$.

    $(2y^2–5y + 1) + (–3y^2 + 6y + 2) = (2y^2–3y^2) + (–5y + 6y) + (1 + 2) = –y^2 + y + 3$

2. **Perform the operation, $(3x^2y + 4xy–5xy^2)–(x^2y–3xy–2xy^2)$.**

    A. $2x^2y–7xy + 3xy^2$

    C. $2x^2y + 7xy–3xy^2$

    B. $2x^2y + 7xy + 3xy^2$

    D. $2x^2y–7xy–3xy^2$

    The correct answer is **C**. The correct solution is $2x^2y + 7xy–3xy^2$.

    $(3x^2y + 4xy–5xy^2)–(x^2y–3xy–2xy^2) = (3x^2y + 4xy–5xy^2) + (–x^2y + 3xy + 2xy^2)$
    $= (3x^2y–x^2y) + (4xy + 3xy) + (–5xy^2 + 2xy^2) = 2x^2y + 7xy–3xy^2$

Multiplying Polynomials

Multiplying polynomials comes in many forms. When multiplying a monomial by a monomial, multiply the coefficients and apply the multiplication rule for the power of an exponent.

> **BE CAREFUL!**
>
> Make sure that you apply the distributive property to all terms in the polynomials.

$$4xy(3x^2y) = 12x^3y^2.$$

When multiplying a monomial by a polynomial, multiply each term of the polynomial by the monomial.

$$4xy(3x^2y-2xy^2) = 4xy(3x^2y) + 4xy(-2xy^2) = 12x^3y^2-8x^2y^3.$$

When multiplying a binomial by a binomial, apply the distributive property and combine like terms.

$$(3x-4)(2x + 5) = 3x(2x + 5)-4(2x + 5) = 6x^2 + 15x-8x-20 = 6x^2 + 7x-20$$

When multiplying a binomial by a trinomial, apply the distributive property and combine like terms.

$$(x + 2)(3x^2-2x + 3) = (x + 2)(3x^2) + (x + 2)(-2x) + (x + 2)(3) = 3x^3 + 6x^2-2x^2-4x + 3x + 6 = 3x^3 + 4x^2-x + 6$$

Examples

1. **Multiply, $3xy^2(2x^2y)$.**

   A. $6x^2y^2$ ⠀⠀⠀⠀⠀ B. $6x^3y^2$ ⠀⠀⠀⠀⠀ C. $6x^3y^3$ ⠀⠀⠀⠀⠀ D. $6x^2y^3$

   The correct answer is **C**. The correct solution is $6x^3y^3$. $3xy^2(2x^2y) = 6x^3y^3$.

2. **Multiply, $-2xy(3xy-4x^2y^2)$.**

   A. $-6x^2y^2 + 8x^3y^3$ ⠀⠀ B. $-6x^2y^2-8x^3y^3$ ⠀⠀ C. $-6xy + 8x^3y^3$ ⠀⠀ D. $-6xy-8x^3y^3$

   The correct answer is **A**. The correct solution is $-6x^2y^2 + 8x^3y^3$.

   $$-2xy(3xy-4x^2y^2) = -2xy(3xy)-2xy(-4x^2y^2) = -6x^2y^2 + 8x^3y^3$$

Polynomial Identities

There are many polynomial identities that show relationships between expressions.

> **BE CAREFUL!**
>
> Pay attention to the details of each polynomial identity and apply them appropriately.

- Difference of two squares: $a^2-b^2 = (a-b)(a + b)$
- Square of a binomial: $(a + b)^2 = a^2 + 2ab + b^2$
- Square of a binomial: $(a-b)^2 = a^2- 2ab + b^2$
- Sum of cubes: $a^3 + b^3 = (a + b)(a^2-ab + b^2)$
- Difference of two cubes: $a^3-b^3 = (a-b)(a^2 + ab + b^2)$

Examples

1. **Apply the polynomial identity to rewrite $x^2 + 6x + 9$.**

   A. $x^2 + 9$ B. $(x^2 + 3)^2$ C. $(x + 3)^2$ D. $(3x)^2$

   The correct answer is **C**. The correct solution is $(x + 3)^2$. The expression $x^2 + 6x + 9$ is rewritten as $(x + 3)^2$ because the value of a is x and the value of b is 3.

2. **Apply the polynomial identity to rewrite $x^3 - 1$.**

   A. $(x - 1)(x^2 + x + 1)$ C. $(x + 1)(x^2 + x + 1)$

   B. $(x - 1)(x^2 - x - 1)$ D. $(x + 1)(x^2 - x - 1)$

   The correct answer is **A**. The expression $x^3 - 1$ can be rewritten with the value a as x and the value of b as 1 using the polynomial identity of the difference of two cubes.

3. **Apply the polynomial identity to rewrite $x^3 - 1$.**

   A. $(x + 1)(x^2 + x + 1)$ C. $(x + 1)(x^2 + x - 1)$

   B. $(x - 1)(x^2 + x - 1)$ D. $(x - 1)(x^2 + x + 1)$

   The correct answer is **D**. The correct solution is $(x - 1)(x^2 + x + 1)$ because the value of a and the value of b is 1. Refer to the polynomial identity for the difference of two cubes equation.

Let's Review!

- Adding, subtracting, and multiplying are commonly applied to polynomials. The key step in applying these operations is combining like terms.
- Polynomial identities require rewriting polynomials into different forms.

RATIOS, PROPORTIONS, AND PERCENTAGES

This lesson reviews percentages and ratios and their application to real-world problems. It also examines proportions and rates of change.

Percentages

A **percent** or **percentage** represents a fraction of some quantity. It is an integer or decimal number followed by the symbol %. The word *percent* means "per hundred." For example, 50% means 50 per 100. This is equivalent to half, or 1 out of 2.

Converting between numbers and percents is easy. Given a number, multiply by 100 and add the % symbol to get the equivalent percent. For instance, 0.67 is equal to $0.67 \times 100 = 67\%$, meaning 67 out of 100. Given a percent, eliminate the % symbol and divide by 100. For instance, 23.5% is equal to $23.5 \div 100 = 0.235$.

Although percentages between 0% and 100% are the most obvious, a percent can be any real number, including a negative number. For example, $1.35 = 135\%$ and $-0.872 = -87.2\%$. An example is a gasoline tank that is one-quarter full: one-quarter is $\frac{1}{4}$ or 0.25, so the tank is 25% full. Another example is a medical diagnostic test that has a certain maximum normal result. If a patient's test exceeds that value, its representation can be a percent greater than 100%. For instance, a reading that is 1.22 times the maximum normal value is 122% of the maximum normal value. Likewise, when measuring increases in a company's profits as a percent from one year to the next, a negative percent can represent a decline. That is, if the company's profits fell by one-tenth, the change was −10%.

Example

If 15 out of every 250 contest entries are winners, what percentage of entries are winners?

   A. 0.06%   B. 6%   C. 15%   D. 17%

The correct answer is **B**. First, convert the fraction $\frac{15}{250}$ to a decimal: 0.06. To get the percent, multiply by 100% (that is, multiply by 100 and add the % symbol). Of all entries, 6% are winners.

Ratios

A **ratio** expresses the relationship between two numbers and is expressed using a colon or fraction notation. For instance, if 135 runners finish a marathon but 22 drop out, the ratio of finishers to non-finishers is 135:22 or $\frac{135}{22}$. These expressions are equal.

> **BE CAREFUL!**
> Avoid confusing standard ratios with odds (such as "3:1 odds"). Both may use a colon, but their meanings differ. In general, a ratio is the same as a fraction containing the same numbers.

Ratios also follow the rules of fractions. Performing arithmetic operations on ratios follows the same procedures as on fractions. Ratios should also generally appear in lowest terms. Therefore, the constituent numbers in a ratio represent the relative quantities of each side, not absolute quantities. For example, because the ratio 1:2 is equal to 2:4, 5:10, and 600:1,200, ratios are insufficient to determine the absolute number of entities in a problem.

Example

If the ratio of women to men in a certain industry is 5:4, how many people are in that industry?

A. 9   B. 20   C. 900   D. Not enough
                                                         information

The correct answer is **D**. The ratio 5:4 is the industry's relative number of women to men. But the industry could have 10 women and 8 men, 100 women and 80 men, or any other breakdown whose ratio is 5:4. Therefore, the question provides too little information to answer. Had it provided the total number of people in the industry, it would have been possible to determine how many women and how many men are in the industry.

> **KEY POINT**
> Mathematically, ratios act just like fractions. For example, the ratio 8:13 is mathematically the same as the fraction $\frac{8}{13}$.

Proportions

A **proportion** is an equation of two ratios. An illustrative case is two equivalent fractions:

$$\frac{21}{28} = \frac{3}{4}$$

This example of a proportion should be familiar: going left to right, it is the conversion of one fraction to an equivalent fraction in lowest terms by dividing the numerator and denominator by the same number (7, in this case).

Equating fractions in this way is correct, but it provides little information. Proportions are more informative when one of the numbers is unknown. Using a question mark (?) to represent an unknown number, setting up a proportion can aid in solving problems involving different scales. For instance, if the ratio of maple saplings to oak saplings in an acre of young forest is 7:5 and that acre contains 65 oaks, the number of maples in that acre can be determined using a proportion:

$$\frac{7}{5} = \frac{?}{65}$$

Note that to equate two ratios in this manner, the numerators must contain numbers that represent the same entity or type, and so must the denominators. In this example, the numerators represent maples and the denominators represent oaks.

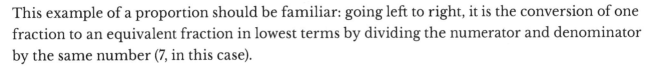

$$\frac{7 \text{ maples}}{5 \text{ oaks}} = \frac{? \text{ maples}}{65 \text{ oaks}}$$

Recall from the properties of fractions that if you multiply the numerator and denominator by the same number, the result is an equivalent fraction. Therefore, to find the unknown in this proportion, first divide the denominator on the right by the denominator on the left. Then, multiply the quotient by the numerator on the left.

$$65 \div 5 = 13$$

$$\frac{7 \times 13}{5 \times 13} = \frac{?}{65}$$

The unknown (?) is $7 \times 13 = 91$. In the example, the acre of forest has 91 maple saplings.

> **DID YOU KNOW?**
> When taking the reciprocal of both sides of a proportion, the proportion still holds. When setting up a proportion, ensure that the numerators represent the same type and the denominators represent the same type.

Example

If a recipe calls for 3 parts flour to 2 parts sugar, how much sugar does a baker need if she uses 12 cups of flour?

A. 2 cups	B. 3 cups	C. 6 cups	D. 8 cups

The correct answer is **D**. The baker needs 8 cups of sugar. First, note that "3 parts flour to 2 parts sugar" is the ratio 3:2. Set up the proportion using the given amount of flour (12 cups), putting the flour numbers in either the denominators or the numerators (either will yield the same answer):

$$\frac{3}{2} = \frac{12}{?}$$

Since $12 \div 3 = 4$, multiply 2×4 to get 8 cups of sugar.

Rates of Change

Numbers that describe current quantities can be informative, but how they change over time can provide even greater insight into a problem. The rate of change for some quantity is the ratio of the quantity's difference over a specific time period to the length of that period. For example, if an automobile increases its speed from 50 mph to 100 mph in 10 seconds, the rate of change of its speed (its acceleration) is

$$\frac{100 \text{ mph} - 50 \text{ mph}}{10 \text{ s}} = \frac{50 \text{ mph}}{10 \text{ s}} = 5 \text{ mph per second} = 5 \text{ mph/s}$$

The basic formula for the rate of change of some quantity is $\frac{x_f - x_i}{t_f - t_i}$.

where t_f is the "final" (or ending) time and t_i is the "initial" (or starting) time. Also, x_f is the (final) quantity at (final) time t_f, and x_i is the (initial) quantity at (initial) time t_i. In the example above, the final time is 10 seconds and the initial time is 0 seconds—hence the omission of the initial time from the calculation.

According to the rules of fractions, multiplying the numerator and denominator by the same number yields an equivalent fraction, so you can reverse the order of the terms in the formula:

$$\frac{x_f - x_i}{t_f - t_i} = \frac{-1}{-1} \times \frac{x_f - x_i}{t_f - t_i} = \frac{x_i - x_f}{t_i - t_f}$$

The key to getting the correct rate of change is to ensure that the first number in the numerator and the first number in the denominator correspond to each other (that is, the quantity from the numerator corresponds to the time from the denominator). This must also be true for the second number.

TEST TIP

To convert a quantity's rate of change to a percent, divide it by the quantity at the *initial* time and multiply by 100%. To convert to a ratio, just skip the multiplication step.

Example

If the population of an endangered frog species fell from 2,250 individuals to 2,115 individuals in a year, what is that population's annual rate of increase?

A. −135%   B. −6%   C. 6%   D. 135%

The correct answer is **B**. The population's rate of increase was −6%. The solution in this case involves two steps. First, calculate the population's annual rate of change using the formula. It will yield the change in the number of individuals.

$$\frac{2,115 - 2,250}{1 \text{ year} - 0 \text{ year}} = -135 \text{ per year}$$

Second, divide the result by the initial population. Finally, convert to a percent.

$$\frac{-135 \text{ per year}}{2,250} = -0.06 \text{ per year}$$

$$(-0.06 \text{ per year}) \times 100\% = -6\% \text{ per year}$$

Since the question asks for the *annual* rate of increase, the "per year" can be dropped. Also, note that the answer must be negative to represent the decreasing population.

Let's Review!

- A percent—meaning "per hundred"—represents a relative quantity as a fraction or decimal. It is the absolute number multiplied by 100 and followed by the % symbol.
- A ratio is a relationship between two numbers expressed using fraction or colon notation (for example, $\frac{3}{2}$ or 3:2). Ratios behave mathematically just like fractions.
- An equation of two ratios is called a proportion. Proportions are used to solve problems involving scale.
- Rates of change are the speeds at which quantities increase or decrease. The formula $\frac{x_f - x_i}{t_f - t_i}$ provides the rate of change of quantity x over the period between some initial (i) time and final (f) time.

POWERS, EXPONENTS, ROOTS, AND RADICALS

This lesson introduces how to apply the properties of exponents and examines square roots and cube roots. It also discusses how to estimate quantities using integer powers of 10.

Properties of Exponents

An expression that is a repeated multiplication of the same factor is a **power**. The **exponent** is the number of times the **base** is multiplied. For example, 6^2 is the same as 6 times 6, or 36. There are many rules associated with exponents.

Property	Definition	Examples
Product Rule (Same Base)	$a^m \times a^n = a^{m+n}$	$4^1 \times 4^4 = 4^{1+4} = 4^5 = 1024$
		$x^1 \times x^4 = x^{1+4} = x^5$
Product Rule (Different Base)	$a^m \times b^m = (a \times b)^m$	$2^2 \times 3^2 = (2 \times 3)^2 = 6^2 = 36$
		$3^3 \times x^3 = (3 \times x)^3 = (3x)^3 = 27x^3$
Quotient Rule (Same Base)	$\frac{a^m}{a^n} = a^{m-n}$	$\frac{4^4}{4^2} = 4^{4-2} = 4^2 = 16$
		$\frac{x^6}{x^3} = x^{6-3} = x^3$
Quotient Rule (Different Base)	$\frac{a^m}{b^m} = \left(\frac{a}{b}\right)^m$	$\frac{4^4}{3^4} = \left(\frac{4}{3}\right)^4$
		$\frac{x^6}{y^6} = \left(\frac{x}{y}\right)^6$
Power of a Power Rule	$(a^m)^n = a^{mn}$	$(2^2)^3 = 2^{2 \times 3} = 2^6 = 64$
		$(x^5)^8 = x^{5 \times 8} = x^{40}$
Zero Exponent Rule	$a^0 = 1$	$64^0 = 1$
		$y^0 = 1$
Negative Exponent Rule	$a^{-m} = \frac{1}{a^m}$	$3^{-3} = \frac{1}{3^3} = \frac{1}{27}$
		$\frac{1}{x^{-3}} = x^3$

For many exponent expressions, it is necessary to use multiplication rules to simplify the expression completely.

Examples

1. **Simplify $(3^2)^3$.**

   A. 18

   C. 243

   B. 216

   D. 729

   The correct answer is **D**. The correct solution is 729 because $(3^2)^3 = 3^{2 \times 3} = 3^6 = 729$.

> **KEEP IN MIND**
>
> The expressions
> $(-2)^2 = (-2) \times (-2) = 4$ and
> $-2^2 = -(2 \times 2) = -4$ have different results because of the location of the negative signs and parentheses. For each problem, focus on each detail to simplify completely and correctly.

2. **Simplify $(2x^2)^4$.**

   A. $2x^8$

   B. $4x^4$

   C. $8x^6$

   D. $16x^8$

   The correct answer is **D**. The correct solution is $16x^8$ because $(2x^2)^4 = 2^4(x^2)^4 = 2^4 x^{2 \times 4} = 16x^8$.

3. Simplify $\left(\frac{x^2}{y^2}\right)^3$.

    A. $\frac{1}{x^6 y^6}$
          B. $\frac{x^6}{y^6}$
          C. $\frac{y^6}{x^6}$
          D. $x^6 y^6$

The correct answer is **A**. The correct solution is $\frac{1}{x^6 y^6}$ because $\left(\frac{x^2}{y^2}\right)^3 = \left(\frac{1}{x^2 y^2}\right)^3 = \frac{1}{x^{2\times3} y^{2\times3}} = \frac{1}{x^6 y^6}$.

Square Root and Cube Roots

The **square** of a number is the number raised to the power of 2. The **square root** of a number, when the number is squared, gives that number. $10^2 = 100$, so the square of 100 is 10, or $\sqrt{100} = 10$. **Perfect squares** are numbers with whole number square roots, such as 1, 4, 9, 16, and 25.

Squaring a number and taking a square root are opposite operations, meaning that the operations undo each other. This means that $\sqrt{x^2} = x$ and $(\sqrt{x})^2 = x$. When solving the equation $x^2 = p$, the solutions are $x = \pm\sqrt{p}$ because a negative value squared is a positive solution.

The **cube** of a number is the number raised to the power of 3. The **cube root** of a number, when the number is cubed, gives that number. $10^3 = 1000$, so the cube of 1,000 is 100, or $\sqrt[3]{1000} = 10$. **Perfect cubes** are numbers with whole number cube roots, such as 1, 8, 27, 64, and 125.

KEEP IN MIND

Most square roots and cube roots are not perfect roots.

Cubing a number and taking a cube root are opposite operations, meaning that the operations undo each other. This means that $\sqrt[3]{x^3} = x$ and $\left(\sqrt[3]{x}\right)^3 = x$. When solving the equation $x^3 = p$, the solution is $x = \sqrt[3]{p}$.

If a number is not a perfect square root or cube root, the solution is an approximation. When this occurs, the solution is an irrational number. For example, $\sqrt{2}$ is the irrational solution to $x^2 = 2$.

Examples

1. Solve $x^2 = 121$.

    A. –10, 10
          B. –11, 11
          C. –12, 12
          D. –13, 13

The correct answer is **B**. The correct solution is –11, 11 because the square root of 121 is 11. The values of –11 and 11 make the equation true.

2. Solve $x^3 = 125$.

    A. 1
          B. 5
          C. 10
          D. 25

The correct answer is **B**. The correct solution is 5 because the cube root of 125 is 5.

Express Large or Small Quantities as Multiples of 10

Scientific notation is a large or small number written in two parts. The first part is a number between 1 and 10. In these problems, the first digit will be a single digit. The number is followed by a multiple to a power of 10. A positive integer exponent means the number is greater than 1, while a negative integer exponent means the number is smaller than 1.

> **KEEP IN MIND**
>
> A positive exponent in scientific notation represents a large number, while a negative exponent represents a small number.

The number 3×10^4 is the same as $3 \times 10,000 = 30,000$.

The number 3×10^{-4} is the same as $3 \times 0.0001 = 0.0003$.

For example, the population of the United States is about 3×10^8, and the population of the world is about 7×10^9. The population of the United States is 300,000,000, and the population of the world is 7,000,000,000. The world population is about 20 times larger than the population of the United States.

Examples

1. **The population of China is about 1×10^9, and the population of the United States is about 3×10^8. How many times larger is the population of China than the population of the United States?**

    A. 2   B. 3   C. 4   D. 5

    The correct answer is **B**. The correct solution is 3 because the population of China is about 1,000,000,000 and the population of the United States is about 300,000,000. So the population is about 3 times larger.

2. **A red blood cell has a length of 8×10^{-6} meter, and a skin cell has a length of 3×10^{-5} meter. How many times larger is the skin cell?**

    A. 1   B. 2   C. 3   D. 4

    The correct answer is **D**. The correct solution is 4 because 3×10^{-5} is 0.00003 and 8×10^{-6} is 0.000008. So, the skin cell is about 4 times larger.

Let's Review!

- The properties and rules of exponents are applicable to generate equivalent expressions.
- Only a few whole numbers out of the set of whole numbers are perfect squares. Perfect cubes can be positive or negative.
- Numbers expressed in scientific notation are useful to compare large or small numbers.

CHAPTER 2 INTERMEDIATE ALGEBRA AND FUNCTIONS
PRACTICE QUIZ 1

1. Multiply, $(5x-3)(5x + 3)$.

   A. $25x^2-9$ C. $25x^2 + 30x-9$

   B. $25x^2 + 9$ D. $25x^2 + 30x + 9$

2. Perform the operation, $(-3x^2-2xy + 4y^2) + (5x^2 + 3xy-3y^2)$.

   A. $2x^2-xy + y^2$ C. $-2x^2 + xy + y^2$

   B. $-2x^2-xy + y^2$ D. $2x^2 + xy + y^2$

3. Apply the polynomial identity to rewrite $x^3 + 125$.

   A. $(x + 5)(x^2-5x + 25)$

   B. $(x-5)(x^2-10x + 25)$

   C. $(x + 5)(x^2 + 10x + 25)$

   D. $(x-5)(x^2 + 10x + 25)$

4. What is 15% of 64?

   A. 5:48   C. 48:5

   B. 15:64   D. 64:15

5. Which proportion yields a number for the unknown that is different from the others?

   A. $\frac{13}{75} = \frac{158}{?}$ C. $\frac{158}{?} = \frac{13}{75}$

   B. $\frac{75}{13} = \frac{?}{158}$ D. $\frac{75}{13} = \frac{158}{?}$

6. If a survey finds that 120 people are in group X and 230 people are in group Y, what is the ratio of people in group Y to people in group X or group Y?

   A. 12:35   C. 23:35

   B. 12:23   D. 35:23

7. Solve the equation by any method, $2x^2-70 = 2$.

   A. ± 2 C. ± 6

   B. ± 4 D. ± 8

8. Solve the equation by completing the square, $x^2-2x-37 = 0$.

   A. $-1 \pm \sqrt{37}$ C. $-1 \pm \sqrt{38}$

   B. $1 \pm \sqrt{37}$ D. $1 \pm \sqrt{38}$

9. Solve the equation by factoring, $x^2 + 3x-88 = 0$.

   A. $-8, -11$

   B. $-8, 11$

   C. $8, -11$

   D. $8, 11$

Chapter 2 Intermediate Algebra and Functions
Practice Quiz 1 – Answer Key

1. A. The correct solution is $25x^2-9$.

$(5x–3)(5x + 3) = 5x(5x + 3)–3 (5x + 3) = 25x^2 + 15x–15x–9 = 25x^2–9$

See Lesson: Polynomials.

2. D. The correct solution is $2x^2 + xy + y^2$.

$(–3x^2–2xy + 4y^2) + (5x^2 + 3xy–3y^2) = (–3x^2 + 5x^2) + (–2xy + 3xy) + (4y^2–3y^2) = 2x^2 + xy + y^2$

See Lesson: Polynomials.

3. A. The correct solution is $(x + 5)(x^2–5x + 25)$.

The expression $x^3 + 125$ is rewritten as $(x + 5)(x^2–5x + 25)$ because the value of a is x and the value of b is 5. **See Lesson: Polynomials.**

4. C. Either set up a proportion or just note that this question is asking for a fraction of a specific number: 15% (or $\frac{3}{20}$) of 64. Multiply $\frac{3}{20}$ by 64 to get $\frac{48}{5}$, or 48:5. **See Lesson: Ratios, Proportions, and Percentages.**

5. D. The correct answer is D. Although solving each proportion is one approach, the easiest approach is to compare them as they are. The proportions in answers A and B yield the same number for the unknown because they keep the same numbers in either the numerators or the denominators. Answer C just reverses the order of the equation in answer A, which does not yield a different number for the unknown. Answer D flips one fraction without flipping the other, which changes the proportion. **See Lesson: Ratios, Proportions, and Percentages.**

6. C. The ratio is 23:35. The first part of the ratio is the number of people in group Y, which is 230. The second part is the number of people in either group, which is the sum 120 + 230 = 350. The ratio is therefore 230:350 = 23:35. **See Lesson: Ratios, Proportions, and Percentages.**

7. C. The correct solutions are ±6. Solve this equation by the square root method. **See Lesson: Solving Quadratic Equations.**

$2x^2 = 72$	Add 70 to both sides of the equation.
$x^2 = ±36$	Divide both sides of the equation by 2.
$x = 6$	Apply the square root to both sides of the equation.

8. D. The correct solutions are $1 \pm \sqrt{38}$. **See Lesson: Solving Quadratic Equations.**

$x^2 - 2x = 37$	Add 37 to both sides of the equation.
$x^2 - 2x + 1 = 37 + 1$	Complete the square, $\left(\frac{2}{2}\right)^2 = 1^2 = 1$.

Add 1 to both sides of the equation.

$x^2 - 2x + 1 = 38$	Simplify the right side of the equation.
$(x-1)^2 = 38$	Factor the left side of the equation.
$x - 1 = \pm\sqrt{38}$	Apply the square root to both sides of the equation.
$x = 1 \pm \sqrt{38}$	Add 1 to both sides of the equation.

9. C. The correct solutions are 8 and –11. See Lesson: Solving Quadratic Equations.

$(x + 11)(x-8) = 0$	Factor the equation.
$(x + 11) = 0$ or $(x-8) = 0$	Set each factor equal to 0.
$x + 11 = 0$	Subtract 11 from both sides of the equation to solve for the first factor.
$x = -11$	
$x - 8 = 0$	Add 8 to both sides of the equation to solve for the second factor.
$x = 8$	

Chapter 2 Intermediate Algebra and Functions
Practice Quiz 2

1. Multiply, $(4y^2 + 3)(2y + 5)$.

   A. $8y^3 + 10y^2 + 16y + 15$

   B. $8y^3 + 20y^2 + 16y + 15$

   C. $8y^3 + 10y^2 + 6y + 15$

   D. $8y^3 + 20y^2 + 6y + 15$

2. Multiply, $(4x + 5)(3x-2)$.

   A. $12x^2-7x + 10$

   C. $12x^2 + 7x-10$

   B. $12x^2 + 7x + 10$

   D. $12x^2-7x-10$

3. Apply the polynomial identity to rewrite $27x^3-8$.

   A. $(3x-2)(9x^2-6x + 4)$

   B. $(3x-2)(9x^2 + 6x + 4)$

   C. $(3x-2)(9x^2 + 6x-4)$

   D. $(3x-2)(9x^2-6x-4)$

4. Which is different from the others?

   A. 0.5

   C. $\frac{1}{2}$

   B. 1:2

   D. 1:2 odds

5. The number 22 is what percent of 54?

   A. 22%

   C. 41%

   B. 29%

   D. 76%

6. If 35% of a cattle herd is Ayrshire and the rest is Jersey, and it has 195 Jerseys, how many cattle are in the herd?

   A. 230

   C. 300

   B. 263

   D. 557

7. Solve the equation by any method, $x^2-23x + 125 = 0$.

   A. –8.81 and –14.2

   C. 8.81 and –14.2

   B. 8.81 and 14.2

   D. –8.81 and 14.2

8. Solve the equation by completing the square, $x^2 + 12x + 10 = 0$.

   A. $6 \pm \sqrt{26}$

   C. $6 \pm \sqrt{10}$

   B. $-6 \pm \sqrt{26}$

   D. $-6 \pm \sqrt{10}$

9. Solve the equation by the square root method, $2x^2 = 162$.

   A. ± 8

   C. ± 10

   B. ± 9

   D. ± 11

CHAPTER 2 INTERMEDIATE ALGEBRA AND FUNCTIONS
PRACTICE QUIZ 2 – ANSWER KEY

1. **D.** The correct solution is $8y^3 + 20y^2 + 6y + 15$.

    $(4y^2 + 3)(2y + 5) = 4y^2(2y + 5) + 3(2y + 5) = 8y^3 + 20y^2 + 6y + 15$

See Lesson: Polynomials.

2. **C.** The correct solution is $12x^2 + 7x - 10$.

    $(4x + 5)(3x-2) = 4x(3x-2) + 5(3x-2) = 12x^2 - 8x + 15x - 10 = 12x^2 + 7x - 10$

See Lesson: Polynomials.

3. **B.** The correct solution is $(3x-2)(9x^2 + 6x + 4)$. The expression $27x^3 - 8$ is rewritten as $(3x-2)(9x^2 + 6x + 4)$ because the value of a is $3x$ and the value of b is 2. **See Lesson: Polynomials.**

4. **D.** The decimal 0.5 is equal to $\frac{1}{2}$, which is also equal to the ratio 1:2. But 1:2 odds are different because odds use colon notation in a different manner. **See Lesson: Ratios, Proportions, and Percentages.**

5. **C.** The fraction $\frac{22}{54}$ is 41%, meaning 22 is 41% of 54. **See Lesson: Ratios, Proportions, and Percentages.**

6. **C.** There are 300 cattle in the herd. Because the herd is only Ayrshire or Jersey, it is 65% Jersey. The equivalent decimals are 0.35 Ayrshire and 0.65 Jersey. Set up a proportion that relates these decimals to the number of cattle of each type:

    $\frac{0.35}{0.65} = \frac{?}{195}$

One approach is to divide 195 by 0.65 to get 300, then multiply by 0.35 to get the number of Ayrshires: 105. Add 195 and 105 to get the total number of cattle in the herd. **See Lesson: Ratios, Proportions, and Percentages.**

7. B. The correct solutions are 8.81 and 14.2. The equation can be solved by the quadratic formula. **See Lesson: Solving Quadratic Equations.**

$$x = \frac{-(-23) \pm \sqrt{(-23)^2 - 4(1)(125)}}{2(1)}$$
Substitute 1 for a, –23 for b, and 125 for c.

$$x = \frac{23 \pm \sqrt{529 - 500}}{2}$$
Apply the exponent and perform the multiplication.

$$x = \frac{23 \pm \sqrt{29}}{2}$$
Perform the subtraction.

$$x = \frac{23 \pm 5.39}{2}$$
Apply the square root.

$$x = \frac{23 + 5.39}{2}, \; x = \frac{23 - 5.39}{2}$$
Separate the problem into two expressions.

$$x = \frac{28.39}{2} = 14.2, \; x = \frac{17.61}{2} = 8.81$$
Simplify the numerator and divide.

8. B. The correct solutions are $-6 \pm \sqrt{26}$. **See Lesson: Solving Quadratic Equations.**

$x^2 + 12x = -10$ Subtract 10 from both sides of the equation.

$x^2 + 12x + 36 = -10 + 36$ Complete the square, $\left(\frac{12}{2}\right)^2 = 6^2 = 36$.

Add 36 to both sides of the equation.

$x^2 + 12x + 36 = 26$ Simplify the right side of the equation.

$(x + 6)^2 = 26$ Factor the left side of the equation.

$x + 6 = \pm\sqrt{26}$ Apply the square root to both sides of the equation.

$x = -6 \pm \sqrt{26}$ Subtract 6 from both sides of the equation.

9. B. The correct solution is ± 9. **See Lesson: Solving Quadratic Equations.**

$x^2 = 81$ Divide both sides of the equation by 2.

$x = \pm 9$ Apply the square root to both sides of the equation.

CHAPTER 3 GEOMETRY AND MEASUREMENT

CONGRUENCE

This lesson discusses basic terms for geometry. Many polygons have the property of lines of symmetry, or rotational symmetry. Rotations, reflections, and translations are ways to create congruent polygons.

Geometry Terms

The terms *point*, *line*, and *plane* help define other terms in geometry. A point is an exact location in space with no size and has a label with a capital letter. A line has location and direction, is always straight, and has infinitely many points that extend in both directions. A plane has infinitely many intersecting lines that extend forever in all directions.

The diagram shows point W, point X, point Y, and point Z. The line is labeled as $\overleftrightarrow{WX}$, and the plane is Plane A or Plane WYZ (or any three points in the plane).

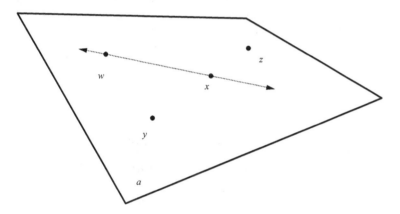

With these definitions, many other geometry terms can be defined. *Collinear* is a term for points that lie on the same line, and *coplanar* is a term for points and/or lines within the same plane. A line segment is a part of a line with two endpoints. For example, $\overline{WX}$ has endpoints W and X. A ray has an endpoint and extends forever in one direction. For example, $\longrightarrow AB$ has an endpoint of A, and $\longrightarrow BA$ has an endpoint of B. The intersection of lines, planes, segment, or rays is a point or a set of points.

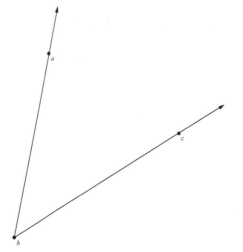

Some key statements that are evident in geometry are

- There is exactly one straight line through any two points.
- There is exactly one plane that contains any three non-collinear points.
- A line with points in the plane lies in the plane.

- Two lines intersect at a point.
- Two planes intersect at a line.

Two rays that share an endpoint form an angle. The vertex is the common endpoint of the two rays that form an angle. When naming an angle, the vertex is the center point. The angle below is named $\angle ABC$ or $\angle CBA$.

An acute angle has a measure between $0°$ and $90°$, and a $90°$ angle is a right angle. An obtuse angle has a measure between $90°$ and $180°$, and a $180°$ angle is a straight angle.

There are two special sets of lines. Parallel lines are at least two lines that never intersect within the same plane. Perpendicular lines intersect at one point and form four angles.

Example

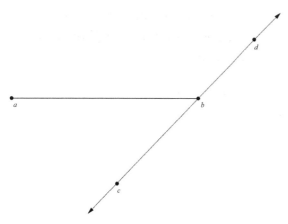

BE CAREFUL!
Lines are always named with two points, a plane can be named with three points, and an angle is named with the vertex as the center point.

Describe the diagram.

A. Points A, B, C, and D are collinear.

B. Points A, C, and D are collinear.

C. $\overline{CD}$ intersects $\overleftrightarrow{AB}$ at point B.

D. $\overline{AB}$ intersects $\overleftrightarrow{CD}$ at point B.

The correct answer is **D**. The correct solution is $\overline{AB}$ intersects $\overleftrightarrow{CD}$ at point B. The segment intersects the line at point B.

Line and Rotational Symmetry

Symmetry is a reflection or rotation of a shape that allows that shape to be carried onto itself. Line symmetry, or reflection symmetry, is when two halves of a shape are reflected onto each other across a line. A shape may have none, one, or several lines of symmetry. A kite has one line of symmetry, and a scalene triangle has no lines of symmetry.

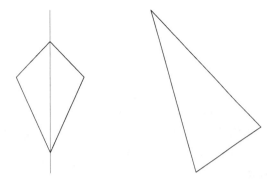

Rotational symmetry is when a figure can be mapped onto itself by a rotation about a point through any angle between 0° and 360°. The order of rotational symmetry is the number of times the object can be rotated. If there is no rotational symmetry, the order is 1 because the object can only be rotated 360° to map the figure onto itself. A square has 90° rotational symmetry and is order 4 because it can be rotated 90°, 180°, 270°, and 360°. A trapezoid has no rotational symmetry and is order 1 because it can only be rotated 360° to map onto itself.

KEEP IN MIND

A polygon can have both, neither, or either reflection and rotational symmetry.

Example

What is the rotational symmetry for a regular octagon?

A. 30°   B. 45°   C. 60°   D. 75°

The correct answer is **B**. The correct solution is 45°. For a regular polygon, divide 360° by the eight sides of the octagon to obtain 45°.

Rotations, Reflections, and Translations

There are three types of transformations: rotations, reflections, and translations. A rotation is a turn of a figure about a point in a given direction. A reflection is a flip over a line of symmetry, and a translation is a slide horizontally, vertically, or both. Each of these transformations produces a congruent image.

A rotation changes ordered pairs (x, y) in the coordinate plane. A 90° rotation counterclockwise about the point becomes $(-y, x)$, a 180° rotation counterclockwise about the point becomes $(-x, -y)$, and a 270° rotation the point becomes $(y, -x)$. Using the point $(6, -8)$,

- 90° rotation counterclockwise about the origin $(8, 6)$
- 180° rotation counterclockwise about the origin $(-6, 8)$
- 270° rotation counterclockwise about the origin $(-8, -6)$

A reflection also changes ordered pairs (x, y) in the coordinate plane. A reflection across the x-axis changes the sign of the y-coordinate, and a reflection across the y-axis changes the sign of the x-coordinate. A reflection over the line $y = x$ changes the points to (y, x), and a reflection over the line $y = -x$ changes the points to $(-y, -x)$. Using the point $(6, -8)$,

- A reflection across the x-axis (6, 8)
- A reflection across the y-axis (−6, −8)
- A reflection over the line $y = x$ (−8, 6)
- A reflection over the line $y = -x$ (8, −6)

A translation changes ordered pairs (x, y) left or right and/or up or down. Adding a positive value to an x-coordinate is a translation to the right, and adding a negative value to an x-coordinate is a translation to the left. Adding a positive value to a y-coordinate is a translation up, and adding a negative value to a y-coordinate is a translation down. Using the point (6, −8),

> **KEEP IN MIND**
>
> A rotation is a turn, a reflection is a flip, and a translation is a slide.

- A translation of $(x + 3)$ is a translation right 3 units (9, −8)
- A translation of $(x − 3)$ is a translation left 3 units (3, −8)
- A translation of $(y + 3)$ is a translation up 3 units (6, −5)
- A translation of $(y − 3)$ is a translation down 3 units (6, −11)

Example

$\triangle ABC$ has points A (3, −2), B (2, −1), and C (−1, 4), which after a transformation become A' (2, 3), B' (1, 2), and C' (−4, −1). What is the transformation between the points?

A. Reflection across the x-axis

B. Reflection across the y-axis

C. Rotation of 90° counterclockwise

D. Rotation of 270° counterclockwise

The correct answer is **C**. The correct solution is a rotation of 90° counterclockwise because the points (x, y) become $(y, -x)$.

Let's Review!

- The terms *point*, *line*, and *plane* help define many terms in geometry.
- Symmetry allows a figure to carry its shape onto itself. This can be reflectional or rotational symmetry.
- Three transformations are rotation (turn), reflection (flip), and translation (slide).

SIMILARITY, RIGHT TRIANGLES, AND TRIGONOMETRY

This lesson defines and applies terminology associated with coordinate planes. It also demonstrates how to find the area of two-dimensional shapes and the surface area and volume of three-dimensional cubes and right prisms.

Coordinate Plane

The **coordinate plane** is a two-dimensional number line with the horizontal axis called the **x-axis** and the vertical axis called the **y-axis**. Each **ordered pair** or **coordinate** is listed as (x, y). The center point is the origin and has an ordered pair of $(0, 0)$. A coordinate plane has four quadrants.

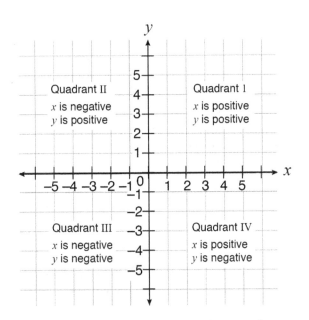

To graph a point in the coordinate plane, start with the x-coordinate. This point states the number of steps to the left (negative) or to the right (positive) from the origin. Then, the y-coordinate states the number of steps up (positive) or down (negative) from the x-coordinate.

Given a set of ordered pairs, points can be drawn in the coordinate plane to create polygons. The length of a segment can be found if the segment has the same first coordinate or the same second coordinate.

Examples

1. Draw a triangle with the coordinates (–2, –1), (–3, 5), (–4, 2).

A.

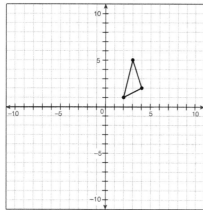

C.

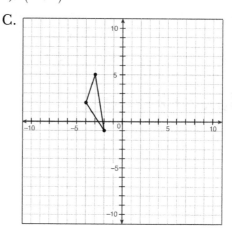

B.

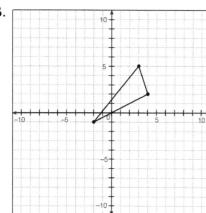

D.

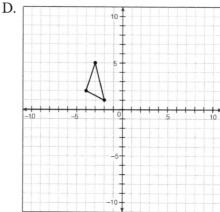

The correct answer is **C**. The first point is in the third quadrant because x is negative and y is negative, and the last two points are in the second quadrant because x is negative and y is positive.

2. Given the coordinates for a rectangle (4, 8), (4, –2), (–1, –2) (–1, 8), find the length of each side of the rectangle.

   A. 3 units and 6 units

   B. 3 units and 10 units

   C. 5 units and 6 units

   D. 5 units and 10 units

   The correct answer is **D**. The correct solution is 5 units and 10 units. The difference between the **x**-coordinates is 4–(–1) = 5 units, and the difference between the **y**-coordinates is 8–(–2) = 10 units.

3. The dimensions for a soccer field are 45 meters by 90 meters. One corner of a soccer field on the coordinate plane is (–45, –30). What could a second coordinate be?

   A. (–45, 30)   B. (–45, 45)   C. (–45, 60)   D. (–45, 75)

   The correct answer is **C**. The correct solution is (–45, 60) because 90 can be added to the y-coordinate, –30 + 90 = 60.

Area of Two-Dimensional Objects

The **area** is the number of unit squares that fit inside a two-dimensional object. A unit square is one unit long by one unit wide, which includes 1 foot by 1 foot and 1 meter by 1 meter. The unit of measurement for area is units squared (or feet squared, meters squared, and so on). The following are formulas for calculating the area of various shapes.

> **BE CAREFUL!**
>
> Make sure that you apply the correct formula for area of each two-dimensional object.

- Rectangle: The product of the length and the width, $A = lw$.
- Parallelogram: The product of the base and the height, $A = bh$.
- Square: The side length squared, $A = s^2$.
- Triangle: The product of one-half the base and the height, $A = \frac{1}{2}bh$.
- Trapezoid: The product of one-half the height and the sum of the bases, $A = \frac{1}{2}h(b_1 + b_2)$.
- Regular polygon: The product of one-half the **apothem** (a line from the center of the regular polygon that is perpendicular to a side) and the sum of the perimeter, $A = \frac{1}{2}ap$.

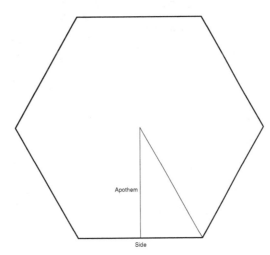

Examples

1. A trapezoid has a height of 3 centimeters and bases of 8 centimeters and 10 centimeters. Find the area in square centimeters.

   A. 18   B. 27   C. 52   D. 55

   The correct answer is **B**. The correct solution is 27. Substitute the values into the formula and simplify using the order of operations, $A = \frac{1}{2}h(b_1 + b_2) = \frac{1}{2}(3)(8 + 10) = \frac{1}{2}(3)(18) = 27$ square centimeters.

2. A regular decagon has a side length of 12 inches and an apothem of 6 inches. Find the area in square inches.

   A. 120   B. 360   C. 720   D. 960

   The correct answer is **B**. The correct solution is 360. Simplify using the order of operations, $A = \frac{1}{2}ap = \frac{1}{2}(6)(12(10)) = 360$ square inches.

3. Two rectangular rooms need to be carpeted. The dimensions of the first room are 18 feet by 19 feet, and the dimensions of the second room are 12 feet by 10 feet. What is the total area to be carpeted in square feet?

   A. 118   B. 236   C. 342   D. 462

   The correct answer is **D**. The correct solution is 462. Substitute the values into the formula and simplify using the order of operations, $A = lw + lw = 18(19) + 12(10) = 342 + 120 = 462$ square feet.

4. A picture frame is in the shape of a right triangle with legs 12 centimeters and 13 centimeters and hypotenuse of 17 centimeters. What is the area in square centimeters?

   A. 78   B. 108   C. 117   D. 156

   The correct answer is **A**. The correct solution is 78. Substitute the values into the formula and simplify using the order of operations, $A = \frac{1}{2}bh = \frac{1}{2}(12)(13) = 78$ square centimeters.

Surface Area and Volume of Cubes and Right Prisms

A three-dimensional object has length, width, and height. **Cubes** are made up of six congruent square faces. A **right prism** is made of three sets of congruent faces, with at least two sets of congruent rectangles.

BE CAREFUL!

Surface area is a two-dimensional calculation, and volume is a three-dimensional calculation.

The **surface area** of any three-dimensional object is the sum of the area of all faces. The formula for the surface area of a cube is $SA = 6s^2$ because there are six congruent faces. For a right rectangular prism, the surface area formula is $SA = 2lw + 2lh + 2hw$ because there are three sets of congruent rectangles. For a triangular prism, the surface area formula is twice the area of the base plus the area of the other three rectangles that make up the prism.

The **volume** of any three-dimensional object is the amount of space inside the object. The volume formula for a cube is $V = s^3$. The volume formula for a rectangular prism is the area of the base times the height, or $V = Bh$.

Examples

1. A cube has a side length of 5 centimeters. What is the surface area in square centimeters?

   A. 20   B. 25   C. 125   D. 150

   The correct answer is **D**. The correct solution is 150. Substitute the values into the formula and simplify using the order of operations, $SA = 6s^2 = 6(5^2) = 6(25) = 150$ square centimeters.

2. A cube has a side length of 5 centimeters. What is the volume in cubic centimeters?

   A. 20   B. 25   C. 125   D. 180

   The correct answer is **C**. The correct solution is 125. Substitute the values into the formula and simplify using the order of operations, $V = s^3 = 5^3 = 125$ cubic centimeters.

3. A right rectangular prism has dimensions of 4 inches by 5 inches by 6 inches. What is the surface area in square inches?

    A. 60   B. 74   C. 120   D. 148

    The correct answer is **D**. The correct solution is 148. Substitute the values into the formula and simplify using the order of operations, $SA = 2lw + 2lh + 2hw = 2(4)(5) + 2(4)(6) + 2(6)(5) = 40 + 48 + 60 = 148$ square inches.

4. A right rectangular prism has dimensions of 4 inches by 5 inches by 6 inches. What is the volume in cubic inches?

    A. 60   B. 62   C. 120   D. 124

    The correct answer is **C**. The correct solution is 120. Substitute the values into the formula and simplify using the order of operations, $V = lwh = 4(5)(6) = 120$ cubic inches.

Let's Review!

- The coordinate plane is a two-dimensional number line that is used to display ordered pairs. Two-dimensional shapes can be drawn on the plane, and the length of the objects can be determined based on the given coordinates.
- The area of a two-dimensional object is the amount of space inside the shape. There are area formulas to use to calculate the area of various shapes.
- For a three-dimensional object, the surface area is the sum of the area of the faces and the volume is the amount of space inside the object. Cubes and right rectangular prisms are common three-dimensional solids.

CIRCLES

This lesson introduces concepts of circles, including finding the circumference and the area of the circle.

Circle Terminology

A **circle** is a figure composed of points that are equidistant from a given point. The **center** is the point from which all points are equidistant. A **chord** is a segment whose endpoints are on the circle, and the **diameter** is a chord that goes through the center of the circle. The **radius** is a segment with one endpoint at the center of the circle and one endpoint on the circle. **Arcs** have two endpoints on the circle and all points on a circle between those endpoints.

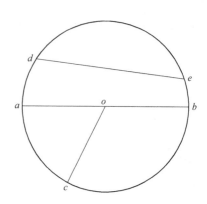

In the circle at the right, O is the center, $\overline{OC}$ is the radius, $\overline{AB}$ is the diameter, $\overline{DE}$ is a chord, and $\overparen{AD}$ is an arc.

Example

Identify a diameter of the circle.

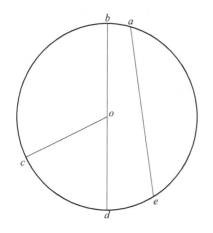

KEEP IN MIND

The radius is one-half the length of the diameter of the circle.

A. $\overline{BD}$ B. $\overline{OC}$ C. $\overline{DO}$ D. $\overline{AE}$

The correct answer is **A**. The correct solution is $\overline{BD}$ because points B and D are on the circle and the segment goes through the center O.

Circumference and Area of a Circle

The **circumference** of a circle is the perimeter, or the distance, around the circle. There are two ways to find the circumference. The formulas are the product of the diameter and pi or the product of twice the radius and pi. In symbol form, the formulas are $C = \pi d$ or $C = 2\pi r$.

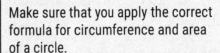

BE CAREFUL!

Make sure that you apply the correct formula for circumference and area of a circle.

The **area** of a circle is the amount of space inside a circle. The formula is the product of pi and the radius squared. In symbol form, the formula is $A = \pi r^2$. The area is always expressed in square units.

Given the circumference or the area of a circle, the radius and the diameter can be determined. The given measurement is substituted into the appropriate formula. Then, the equation is solved for the radius or the diameter.

Examples

1. Find the circumference in centimeters of a circle with a diameter of 8 centimeters. Use 3.14 for π.

   A. 12.56   B. 25.12   C. 50.24   D. 100.48

   The correct answer is **B**. The correct solution is 25.12 because $C = \pi d \approx 3.14(8) \approx 25.12$ centimeters.

2. Find the area in square inches of a circle with a radius of 15 inches. Use 3.14 for π.

   A. 94.2   B. 176.63   C. 706.5   D. 828.96

   The correct answer is **C**. The correct solution is 706.5 because $A = \pi r^2 \approx 3.14(15)^2 \approx$

   $3.14(225) \approx 706.5$ square inches.

3. A circle has a circumference of 70 centimeters. Find the diameter to the nearest tenth of a centimeter. Use 3.14 for π.

   A. 11.1   B. 22.3   C. 33.5   D. 44.7

   The correct answer is **B**. The correct solution is 22.3 because $C = \pi d; 70 = 3.14d; d \approx 22.3$ centimeters.

4. A circle has an area of 95 square centimeters. Find the radius to the nearest tenth of a centimeter. Use 3.14 for π.

   A. 2.7   B. 5.5   C. 8.2   D. 10.9

   The correct answer is **B**. The correct solution is 5.5 because
   $A = \pi r^2; 95 = 3.14 r^2; 30.25 = r^2; r \approx 5.5$ centimeters.

Finding Circumference or Area Given the Other Value

Given the circumference of a circle, the area of the circle can be found. First, substitute the circumference into the formula and find the radius. Substitute the radius into the area formula and simplify.

Reverse the process to find the circumference given the area. First, substitute the area into the area formula and find the radius. Substitute the radius into the circumference formula and simplify.

BE CAREFUL!

Pay attention to the details with each formula and apply them in the correct order.

Examples

1. The circumference of a circle is 45 inches. Find the area of the circle in square inches. Round to the nearest tenth. Use 3.14 for π.

   A. 51.8   B. 65.1   C. 162.8   D. 204.5

   The correct answer is **C**. The correct solution is 162.8.

   $C = 2\pi r; 45 = 2(3.14)r; 45 = 6.28r; r \approx 7.2$ inches. $A = \pi r^2 \approx 3.14(7.2)^2 \approx 3.14(51.84) \approx 162.8$ square inches.

2. The area of a circle is 60 square centimeters. Find the circumference of the circle in centimeters. Round to the nearest tenth. Use 3.14 for π.

   A. 4.4   B. 13.8   C. 19.1   D. 27.6

   The correct answer is **D**. The correct solution is 27.6.

   $A = \pi r^2; 60 = 3.14 r^2; 19.11 = r^2; r \approx 4.4$ centimeters. $C = 2\pi r; C = 2(3.14)4.4 \approx 27.6$ centimeters.

Let's Review!

- Key terms related to circles are *radius, diameter, chord,* and *arc*. Note that the diameter is twice the radius.
- The circumference or the perimeter of a circle is the product of pi and the diameter or twice the radius and pi.
- The area of the circle is the product of pi and the radius squared.

MEASUREMENT AND DIMENSION

This lesson applies the formulas of volume for cylinders, pyramids, cones, and spheres to solve problems.

Volume of a Cylinder

A **cylinder** is a three-dimensional figure with two identical circular bases and a rectangular lateral face.

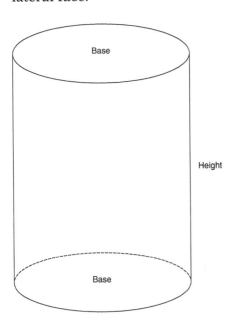

KEEP IN MIND

The volume of a cylinder can be expressed in terms of π, and the volume is measured in cubic units.

The volume of a cylinder equals the product of the area of the base and the height of the cylinder. This is the same formula used to calculate the volume of a right prism. In this case, the area of a base is a circle, so the formula is $V = Bh = \pi r^2 h$. The height is the perpendicular distance between the two circular bases.

Example

Find the volume of a cylinder in cubic centimeters with a radius of 13 centimeters and a height of 12 centimeters.

   A. 156π B. 312π C. $1,872\pi$ D. $2,028\pi$

The correct answer is **D**. The correct solution is $2,028\pi$. Substitute the values into the formula and simplify using the order of operations, $V = \pi r^2 h = \pi 13^2(12) = \pi(169)(12) = 2,028\pi$ cubic centimeters.

Volume of a Pyramid and a Cone

A **pyramid** is a three-dimensional solid with
one base and all edges from the base meeting
at the top, or apex. Pyramids can have any two-
dimensional shape as the base. A **cone** is similar to
a pyramid, but it has a circle instead of a polygon
for the base.

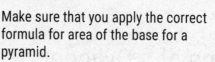

BE CAREFUL!

Make sure that you apply the correct
formula for area of the base for a
pyramid.

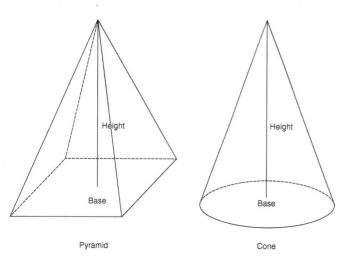

The formula for the volume of a pyramid is similar to a prism, $V = \frac{1}{3}Bh$ where B is the area of
the base; in the case of a hexagonal pyramid B is = to $\frac{1}{2}(apothem)(perimeter)$. The base is a circle
for a cone, and the formula for the volume is $V = \frac{1}{3}Bh = \frac{1}{3}\pi r^2 h$.

Examples

1. A regular hexagonal pyramid has base with side lengths of 5 centimeters and an apothem
    of 3 centimeters. If the height is 6 centimeters, find the volume in cubic centimeters.

    A. 90   B. 180   C. 270   D. 360

    The correct answer is **A**. The correct solution is 90. Substitute the values into the formula
    and simplify using the order of operations, $V = \frac{1}{3}Bh = \frac{1}{3}(\frac{1}{2}ap)h = \frac{1}{3}(\frac{1}{2}(3)(30))6 = 90$ cubic
    centimeters.

2. A cone has a radius of 10 centimeters and a height of 9 centimeters. Find the volume in
    cubic centimeters.

    A. 270π B. 300π C. 810π D. 900π

    The correct answer is **B**. The correct solution is 300π. Substitute the values into the formula
    and simplify using the order of operations, $V = \frac{1}{3}\pi r^2 h = \frac{1}{3}\pi 10^2(9) = \frac{1}{3}\pi(100)(9) = 300\pi$ cubic
    centimeters.

Volume of a Sphere

A **sphere** is a round, three-dimensional solid, with every point on its surface equidistant to the center. The formula for the volume of a sphere is represented by just the radius of the sphere. The volume of a sphere is $V = \frac{4}{3}\pi r^3$. The volume of a hemi (half) of a sphere is $V = \left(\frac{1}{2}\right)\frac{4}{3}\pi r^3 = \frac{2}{3}\pi r^3$.

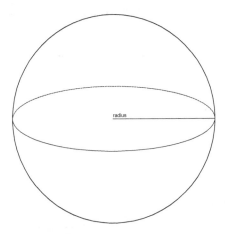

BE CAREFUL!

The radius is cubed, not squared, for the volume of a sphere.

Example

A sphere has a radius of 3 centimeters. Find the volume of a sphere in cubic centimeters.

A. 18π B. 27π C. 36π D. 45π

The correct answer is **C**. The correct solution is 36π. Substitute the values into the formula and simplify using the order of operations, $V = \frac{4}{3}\pi r^3 = \frac{4}{3}\pi 3^3 = \frac{4}{3}\pi(27) = 36\pi$ cubic centimeters.

Let's Review!

- The volume is the capacity of a three-dimensional object and is expressed in cubic units.
- The volume formula for a cylinder is the product of the area of the base (which is a circle) and the height of the cylinder.
- The volume formula for a pyramid or cone is one-third of the product of the area of the base (a circle in the case of the cone) and the height of the pyramid or cone.
- The volume formula for a sphere is $V = \frac{4}{3}\pi r^3$.

CHAPTER 3 GEOMETRY AND MEASUREMENT PRACTICE QUIZ 1

1. A circular dinner plate has a diameter of 13 inches. A ring is placed along the edge of the plate. Find the circumference of the ring in inches. Use 3.14 for π.

   A. 31.4

   B. 40.82

   C. 62.8

   D. 81.64

2. The area of a half circle is 48 square centimeters. Find the circumference of the curved portion of the half circle to the nearest tenth of a centimeter. Use 3.14 for π.

   A. 17.3

   B. 24.5

   C. 34.5

   D. 49.0

3. Identify the diameter of the circle.

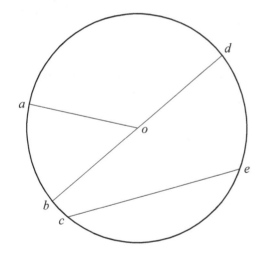

   A. $\overline{AO}$

   B. $\overline{BD}$

   C. $\overline{CE}$

   D. $\overline{AC}$

4. What is the intersection of two walls in a room?

   A. A ray

   B. A line

   C. A point

   D. A plane

5. What points in the diagram are collinear?

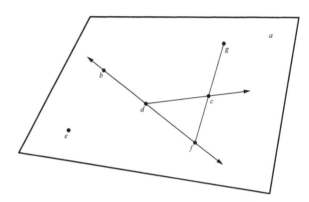

   A. Points D, C, and F

   B. Points B, D, and F

   C. Points B, C, and E

   D. Points B, C, and D

6. What is the order of rotational symmetry for a parallelogram?

   A. 1

   B. 2

   C. 3

   D. 4

7. A rectangular pyramid has a length of 10 centimeters, a width of 11 inches, and a height of 12 inches. Find the volume in cubic inches.

   A. 220

   B. 440

   C. 660

   D. 880

8. A sphere has a volume of 972π cubic millimeters. Find the radius in millimeters.

   A. 3

   B. 9

   C. 27

   D. 81

9. Find the height in centimeters of a cylinder with a volume of 800π cubic centimeters and a radius of 10 centimeters.

   A. 8

   B. 10

   C. 40

   D. 80

10. A regular hexagon has a side length of 5 inches and an apothem of 2 inches. Find the area in square inches.

    A. 30

    B. 40

    C. 50

    D. 60

11. Given the coordinates for a square $(-3, -5), (-3, 4), (6, 4)(6, -5)$, find the length of each side of the square.

    A. 3 units

    B. 6 units

    C. 9 units

    D. 12 units

12. A stop sign is a regular octagon with an area of 27,000 square centimeters and an apothem of 90 centimeters. What is the length in centimeters of one side?

    A. 38

    B. 75

    C. 300

    D. 600

CHAPTER 3 GEOMETRY AND MEASUREMENT PRACTICE QUIZ 1 – ANSWER KEY

1. B. The correct solution is 40.82 because $C = \pi d \approx 3.14(13) \approx 40.82$ inches. **See Lesson: Circles.**

2. A. The correct solution is 17.3. $A = \frac{1}{2}\pi r^2; 48 = \frac{1}{2}(3.14)r^2; 48 = 1.57 r^2; 30.57 = r^2; r \approx 5.5$ centimeters. $C = \frac{1}{2}(2\pi r); C = \frac{1}{2}(2)(3.14)(5.5) \approx 17.3$ centimeters. **See Lesson: Circles.**

3. B. The correct solution is $\overline{BD}$ because B and D are on the circle and the segment goes through the center of the circle. **See Lesson: Circles.**

4. B. The correct solution is a line. The walls are two planes, and two planes intersect at a line. **See Lesson: Congruence.**

5. B. The correct solution is points B, D, and F because these points are line $\overleftrightarrow{BF}$. **See Lesson: Congruence.**

6. B. The correct solution is 2. For a parallelogram, there is rotational symmetry every 180°. **See Lesson: Congruence.**

7. B. The correct solution is 440. Substitute the values into the formula and simplify using the order of operations, $V = \frac{1}{3}Bh = \frac{1}{3}lwh = \frac{1}{3}(10)(11)12 = 440$ cubic inches. **See Lesson: Measurement and Dimension.**

8. B. The correct solution is 9 millimeters. Substitute the values into the formula, $972\pi = \frac{4}{3}\pi r^3$, then multiply by the reciprocal, $729 = r^3$, and apply the cube root, $r = 9$ millimeters. **See Lesson: Measurement and Dimension.**

9. A. The correct solution is 8. Substitute the values into the formula, $800\pi = \pi 10^2 h$, and apply the exponent, $800\pi = \pi(100)h$. Then, divide both sides of the equation by 100π, $h = 8$ centimeters. **See Lesson: Measurement and Dimension.**

10. A. The correct solution is 30. Substitute the values into the formula and simplify using the order of operations, $A = \frac{1}{2}ap = \frac{1}{2}(2)(6(5)) = 30$ square inches. **See Lesson: Similarity, Right Triangles, and Trigonometry.**

11. C. The correct solution 9 units. The difference between the x-coordinates is $6-(-3) = 9$ units, and the difference between the y-coordinates is $4-(-5) = 9$ units. **See Lesson: Similarity, Right Triangles, and Trigonometry.**

12. B. The correct solution is 75. Substitute the values into the formula, $27{,}000 = \frac{1}{2}(90)p$ and simplify using the order of operations, $27{,}000 = 45p$. Divide both sides of the equation by 45 to find the perimeter, $p = 600$ centimeters. Divide the perimeter by 8 to find the length of 75 centimeters for each side. **See Lesson: Similarity, Right Triangles, and Trigonometry.**

CHAPTER 3 GEOMETRY AND MEASUREMENT PRACTICE QUIZ 2

1. A half circle has an area of 45 square centimeters. Find the diameter to the nearest tenth of a centimeter. Use 3.14 for π.

   A. 2.7   C. 10.8

   B. 5.4   D. 16.2

2. Find the area in square centimeters of a circle with a diameter of 16 centimeters. Use 3.14 for π.

   A. 25.12   C. 100.48

   B. 50.24   D. 200.96

3. A dime has a radius of 8.5 millimeters. Find the circumference in millimeters of the dime. Use 3.14 for π.

   A. 11.64   C. 53.38

   B. 26.69   D. 106.76

4. Select the square with the correct lines of symmetry.

   A.

   B.

   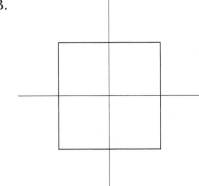

   C.

   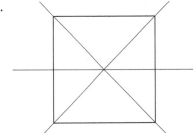

   D.

   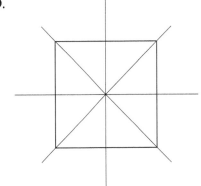

5. **Identify the coplanar points in the diagram.**

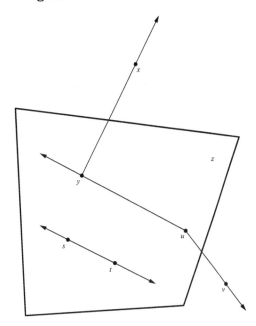

   A. Points S, T, U, and Y

   B. Points X, V, S, and Z

   C. Points X, Y, U, and V

   D. Points U, Y, Z, and T

6. **What shape is used to measure the distance between two cities on a map?**

   A. A ray   C. A point

   B. A line   D. A line segement

7. **A package of a toy is a cylinder with a cone on top. The radius of the figure is 2 feet, the height of the cylinder is 3 feet, and the height of the cone is 3 feet. Find the volume to the nearest cubic foot. Use 3.14 for π.**

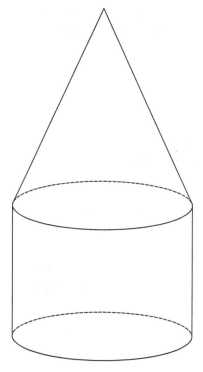

   A. 12   C. 50

   B. 38   D. 76

8. **Find the radius in meters of a cone with a volume of $\frac{640}{3}\pi$ cubic meters and a height of 8 meters.**

   A. 2   C. 6

   B. 4   D. 8

9. **A square pyramid has a volume of 189 cubic feet and a height of 7 feet. Find the length in feet of a side of the base.**

   A. 3   C. 12

   B. 9   D. 18

10. A wedge of cheese is in the shape of a right triangular prism. The area of the base is 30 square inches. What is the height in inches of the cheese if the volume is 150 cubic inches?

   A. 2.5 C. 7.5

   B. 5 D. 10

11. A house is located at (15,30). The next house is 100 meters away. What could be the coordinate of the second house?

   A. (15, 30) C. (115, 15)

   B. (30, 15) D. (115, 30)

12. A trapezoid has bases of 8 inches and 12 inches and a height of 6 inches. Find the area in square inches.

   A. 18 C. 60

   B. 20 D. 72

CHAPTER 3 GEOMETRY AND MEASUREMENT PRACTICE QUIZ 2 – ANSWER KEY

1. C. The correct solution is 10.8 because $A = \frac{1}{2}\pi r^2; 45 = \left(\frac{1}{2}\right)3.14\,r^2; 45 = 1.57\,r^2 = 28.66 = r^2; r \approx 5.4$. The diameter is twice the radius, or about 10.8 centimeters. **See Lesson: Circles.**

2. D. The correct solution is 200.96. The radius is 8 centimeters and $A = \pi r^2 \approx 3.14(8)^2 \approx 3.14(64) \approx 200.96$ square centimeters. **See Lesson: Circles.**

3. C. The correct solution is 53.38 because $C = 2\pi r \approx (2)3.14(8.5) \approx 53.38$ millimeters. **See Lesson: Circles.**

4. D. The correct solution is the square with four lines of symmetry. There is a horizontal line, a vertical line, and two diagonals of symmetry that map the rectangle onto itself. **See Lesson: Congruence.**

5. A. The correct solution is points S, T, U, and Y because these four points are in plane Z. **See Lesson: Congruence.**

6. D. The correct solution is line segment because the cities represent the endpoints and the segment is the distance between the two points. **See Lesson: Congruence.**

7. C. The correct solution is 50 cubic feet. Substitute the values into the formula and simplify using the order of operations, $V = \pi r^2 h + \frac{1}{3}\pi r^2 h = \frac{4}{3}\pi r^2 h = \frac{4}{3}(3.14)\,2^2(3) = \frac{4}{3}(3.14)(4)(3) = 50$ cubic feet. **See Lesson: Measurement and Dimension.**

8. D. The correct solution is 8 meters. Substitute the values into the formula, $\frac{640}{3}\pi = \frac{1}{3}\pi r^2 (8)$ and simplify the right side of the equation, $\frac{640}{3}\pi = \frac{8}{3}\pi r^2$. Multiply by the reciprocal of $\frac{3}{8\pi}$ with a result of $64 = r^2$, and apply the square root, $r = 8$ meters. **See Lesson: Measurement and Dimension.**

9. B. The correct solution is 9. Substitute the values into the formula, $189 = \frac{1}{3}s^2(7)$ and simplify the right side of the equation, $189 = \frac{7}{3}s^2$. Multiply both sides by the reciprocal and apply the square root, $81 = s^2, s = 9$ feet. **See Lesson: Measurement and Dimension.**

10. B. The correct solution is 5. Substitute the values into the formula, $150 = 30h$. Divide both sides of the equation by 30, $h = 5$ inches. **See Lesson: Similarity, Right Triangles, and Trigonometry.**

11. D. The correct solution is (115, 30) because 100 can be added to the x-coordinate, $15 + 100 = 115$. **See Lesson: Similarity, Right Triangles, and Trigonometry.**

12. C. The correct solution is 60. Substitute the values into the formula and simplify using the order of operations, $A = \frac{1}{2}h(b_1 + b_2) = \frac{1}{2}(6)(8 + 12) = \frac{1}{2}(6)(20) = 60$ square inches. **See Lesson: Similarity, Right Triangles, and Trigonometry.**

CHAPTER 4 DATA ANALYSIS, STATISTICS, AND PROBABILITY

INTERPRETING GRAPHICS

This lesson discusses how to create a bar, line, and circle graph and how to interpret data from these graphs. It also explores how to calculate and interpret the measures of central tendency.

Creating a Line, Bar, and Circle Graph

A line graph is a graph with points connected by segments that examines changes over time. The horizontal axis contains the independent variable (the input value), which is usually time. The vertical axis contains the dependent variable (the output value), which is an item that measures a quantity. A line graph will have a title and an appropriate scale to display the data. The graph can include more than one line.

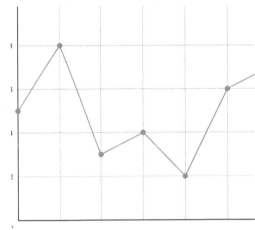

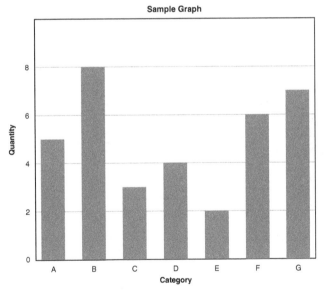

A bar graph uses rectangular horizontal or vertical bars to display information. A bar graph has categories on the horizontal axis and the quantity on the vertical axis. Bar graphs need a title and an appropriate scale for the frequency. The graph can include more than one bar.

BE CAREFUL

Make sure to use the appropriate scale for each type of graph.

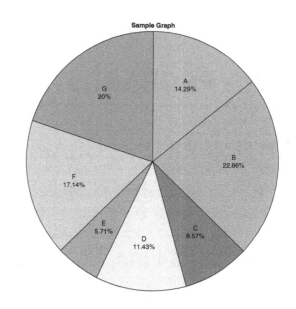

A circle graph is a circular chart that is divided into parts, and each part shows the relative size of the value. To create a circle graph, find the total number and divide each part by the total to find the percentage. Then, to find the part of the circle, multiply each percent by 360°. Draw each part of the circle and create a title.

Examples

1. The table shows the amount of rainfall in inches. Select the line graph that represents this data.

Day	1	2	3	4	5	6	7	8	9	10	11	12
Rainfall Amount	0.5	0.2	0.4	1.1	1.6	0.9	0.7	1.3	1.5	0.8	0.5	0.1

A.

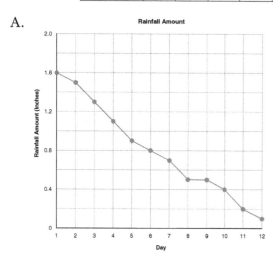

C.

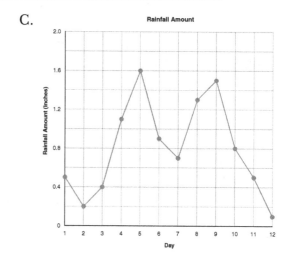

B.

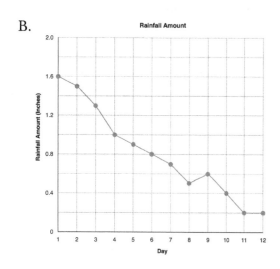

D.

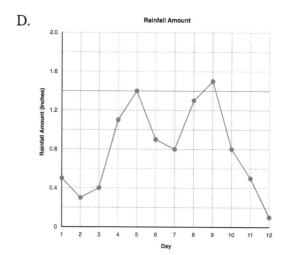

The correct answer is **C**. The graph is displayed correctly for the days with the appropriate labels.

2. **Students were surveyed about their favorite pet, and the table shows the results. Select the bar graph that represents this data.**

Pet	Quantity
Dog	14
Cat	16
Fish	4
Bird	8
Gerbil	7
Pig	3

A.
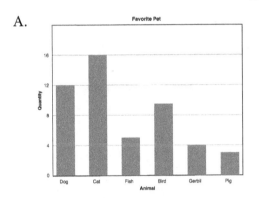

C.
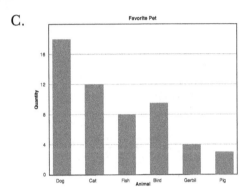

B.
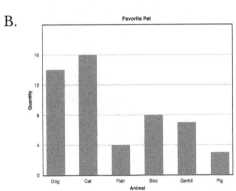

D.
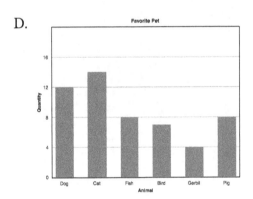

The correct answer is **B**. The bar graph represents each pet correctly and is labeled correctly.

3. The table shows the amount a family spends each month. Select the circle graph that represents the data.

Item	Food/Household Items	Bills	Mortgage	Savings	Miscellaneous
Amount	$700	$600	$400	$200	$100

A.

C.

B.

D.

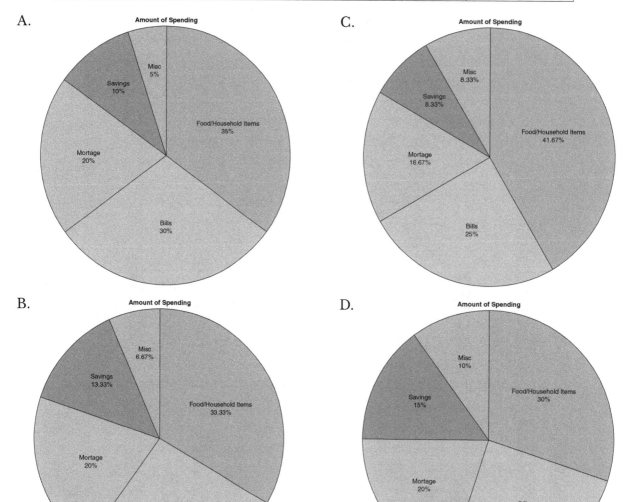

The correct answer is **A**. The total amount spent each month is $2,000. The section of the circle for food and household items is $\frac{700}{2,000} = 0.35 = 35\%$. The section of the circle for bills is $\frac{600}{2,000} = 0.30 = 30\%$. The section of the circle for mortgage is $\frac{400}{2,000} = 0.20 = 20\%$. The section of the circle for savings is $\frac{200}{2,000} = 0.10 = 10\%$. The section of the circle for miscellaneous is $\frac{100}{2,000} = 0.05 = 5\%$.

Interpreting and Evaluating Line, Bar, and Circle Graphs

Graph and charts are used to create visual examples of information, and it is important to be able to interpret them. The examples from Section 1 can show a variety of conclusions.

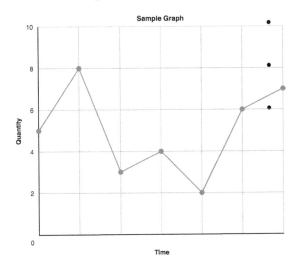

The minimum value is 2, and the maximum value is 8.

The largest decrease is between the second and third points.

The largest increase is between the fifth and sixth points.

KEEP IN MIND

Read and determine the parts of the graph before answering questions related to the graph.

- Category B is the highest with 8.
- Category E is the lowest with 2.
- There are no categories that are the same.

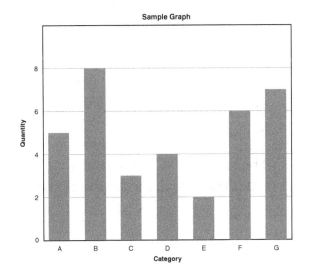

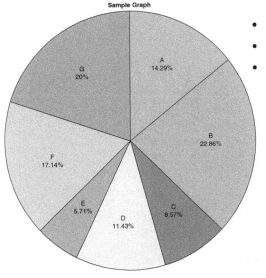

- Category B is the largest with 22.86%.
- Category E is the smallest with 5.71%.
- All of the categories are less than one-fourth of the graph.

Examples

1. The line chart shows the number of minutes a commuter drove to work during a month. Which statement is true for the line chart?

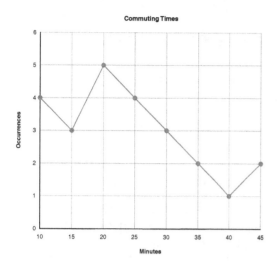

A. The commuter drove 25 minutes to work the most times

B. The commuter drove 25 minutes to work the fewest times.

C. The commuter took 10 minutes and 25 minutes twice during the month.

D. The commuter took 35 minutes and 45 minutes twice during the month.

The correct answer is **D**. The commuter took 35 minutes and 45 minutes twice during the month.

2. The bar chart shows the distance different families traveled for summer vacation. Which statement is true for the bar chart?

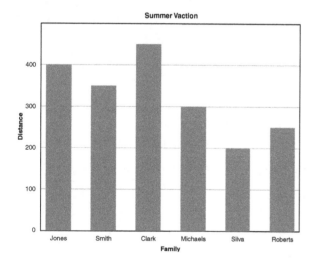

A. All families drove more than 200 miles.

B. The Clark family traveled 250 miles more than the Silva family.

C. The Roberts family traveled more miles than the Michaels family.

D. The Jones family is the only family that traveled 400 miles or more.

The correct answer is **B**. The correct solution is the Clark family traveled 250 miles more than the Silva family. The Clark family traveled 450 miles, and the Silva family traveled 200 miles, making the difference 250 miles.

3. **Students were interviewed about their favorite subject in school. The circle graph shows the results. Which statement is true for the circle graph?**

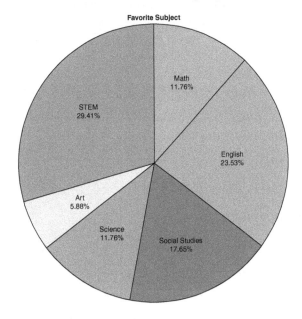

A. Math is the smallest percent for favorite subject.

B. The same number of students favor science and social studies.

C. English and STEM together are more than half of the respondents.

D. English and social students together are more than half of the respondents.

The correct answer is **C**. The correct solution is English and STEM together are more than half of the respondents because these values are more than 50% combined.

Mean, Median, Mode, and Range

The mean, median, mode, and range are common values related to data sets. These values can be calculated using the data set 2, 4, 7, 6, 8, 5, 6, and 3.

The mean is the sum of all numbers in a data set divided by the number of elements in the set. The sum of items in the data set is 41. Divide the value of 41 by the 8 items in the set. The mean is 5.125.

The median is the middle number of a data set when written in order. If there are an odd number of items, the median is the middle number. If there are an even number of items, the median is the mean of the middle two numbers. The

KEEP IN MIND

The mean, median, mode, and range can have the same values, depending on the data set.

numbers in order are 2, 3, 4, 5, 6, 6, 7, 8. The middle two numbers are 5 and 6. The mean of the two middle numbers is 5.5, which is the median.

The mode is the number or numbers that occur most often. There can be no modes, one mode, or many modes. In the data set, the number 6 appears twice, making 6 the mode.

The range is the difference between the highest and lowest values in a data set. The highest value is 8 and the lowest value is 2, for a range of 6.

Examples

1. Find the mean and the median for the data set 10, 20, 40, 20, 30, 50, 40, 60, 30, 10, 40, 20, 50, 70, and 80.

   A. The mean is 40, and the median is 38.

   B. The mean is 38, and the median is 40.

   C. The mean is 36, and the median is 50.

   D. The mean is 50, and the median is 36.

   The correct answer is **B**. The correct solution is the mean is 38 and the median is 40. The sum of all items is 570 divided by 15, which is 38. The data set in order is 10, 10, 20, 20, 20, 30, 30, 40, 40, 40, 50, 50, 60, 70, 80. The median number is 40.

2. Find the mode and the range for the data set 10, 20, 40, 20, 30, 50, 40, 60, 30, 10, 40, 20, 50, 70, and 80.

   A. The mode is 20, and the range is 70.

   B. The mode is 40, and the range is 70.

   C. The modes are 20 and 40, and the range is 70.

   D. The modes are 20, 40, and 70, and the range is 70.

   The correct answer is **C**. The correct solution is the modes are 20 and 40 and the range is 70. The modes are 20 and 40 because each of these numbers appears three times. The range is the difference between 80 and 10, which is 70.

Let's Review!

- A bar graph, line graph, and circle graph are different ways to summarize and represent data.
- The mean, median, mode, and range are values that can be used to interpret the meaning of a set of numbers.

STATISTICAL MEASURES

This lesson explores the different sampling techniques using random and non-random sampling. The lesson also distinguishes among different study techniques. In addition, it provides simulations that compare results with expected outcomes.

Probability and Non-Probability Sampling

A population includes all items within a set of data, while a sample consists of one or more observations from a population.

The collection of data samples from a population is an important part of research and helps researcher draw conclusions related to populations. Probability sampling creates a sample from a population by using random sampling techniques.

> **KEEP IN MIND**
> Probability sampling is random, and non-probability sampling is not random.

Every person within a population has an equal chance of being selected for a sample. Non-probability sampling creates a sample from a population without using random sampling techniques.

There are four types of probability sampling. Simple random sampling is assigning a number to each member of a population and randomly selecting numbers. Stratified sampling uses simple random sampling after the population is split into equal groups. Systematic sampling chooses every n^{th} member from a list or a group. Cluster random sampling uses natural groups in a population: the population is divided into groups, and random samples are collected from groups.

Each type of probability sampling has an advantage and a disadvantage when finding an appropriate sample.

Probability Sampling	Advantage	Disadvantage
Simple random sampling	Most cases have a sample representative of a population	Not efficient for large samples
Stratified random sampling	Creates layers of random samples from different groups representative of a population	Not efficient for large samples
Systematic sampling	Creates a sample representative of population without a random number selection	Not as random as simple random sampling
Cluster random sampling	Relatively easy and convenient to implement	Might not work if clusters are different from one another

There are four types of non-probability sampling. Convenience sampling produces samples that are easy to access. Volunteer sampling asks for volunteers or recommendations for a sample. Purposive sampling bases samples on specific characteristics by selecting samples from a group that meets the qualifications of the study. Quota sampling is choosing samples of groups of the subpopulation.

Examples

1. A factory is studying the quality of beverage samples. There are 50 bottles randomly chosen from one shipment every 60 minutes. What type of sampling is used?

   A. Systematic sampling

   B. Simple random sampling

   C. Cluster random sampling

   D. Stratified random sampling

   The correct answer is **C**. The correct solution is cluster random sampling because bottles of beverage are selected within specific boundaries.

2. A group conducting a survey asks a person for his or her opinion. Then, the group asks the person being surveyed for the names of 10 friends to obtain additional options. What type of sampling is used?

   A. Quota sampling

   B. Volunteer sampling

   C. Purposive sampling

   D. Convenience sampling

   The correct answer is **B**. The correct solution is volunteer sampling because the group is looking for recommendations.

Census, Surveys, Experiments, Observational Studies

Various sampling techniques are used to collect data from a population. These are in the form of a census, a survey, observational studies, or experiments.

KEEP IN MIND

A census includes everyone within a population, and a survey includes every subject of a sample. An observational study involves watching groups randomly, and an experiment involves assigning groups.

A census collects data by asking everyone in a population the same question. Asking everyone at school or everyone at work are examples of a census. A survey collects data on every subject within a sample. The subjects can be determined by convenience sampling or by simple random sampling. Examples of surveys are asking sophomores at school or first shift workers at work.

In an observational study, data collection occurs by watching or observing an event. Watching children who play outside and observing if they drink water or sports drinks is an example. An experiment is way of finding information by assigning people to groups and collecting data on observations. Assigning one group of children to drink water and another group to drink sports drinks after playing and making comparisons is an example of an experiment.

Examples

1. **A school wants to create a census to identify students' favorite subject in school. Which group should the school ask?**

   A. All staff

   B. All students

   C. All sophomores

   D. All male students

   The correct answer is **B**. The correct solution is all students because this gathers information on the entire population.

2. **A researcher records the arrival time of employees at a job based on their actual start time. What type of study is this?**

   A. Census

   B. Survey

   C. Experiment

   D. Observational study

   The correct answer is **D**. The correct solution is observational study because the researcher is observing the time the employees arrive at work.

3. **The local county wants to test the water quality of a stream by collecting samples. What should the county collect?**

   A. The water quality at one spot

   B. The water quality under trees

   C. The water quality under bridges

   D. The water quality at different spots

   The correct answer is **D**. The correct solution is the water quality at different spots because this survey allows for the collection of different samples.

Simulations

A simulation enables researchers to study real-world events by modeling events. Advantages of simulations are that they are quick, easy, and inexpensive; the disadvantage is that the results are approximations. The steps to complete a simulation are as follows:

KEEP IN MIND

A simulation is only useful if the results closely mirror real-world outcomes.

- Describe the outcomes.
- Assign a random value to the outcomes.
- Choose a source to generate the outcomes.
- Generate values for the outcomes until a consistent pattern emerges.
- Analyze the results.

Examples

1. **A family has two children and wants to simulate the gender of the children. Which object would be beneficial to use for the simulation?**

   A. Coin

   B. Four-section spinner

   C. Six-sided number cube

   D. Random number generator

   The correct answer is **B**. The correct solution is a four-section spinner because there are four possible outcomes of the event (boy/boy, boy/girl, girl/boy, and girl/girl).

2. **There are six options from which to choose a meal at a festival. A model using a six-sided number cube is used to represent the simulation.**

Hamburger	Chicken	Hot Dog	Bratwurst	Pork Chop	Fish	Total
1	2	3	4	5	6	
83	82	85	89	86	75	500

   Choose the statement that correctly answers whether the simulation of using a six-sided number cube is consistent with the actual number of dinners sold and then explains why or why not.

   A. The simulation is consistent because it has six equally likely outcomes.

   B. The simulation is consistent because it has two equally likely outcomes.

   C. The simulation is not consistent because of the limited number of outcomes.

   D. The simulation is not consistent because of the unlimited number of outcomes.

   The correct answer is **A**. The correct solution is the simulation is consistent because it has six equally likely outcomes. The six-sided number cube provides consistent outcomes because there is an equal opportunity to select any dinner.

Let's Review!

- Probability (random) sampling and non-probability (not random) sampling are ways to collect data.
- Censuses, surveys, experiments, and observational studies are ways to collect data from a population.
- A simulation is way to model random events and compare the results to real-world outcomes.

STATISTICS & PROBABILITY: THE RULES OF PROBABILITY

This lesson explores a sample space and its outcomes and provides an introduction to probability, including how to calculate expected values and analyze decisions based on probability.

Sample Space

A **sample space** is the set of all possible outcomes. Using a deck of cards labeled 1–10, the sample space is 1, 2, 3, 4, 5, 6, 7, 8, 9, and 10. An **event** is a subset of the sample space. For example, if a card is drawn and the outcome of the event is an even number, possible results are 2, 4, 6, 8, 10.

The **union** of two events is everything in both events, and the notation is $A \bigcup B$. The union of events is associated with the word *or*. For example, a card is drawn that is either a multiple of 3 or a multiple of 4. The set containing the multiples of 3 is 3, 6, and 9. The set containing the multiples of 4 is 4 and 8. The union of the set is 3, 4, 6, 8, and 9.

> **KEEP IN MIND**
> The intersection of an event can have no values. The intersection of drawing a card that is even and odd is a set with no values because a card cannot be both even and odd. The complement of an event is the "not," or the opposite of, the event.

The **intersection** of two events is all of the events in both sets, and the notation is $A \bigcap B$. The intersection of events is associated with the word *and*. For example, a card is drawn that is even and a multiple of 4. The set containing even numbers is 2, 4, 6, 8, and 10. The set containing the multiples of 4 is 4 and 8. The intersection is 4 and 8 because these numbers are in both sets.

The **complement** of an event is an outcome that is not part of the set. The complement of an event is associated with the word *not*. A card is drawn and is not a multiple of 5. The set not containing multiples of 5 is 1, 2, 3, 4, 6, 7, 8, and 9. The complement of not a multiple of 5 is 1, 2, 3, 4, 6, 7, 8, and 9.

Examples

Use the following table of the results when rolling two six-sided number cubes.

1, 1	1, 2	1, 3	1, 4	1, 5	1, 6
2, 1	2, 2	2, 3	2, 4	2, 5	2, 6
3, 1	3, 2	3, 3	3, 4	3, 5	3, 6
4, 1	4, 2	4, 3	4, 4	4, 5	4, 6
5, 1	5, 2	5, 3	5, 4	5, 5	5, 6
6, 1	6, 2	6, 3	6, 4	6, 5	6, 6

1. **How many possible outcomes are there for the union of rolling a sum of 3 or a sum of 5?**

   A. 2   B. 4   C. 6   D. 8

   The correct answer is **C**. The correct solution is 6 possible outcomes. There are two options for the first event (2, 1) and (1, 2). There are 4 options for the second event (4, 1), (3, 2), (2, 3), and (1, 4). The union of two events is six possible outcomes.

2. **How many possible outcomes are there for the intersection of rolling a double and a multiple of 3?**

   A. 0   B. 2   C. 4   D. 6

   The correct answer is **B**. The correct solution is 2 possible outcomes. There are six options for the first event (1, 1), (2, 2), (3, 3), (4, 4), (5, 5), and (6, 6). There are 12 options for the second event of the multiple of three. The intersection is (3, 3) and (6, 6) because these numbers meet both requirements.

3. **How many possible outcomes are there for the complement of rolling a 3 and a 5?**

   A. 16   B. 18   C. 27   D. 36

   The correct answer is **A**. The correct solution is 16 possible outcomes. There are 16 options of not rolling a 3 or a 5.

Probability

The **probability** of an event is the number of favorable outcomes divided by the total number of possible outcomes.

$$Probability = \frac{number\ of\ favorable\ outcomes}{number\ of\ possible\ outcomes}$$

Probability is a value between 0 (event does not happen) and 1 (event will happen). For example, the probability of getting heads when a coin is flipped is $\frac{1}{2}$ because heads is 1 option out of 2 possibilities.

> **BE CAREFUL!**
> Make sure that you apply the correct formula for the probability of an event.

The probability of rolling an odd number on a six-sided number cube is $\frac{3}{6} = \frac{1}{2}$ because there are three odd numbers, 1, 3, and 5, out of 6 possible numbers.

The probability of an "or" event happening is the sum of the events happening. For example, the probability of rolling an odd number or a 4 on a six-sided number cube is $\frac{4}{6}$. The probability of rolling an odd number is $\frac{3}{6}$, and the probability of rolling a 4 is $\frac{1}{6}$. Therefore, the probability is $\frac{3}{6} + \frac{1}{6} = \frac{4}{6} = \frac{2}{3}$.

The probability of an "and" event happening is the product of the probability of two or more events. The probability of rolling 6 three times in a row is $\frac{1}{216}$. The probability of a single event is $\frac{1}{6}$, and this fraction is multiplied three times to find the probability, $\frac{1}{6} \times \frac{1}{6} \times \frac{1}{6}$. There are cases of "with replacement" when the item is returned to the pile and "without replacement" when the item is not returned to the pile.

The probability of a "not" event happening is 1 minus the probability of the event occurring. For example, the probability of not rolling 6 three times in a row is $1-\frac{1}{216}=\frac{215}{216}$.

Examples

1. **A deck of cards contains 40 cards divided into 4 colors: red, blue, green, and yellow. Each group has cards numbered 0–9. What is the probability of selecting an 8?**

   A. $\frac{1}{10}$ B. $\frac{1}{8}$ C. $\frac{1}{4}$ D. $\frac{1}{2}$

   The correct answer is **A**. The correct solution is $\frac{1}{10}$. There are 4 cards out of 40 that contain the number 8, making the probability $\frac{4}{40}=\frac{1}{10}$.

2. **A deck of cards contains 40 cards divided into 4 colors: red, blue, green, and yellow. Each group has cards numbered 0–9. What is the probability of selecting an even or a red card?**

   A. $\frac{1}{4}$ B. $\frac{3}{8}$ C. $\frac{5}{8}$ D. $\frac{3}{4}$

   The correct answer is **C**. The correct solution is $\frac{5}{8}$. There are 20 even cards and 10 red cards. The overlap of 5 red even cards is subtracted from the probability, $\frac{20}{40}+\frac{10}{40}-\frac{5}{40}=\frac{25}{40}=\frac{5}{8}$.

3. **A deck of cards contains 40 cards divided into 4 colors: red, blue, green, and yellow. Each group has cards numbered 0–9. What is the probability of selecting a blue card first, replacing the card, and selecting a 9?**

   A. $\frac{1}{100}$ B. $\frac{1}{80}$ C. $\frac{1}{40}$ D. $\frac{1}{20}$

   The correct answer is **C**. The correct solution is $\frac{1}{40}$. There are 10 blue cards and 4 cards that contain the number 9. The probability of the event is $\frac{10}{40}\times\frac{4}{40}=\frac{40}{1600}=\frac{1}{40}$.

4. **A deck of cards contains 40 cards divided into 4 colors: red, blue, green, and yellow. Each group has cards numbered 0–9. What is the probability of NOT selecting a green card?**

   A. $\frac{1}{4}$ B. $\frac{3}{8}$ C. $\frac{1}{2}$ D. $\frac{3}{4}$

   The correct answer is **D**. The correct solution is $\frac{3}{4}$. There are 10 cards that are green, making the probability of NOT selecting a green card $1-\frac{10}{40}=\frac{30}{40}=\frac{3}{4}$.

Calculating Expected Values and Analyzing Decisions Based on Probability

The **expected value** of an event is the sum of the products of the probability of an event times the payoff of an event. A good example is calculating the expected value for buying a lottery ticket. There is a one in a hundred million chance that a person would win $50 million. Each ticket costs $2. The expected value is

$$\frac{1}{100,000,000}(50,000,000-2)+\frac{99,999,999}{100,000,000}(-2)=\frac{49,999,998}{100,000,000}-\frac{199,999,998}{100,000,000}=-\frac{150,000,000}{100,000,000}=-\$1.50$$

On average, one should expect to lose $1.50 each time the game is played. Analyzing the

BE CAREFUL!

The expected value will not be the same as the actual value unless the probability of winning is 100%.

information, the meaning of the data shows that playing the lottery would result in losing money every time.

Examples

1. **What is the expected value of an investment if the probability is $\frac{1}{5}$ of losing \$1,000, $\frac{1}{4}$ of no gain, $\frac{2}{5}$ of making \$1,000, and $\frac{3}{20}$ of making \$2,000?**

   A. \$0   B. \$200   C. \$500   D. \$700

   The correct answer is **C**. The correct solution is \$500. The expected value is $\frac{1}{5}(-1,000) + \frac{1}{4}(0) + \frac{2}{5}(1,000) + \frac{3}{20}(2,000) = -200 + 0 + 400 + 300 = \$500$.

2. **The table below shows the value of the prizes and the probability of winning a prize in a contest.**

Prize	\$10	\$100	\$5,000	\$50,000
Probability	1 in 50	1 in 1,000	1 in 50,000	1 in 250,000

   Calculate the expected value.

   A. \$0.10   B. \$0.20   C. \$0.50   D. \$0.60

   The correct answer is **D**. The correct solution is \$0.60. The probability for each event is

Prize	\$10	\$100	\$5,000	\$50,000	Not Winning
Probability	1 in 50 = 0.02	1 in 1,000 = 0.001	1 in 50,000 = 0.00002	1 in 250,000 = 0.000004	0.978976

   The expected value is $0.02(10) + 0.001(100) + 0.00002(5,000) + 0.000004(50,000) + 0.978976(0) = 0.2 + 0.1 + 0.1 + 0.2 + 0 = \$0.60$.

3. **Which option results in the largest loss on a product?**

   A. 40% of gaining \$100,000 and 60% of losing \$100,000

   B. 60% of gaining \$250,000 and 40% of losing \$500,000

   C. 30% of gaining \$400,000 and 70% of losing \$250,000

   D. 60% of gaining \$250,000 and 40% of losing \$450,000

   The correct answer is **C**. The correct solution is 30% of gaining \$400,000 and 70% of losing \$250,000. The expected value is $0.30(400,000) + 0.7(-250,000) = 120,000 + (-175,000) = -55,000$.

Let's Review!

- The sample space is the number of outcomes of an event. The union, the intersection, and the complement are related to the sample space.
- The probability of an event is the number of possible events divided by the total number of outcomes. There can be "and," "or," and "not" probabilities.
- The expected value of an event is based on the payout and probability of an event occurring.

CHAPTER 4 DATA ANALYSIS, STATISTICS, AND PROBABILITY
PRACTICE QUIZ 1

1. Find the median for the data set 34, 31, 37, 35, 38, 33, 39, 32, 36, 35, 37, and 33.

    A. 34   C. 36

    B. 35   D. 37

2. The bar chart shows the number of items collected for a charity drive. What is the total number of items collected for the three highest classes?

    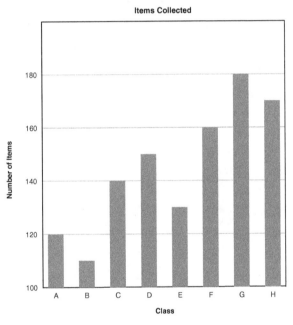

    Items Collected

    A. 500   C. 520

    B. 510   D. 530

3. Find the range for the data set 34, 45, 27, 29, 36, 60, 52, 48, 41, 65, 44, 50, 64, 58, 47, and 31.

    A. 3   C. 36

    B. 5   D. 38

4. A factory is investigating defects in screwdrivers that have been placed in containers to be shipped to stores. Random containers are selected for the team leader to review. What type of sampling is used?

    A. Systematic sampling

    B. Simple random sampling

    C. Cluster random sampling

    D. Stratified random sampling

5. There is an election at a school where 4 candidates out of 10 will be elected. Which object and results are the most appropriate for a simulation?

    A. Toss a coin

    B. Ten-sided number cube and use multiples of 2

    C. Eight-section spinner and use the odd numbers

    D. Throw two six-sided number cubes and use the results of 1 and 6

6. A survey group wants to know the percentage of voters in a town who favor building a new shopping center. What is the survey group's population?

    A. All eligible voters in the town

    B. All people who live in the town

    C. All interviewed people in the town

    D. All voters 35 years and older in the town

7. A bag contains 10 red marbles, 8 black marbles, and 7 white marbles. What is the probability of selecting a black marble first and a red marble second with no replacement?

   A. $\frac{8}{25}$ C. $\frac{2}{15}$

   B. $\frac{16}{125}$ D. $\frac{7}{75}$

8. If a letter is chosen at random from the word SUBSTITUTE, what is the probability that the letter chosen is "S" or "T"?

   A. $\frac{1}{5}$ C. $\frac{2}{5}$

   B. $\frac{3}{10}$ D. $\frac{1}{2}$

9. A spinner contains numbers 1–20. What is the probability of spinning a multiple of 3 or a multiple of 5?

   A. $\frac{3}{10}$ C. $\frac{9}{20}$

   B. $\frac{1}{5}$ D. $\frac{11}{20}$

CHAPTER 4 DATA ANALYSIS, STATISTICS, AND PROBABILITY
PRACTICE QUIZ 1 – ANSWER KEY

1. B. The correct solution is 35. The data set in order is 31, 32, 33, 33, 34, 35, 35, 36, 37, 37, 38, 39, and the middle numbers are both 35. Therefore, the median is 35. **See Lesson: Interpreting Graphics.**

2. B. The correct solution is 510 items because the three largest classes collected 180, 170, and 160 items. **See Lesson: Interpreting Graphics.**

3. D. The correct solution is 38. The difference between the highest value of 65 and the lowest value of 27 is 38. **See Lesson: Interpreting Graphics.**

4. D. The correct solution is stratified random sampling because the screwdrivers are placed into containers and the containers are randomly selected. **See Lesson: Statistical Measures.**

5. B. The correct solution is ten-sided number cube and use multiples of 2 because there are 4 results out of 10 that would match the probability of the actual event. **See Lesson: Statistical Measures.**

6. A. The correct solution is all eligible voters in the town because this is the population for the entire survey. **See Lesson: Statistical Measures.**

7. C. The correct solution is $\frac{2}{15}$. There are 8 marbles out of 25 for the first event and 10 marbles out of 24 for the second event. The probability of the event is $\frac{8}{25} \times \frac{10}{24} = \frac{80}{600} = \frac{2}{15}$. **See Lesson: Statistics & Probability: The Rules of Probability.**

8. D. The correct solution is $\frac{1}{2}$. There are 3 S's and 2 T's in the word SUBTITUTE out of 10 letters. The probability is $\frac{3}{10} + \frac{2}{10} = \frac{5}{10} = \frac{1}{2}$. **See Lesson: Statistics & Probability: The Rules of Probability.**

9. C. The correct solution is $\frac{9}{20}$. There are six multiples of 3 and four multiples of 5. The overlap of 15 is subtracted from the probability, $\frac{6}{20} + \frac{4}{20} - \frac{1}{20} = \frac{9}{20}$. **See Lesson: Statistics & Probability: The Rules of Probability.**

CHAPTER 4 DATA ANALYSIS, STATISTICS, AND PROBABILITY
PRACTICE QUIZ 2

1. The data set represents the number of weekly pop-up ads for 12 families: 125, 145, 150, 130, 150, 120, 170, 165, 175, 145, 150, and 130. Find the median.

   A. 145

   B. 145.5

   C. 147

   D. 147.5

2. Find the mode for the data set 42, 45, 44, 44, 45, 42, 45, 44, 45, 46, 42, 44, 41, 48, 47, 46, 45, 42, 42, and 44.

   A. 42, 43

   B. 44, 45

   C. 42, 44, 45

   D. 42, 43, 44, 45

3. Find the mean for the data set 16, 18, 17, 15, 19, 14, 12, 11, 10, 16, 18, and 17.

   A. 14.25

   B. 15.25

   C. 16

   D. 17

4. A group is conducting a survey at a mall asking shoppers their opinion of the mall. What type of sampling is used?

   A. Quota sampling

   B. Volunteer sampling

   C. Purposive sampling

   D. Convenience sampling

5. At the grocery store, a researcher asks random people about the number of text messages they send daily. What type of study is this?

   A. Census

   B. Survey

   C. Experiment

   D. Observational study

6. At a school, the probability a student has a study hall is two-thirds. What object and results could be used for a simulation of 1,000 times?

   A. Flipping a coin

   B. Playing rock, paper, scissors and looking for rock

   C. Using a four-sided spinner and spinning 1, 2, or 3

   D. Throwing a six-sided number cube and looking for 1, 2, 3, or 4

7. Which option results in the greatest gain on an investment?

   A. 100% of gaining $1,000

   B. 60% of gaining $2,500 and 40% of gaining $0

   C. 75% of gaining $1,000 and 25% of gaining $1,500

   D. 70% of gaining $1,500 and 30% of gaining $1,000

8. In a deck of 20 number cards, cards 1–5 are green, cards 6–10 are red, cards 11–15 are yellow, and cards 16–20 are blue. Describe the complement of even cards.

   A. Odd number cards

   B. Even number cards

   C. Green and red cards

   D. Yellow and blue cards

9. **Which option is the greatest gain on a sale?**

   A. 50% of gaining $8 million and 50% of gaining $7 million

   B. 60% of gaining $9 million and 40% of gaining $6 million

   C. 70% of gaining $10 million and 30% of gaining $5 million

   D. 80% of gaining $11 million and 20% of gaining $4 million

Chapter 4 Data Analysis, Statistics, and Probability
Practice Quiz 2 – Answer Key

1. D. The correct solution is 147.5. The data set written in order is 120, 125, 130, 130, 145, 145, 150, 150, 150, 165, 170, 175. The middle two numbers are 145 and 150, and the mean of the numbers is 147.5. **See Lesson: Interpreting Graphics.**

2. C. The correct solution is 42, 44, and 45. The modes are 42, 44, and 45 because these values appear four times in the data set. **See Lesson: Interpreting Graphics.**

3. B. The correct solution is 15.25. The sum of all items is 183, and 183 and divided by 12 gives a mean of 15.25. **See Lesson: Interpreting Graphics.**

4. D. The correct solution is convenience sampling because the group is at a mall asking shoppers at the mall for their opinions. **See Lesson: Statistical Measures.**

5. B. The correct solution is a survey because the sampling is convenient and only the results are recorded. **See Lesson: Statistical Measures.**

6. D. The correct solution is throwing a six-sided number cube and looking for 1, 2, 3, or 4 because the dice has 4 out of 6, or two-thirds, options to match the probability of the event. **See Lesson: Statistical Measures.**

7. B. The correct solution is 60% of gaining $2,500 and 40% of gaining $0. The expected value is $0.60(2,500) + 0.40(0) = \$1,500$. **See Lesson: Statistics & Probability: The Rules of Probability.**

8. A. The correct solution is odd number cards. The complement of even number cards is odd. **See Lesson: Statistics & Probability: The Rules of Probability.**

9. D. The correct solution is 80% of gaining $11 million and 20% of gaining $4 million. The expected value is $0.80(11) + 0.20(4) = 8.8 + 0.8 = \$9.6$ million. **See Lesson: Statistics & Probability: The Rules of Probability.**

SECTION II
READING

Reading: 24 questions, untimed

Areas assessed: Literary Analysis, Making Inferences & Evaluating an Argument, and The Author's Use of Language

READING TIPS

- If the question doesn't reference something in one of the answers, that answer is probably incorrect. Check to see what is/isn't referenced and choose the best answer from there.
- Do not assume facts about questions. Often, if information is not provided in the question, it will not be relevant. Stick to the facts that are provided.
- Some questions will focus on your ability to determine the difference between opinion and fact. Practice recognizing the difference between fact (the grass is green) and opinion (the grass smells nice).
- Read carefully and slowly. Questions may be confusing if you read too quickly.
- If you think that 2 answers could be correct, ask yourself, "What is it REALLY asking?"
- Study and know different types of writing styles. You may be asked to identify. i.e. narrative, expository, entertaining, analytical, or persuasive writing.
- Know how to identify first person (I), second person (You), third person (Narration).
- Use only the information you are given, if it is not stated in the text then don't assume it to be relevant.
- Use Process of Elimination. Eliminate answers you know are wrong and work your way to one, final answer.
- Know how to use an index, dictionary, almanac, encyclopedia, and glossary.
- Try to improve your reading speed and comprehension in advance. You want to ensure that you can finish the section before the time is up.
- Pay attention to the wording in questions. The wording in the question itself will usually provide helpful hints that can lead you toward the correct answer.

CHAPTER 5 LITERARY ANALYSIS

MAIN IDEAS, TOPIC SENTENCES, AND SUPPORTING DETAILS

To read effectively, you need to know how to identify the most important information in a text. You must also understand how ideas within a text relate to one other.

Main Ideas

The central or most important idea in a text is the **main idea**. As a reader, you need to avoid confusing the main idea with less important details that may be interesting but not central to the author's point.

The **topic** of a text is slightly different than the main idea. The topic is a word or phrase that describes roughly what a text is about. A main idea, in contrast, is a complete sentence that states the topic and explains what an author wants to say about it.

All types of texts can contain main ideas. Read the following informational paragraph and try to identify the main idea:

> The immune system is the body's defense mechanism. It fights off harmful bacteria, viruses, and substances that attack the body. To do this, it uses cells, tissues, and organs that work together to resist invasion.

The topic of this paragraph is the immune system. The main idea can be expressed in a sentence like this: "This paragraph defines and describes the immune system." Ideas about organisms and substances that invade the body are not the central focus. The topic and main idea must always be directly related to every sentence in the text, as the immune system is here.

Read the persuasive paragraph below and consider the topic and main idea:

> Football is not a healthy activity for kids. It causes head injuries that harm the ability to learn and achieve. It causes painful bodily injuries that can linger into adulthood. It teaches aggressive behavioral habits that make life harder for players after they have left the field.

The topic of this paragraph is youth football, and the main idea is that kids should not play the game. Note that if you are asked to state the main idea of a persuasive text, it is your job to be objective. This means you should describe the author's opinion, not make an argument of your own in response.

Both of the example paragraphs above state their main idea explicitly. Some texts have an implicit, or suggested, main idea. In this case, you need to figure out the main idea using the details as clues.

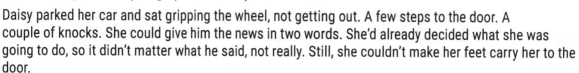

> **FOR EXAMPLE**
>
> The following fictional paragraph has an implicit main idea:
>
> Daisy parked her car and sat gripping the wheel, not getting out. A few steps to the door. A couple of knocks. She could give him the news in two words. She'd already decided what she was going to do, so it didn't matter what he said, not really. Still, she couldn't make her feet carry her to the door.
>
> The main idea here is that Daisy feels reluctant to speak to someone. This point is not stated outright, but it is clear from the details of Daisy's thoughts and actions.

Topic Sentences

Many paragraphs identify the topic and main idea in a single sentence. This is called a **topic sentence,** and it often appears at the beginning of a paragraph. However, a writer may choose to place a topic sentence anywhere in the text.

Some paragraphs contain an introductory sentence to grab the reader's attention before clearly stating the topic. A paragraph may begin by asking a rhetorical question, presenting a striking idea, or showing why the topic is important. When authors use this strategy, the topic sentence usually comes second:

> Have you ever wondered how your body fights off a nasty cold? **It uses a complex defense mechanism called the immune system.** The immune system fights off harmful bacteria, viruses, and substances that attack the body. To do this, it uses cells, tissues, and organs that work together to resist invasion.

Here, the first sentence grabs the attention, and the second, **boldfaced** topic sentence states the main idea. The remaining sentences provide further information, explaining what the immune system does and identifying its basic components.

> **COMPARE!**
>
> The informational paragraph above contains a question that grabs the attention at the beginning. The writer could convey the same information with a little less flair by omitting this device. The version you read in Section 1 does exactly this. (The topic sentence below is **boldfaced.**)
>
> > **The immune system is the body's defense mechanism.** It fights off harmful bacteria, viruses, and substances that attack the body. To do this, it uses cells, tissues, and organs that work together to resist invasion.
>
> Look back at the football paragraph from Section 1. Which sentence is the topic sentence?

Sometimes writers wait until the end of a paragraph to reveal the main idea in a topic sentence. When you're reading a paragraph that is organized this way, you may feel like you're reading a bit of a puzzle. It's not fully clear what the piece is about until you get to the end:

It causes head injuries that harm the ability to learn and achieve. It causes painful bodily injuries that can linger through the passage of years. It teaches aggressive behavioral habits that make life harder for players after they have left the field. **Football is not a healthy activity for kids.**

Note that the topic—football—is not actually named until the final, **boldfaced** topic sentence. This is a strong hint that this final sentence is the topic sentence. Other paragraphs with this structure may contain several examples or related ideas and then tie them together with a summary statement near the end.

Supporting Details

The **supporting details** of a text develop the main idea, contribute further information, or provide examples.

All of the supporting details in a text must relate back to the main idea. In a text that sets out to define and describe the immune system, the supporting details could explain how the immune system works, define parts of the immune system, and so on.

> **Main Idea:** The immune system is the body's defense mechanism.

> **Supporting Detail:** It fights off harmful bacteria, viruses, and substances that attack the body.

> **Supporting Detail:** To do this, it uses cells, tissues, and organs that work together to resist invasion.

The above text could go on to describe white blood cells, which are a vital part of the body's defense system against disease. However, the supporting details in such a text should *not* drift off into descriptions of parts of the body that make no contribution to immune response.

Supporting details may be facts or opinions. A single text can combine both facts and opinions to develop a single main idea.

> **Main Idea:** Football is not a healthy activity for kids.

> **Supporting Detail:** It teaches aggressive behavioral habits that make life harder for players after they have left the field.

> **Supporting Detail:** In a study of teenage football players by Dr. Sophia Ortega at Harvard University, 28% reported involvement in fights or other violent incidents, compared with 19% of teenage boys who were not involved in sports.

The first supporting detail above states an opinion. The second is still related to the main idea, but it provides factual information to back up the opinion. Further development of this paragraph could contain other types of facts, including information about football injuries and anecdotes about real players who got hurt playing the game.

Let's Review!

- The main idea is the most important piece of information in a text.
- The main idea is often expressed in a topic sentence.
- Supporting details develop the main idea, contribute further information, or provide examples.

SUMMARIZING TEXT AND USING TEXT FEATURES

Effective readers need to know how to identify and restate the main idea of a text through summary. They must also follow complex instructions, figure out the sequence of events in a text that is not presented in order, and understand information presented in graphics.

Summary Basics

A **summary** is a text that restates the ideas from a different text in a new way. Every summary needs to include the main idea of the original. Some summaries may include information about the supporting details as well.

The content and level of detail in a summary vary depending on the purpose. For example, a journalist may summarize a recent scientific study in a newspaper profile of its authors. A graduate student might briefly summarize the same study in a paper questioning its conclusions. The journalist's version would likely use fairly simple language and restate only the main points. The student's version would likely use specialized scientific vocabulary and include certain supporting details, especially the ones most applicable to the argument the student intends to make later.

The language of a summary must be substantially different from the original. It should not retain the structure and word choice of the source text. Rather, it should provide a completely new way of stating the ideas.

Read the passage below and the short summary that follows:

Original: There is no need for government regulations to maintain a minimum wage because free market forces naturally adjust wages on their own. Workers are in short supply in our thriving economy, and businesses must offer fair wages and working conditions to attract labor. Business owners pay employees well because common sense dictates that they cannot succeed any other way.

Effective Summary: The author argues against minimum wage laws. He claims free market forces naturally keep wages high in a healthy economy with a limited labor supply.

KEY POINT!

Many ineffective summaries attempt to imitate the structure of the original text and change only individual words. This makes the writing process difficult, and it can lead to unintentional plagiarism.

Ineffective Summary (Plagiarism): It is unnecessary for government regulations to create a minimum wage because capitalism adjusts wages without help. Good labor is rare in our excellent economy, and businesses need to offer fair wages and working conditions in order to attract workers.

The above text is an example of structural plagiarism. Summary writing does not just involve rewriting the original words one by one. An effective summary restates the main ideas of the text in a wholly original way.

The effective summary above restates the main ideas in a new but objective way. Objectivity is a key quality of an effective summary. A summary does not exaggerate, judge, or distort the author's original ideas.

> **Not a Summary:** The author makes a wild and unsupportable claim that minimum wage laws are unnecessary because market forces keep wages high without government intervention.

Although the above text might be appropriate in persuasive writing, it makes its own claims and judgments rather than simply restating the original author's ideas. It would not be an effective sentence in a summary.

In some cases, particularly dealing with creative works like fiction and poetry, summaries may mention ideas that are clearly implied but not stated outright in the original text. For example, a mobster in a thriller novel might turn to another character and say menacingly, "I wouldn't want anything to happen to your sweet little kids." A summary of this passage could objectively say the mobster had threatened the other character. But everything in the summary needs to be clearly supportable in the text. The summary could not go on to say how the other character feels about the threat unless the author describes it.

Attending to Sequence and Instructions

Events happen in a sequence. However, many written texts present events out of order to create an effect on the reader. Nonfiction writers such as journalists and history writers may use this strategy to create surprise or bring particular ideas to the forefront. Fiction writers may interrupt the flow of a plot to interweave bits of a character's history or to provide flashes of insight into future events. Readers need to know how to untangle this presentation of events and figure out what actually happened first, second, and third. Consider the following passage:

> The man in dark glasses was looking for something. He checked his pockets. He checked his backpack. He walked back to his car, unlocked the doors, and inspected the area around the seats. Shaking his head, he re-locked the doors and rubbed his forehead in frustration. When his hand bumped his sunglasses, he finally realized where he had put them.

This passage does not mention putting the sunglasses on until the end, but it is clear from context that the man put them on first, before beginning his search. You can keep track of sequence by paying attention to time words like *when* and *before*, noticing grammatical constructions *he had* that indicate when events happened, and making common sense observations like the fact that the man is wearing his dark glasses in the first sentence.

Sequence is also an important aspect of reading technical and functional documents such as recipes and other instructions. If such documents present many steps in a large text block without illustrations or visual breaks, you may need to break them down and categorize them yourself. Always read all the steps first and think about how to follow them before jumping in. To see why, read the pancake recipe below:

Combine flour, baking powder, sugar, and salt. Break the eggs into a separate bowl. Add milk and oil to the beaten eggs. Combine dry and liquid ingredients and stir. While you are doing the above, put a small amount of oil into a pan and heat it on medium heat. When it is hot, spoon batter onto the pan.

To follow directions like these effectively, a reader must break them down into categories, perhaps even rewriting them in a numbered list and noting when to start steps like heating the pan, which may be worth doing in a different order than it appears above.

Interpreting Graphics

Information is often presented in pictures, graphs, or diagrams. These **graphic elements** may provide information to back up an argument, illustrate factual information or instructions, or present key facts and statistics.

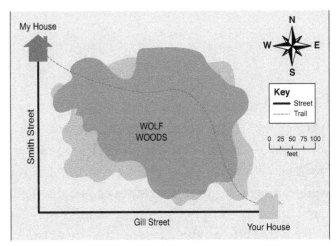

When you read charts and graphs, it is important to look carefully at all the information presented, including titles and labels, to be sure that you are interpreting the visuals correctly.

Diagram

A diagram presents a picture with labels that shows the parts of an object or functions of a mechanism. The diagram of a knee joint below shows the parts of the knee. Like many diagrams, it is placed in relation to a larger object—in this case, a leg—to clarify how the labeled parts fit into a larger context.

Flowchart

A flowchart shows a sequence of actions or decisions involved in a complex process. A flowchart usually begins with an oval-shaped box that asks a yes-no question or gives an instruction. Readers follow arrows indicating possible responses. This helps readers figure out how to solve a problem, or it illustrates how a complex system works.

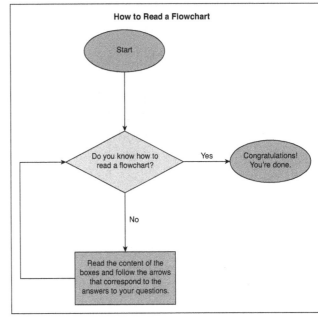

Bar Graph

A bar graph uses bars of different sizes to represent numbers. Larger bars show larger numbers to convey the magnitude of differences between two numeric values at a glance. In this case, each rectangle shows the number of candy bars of different types that a particular group of people ate.

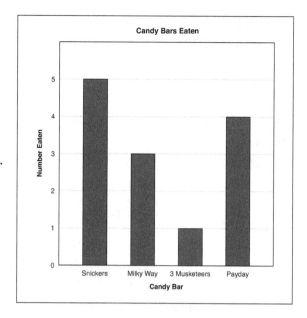

Pie Chart

A pie chart is useful for representing all of something—in this case, the whole group of people surveyed about their favorite kind of pie. Larger wedges mean larger percentages of people liked a particular kind of pie. Percentage values may be written directly on the chart or in a key to the side.

Let's Review!

- A summary restates the main ideas of a text in different words.
- A summary should objectively restate ideas in the present tense and give credit to the original author.
- Effective readers need to mentally reconstruct the basic sequence of events authors present out of order.
- Effective readers need to approach complex instructions by grouping steps into categories or considering how best to approach the steps.
- Information may be presented graphically in the form of diagrams, flowcharts, graphs, or charts.

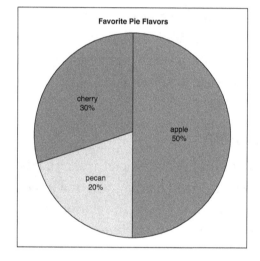

EVALUATING AND INTEGRATING DATA

Effective readers do more than absorb and analyze the content of sentences, paragraphs, and chapters. They recognize the importance of features that stand out in and around the text, and they understand and integrate knowledge from visual features like maps and charts.

Text Features

Elements that stand out from a text are called **text features**. Text features perform many vital functions.

- **Introducing the Topic and Organizing Information**

> **COMPARE!**
> The title on a fictional work does not always state the topic explicitly. While some titles do this, others are more concerned with hinting at a theme or setting up the tone.

- *Titles* – The title of a nonfiction text typically introduces the topic. Titles are guiding features of organization because they give clues about what is and is not covered. The title of this section, "Text Features," covers exactly that—not, for example, implicit ideas.
- *Headings and Subheadings* – Headings and subheadings provide subtopic information about supporting points and let readers scan to see how information is organized. The subheadings of this page organize text features according to the functions they perform.

- **Helping the Reader Find Information**

- *Table of Contents* – The table of contents of a long work lists chapter titles and other large-scale information so readers can predict the content. This helps readers to determine whether or not a text will be useful to them and to find sections relevant to their research.
- *Index* – In a book, the index is an alphabetical list of topics covered, complete with page numbers where the topics are discussed. Readers looking for information on one small subtopic can check the index to find out which pages to view.
- *Footnotes and Endnotes* – When footnotes and endnotes list sources, they allow the reader to find and evaluate the information an author is citing.

- **Emphasizing Concepts**

- *Formatting Features* – Authors may use formatting features such as *italics*, **boldfacing** or underlining to emphasize a word, phrase, or other important information in a text.
- *Bulleting and numbering* – Bullet points and numbered lists set off information and allow readers to scan for bits of information they do not know. It also helps to break down a list of steps.

- **Presenting Information and Illustrating Ideas**

  - *Graphic Elements* – Charts, graphs, diagrams, and other graphic elements present data succinctly, illustrate complex ideas, or otherwise convey information that would be difficult to glean from text alone.

- **Providing Peripheral Information**

  - *Sidebars* – Sidebars are text boxes that contain information related to the topic but not essential to the overall point.

  - *Footnotes and Endnotes* – Some footnotes and endnotes contain information that is not essential to the development of the main point but may nevertheless interest readers and researchers.[1]

FUN FACT!

Online, a sidebar is sometimes called a *doobly doo*.

P.S. This is an example of a sidebar.

Maps and Charts

To read maps and charts, you need to understand what the labels, symbols, and pictures mean. You also need to know how to make decisions using the information they contain.

Maps

Maps are stylized pictures of places as seen from above. A map may have a box labeled "Key" or "Legend" that provides information about the meanings of colors, lines, or symbols. On the map below, the key shows that a solid line is a road and a dotted line is a trail.

There may also be a line labeled "scale" that helps you figure out how far you need to travel to get from one point on the map to another. In the example below, an inch is only 100 feet, so a trip from one end to the other is not far.

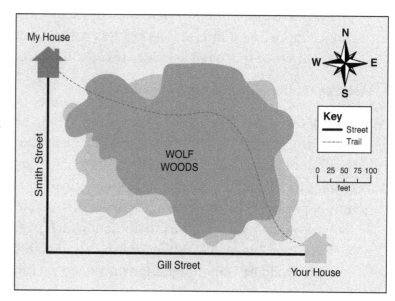

Some maps, including the example above, have compasses that show directions. If no compass is pictured, assume the top of the map is north.

---

[1] Anthony Grafton's book *The Footnote: A Curious History* is an in-depth history of the origins and development of the footnote. (Also, this is an example of a footnote.)

Charts

Nutrition Facts Labels

Nutrition facts labels are charts many people see daily, but not everyone knows how to read them. The top third of the label lists calorie counts, serving sizes, and amount of servings in a package. If a package contains more than one serving, a person who eats the entire contents of the package may be consuming many times the number of calories listed per serving.

The label below lists the content of nutrients such as fats and carbohydrates, and so on. According to the label, a person who eats one serving of the product in the package will ingest 30 mg of cholesterol, or 10% of the total cholesterol he or she should consume in a day.

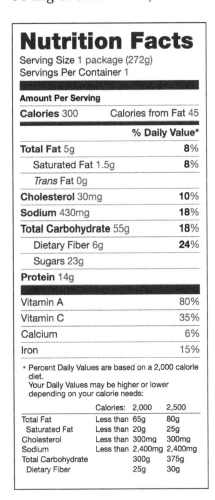

KEEP IN MIND . . .

The percentages on a Nutrition Facts label do not (and are not meant to) add up to 100. Instead, they show how much of a particular nutrient is contained in a serving of the product, as a proportion of a single person's Daily Value for that nutrient. The Daily Value is the total amount of a nutrient a person is supposed to eat in a day, based on a 2000-calorie diet.

In general, a percentage of 5% or less is considered low, whereas a percentage of 20% or more is considered high. A higher percentage can be good or bad, depending on whether or not a person should be trying to get more of a particular ingredient. People need to get plenty of vitamins, minerals, and fiber. In contrast, most people need to limit their intake of fat, cholesterol, and sodium.

Tables

Tables organize information into vertical columns and horizontal rows. Below is a table that shows how much water falls on areas of various sizes when it rains one inch. It shows, for instance, that a 40'x70' roof receives 1,743 gallons of rain during a one-inch rainfall event.

Area	Area (square miles)	Area (square kilometers)	Amount of water (gallons)	Amount of water (liters)
My roof 40x70 feet	.0001	.000257	1,743 gallons	6,601 liters
1 acre (1 square mile = 640 acres)	.00156	.004	27,154 gallons	102,789 liters
1 square mile	1	2.6	17.38 million gallons	65.78 million liters
Atlanta, Georgia	132.4	342.9	2.293 billion gallons	8.68 billion liters
United States	3,537,438	9,161,922	61,474 billion gallons	232,700 billion liters

Let's Review!

- Readers must understand how and why text features make certain information stand out from the text.
- Readers must understand and interpret the content of maps and charts.

CHAPTER 5 LITERARY ANALYSIS PRACTICE QUIZ 1

1. What are graphic elements in a text?

   A. Ideas arranged sequentially

   B. Main ideas restated differently

   C. Information presented visually

   D. White space between paragraphs

2. Which of the following statements accurately describes a summary?

   A. A summary makes a judgment about the original text.

   B. A summary leaves out the main idea of the original text.

   C. A summary restates implicit ideas from the original text.

   D. A summary copies words and phrases from the original text.

3. If a map does not have a compass, north is:

   A. up.   C. right.

   B. down.   D. left.

4. The purpose of an index is to tell readers:

   A. how to find sources that back up key ideas in the text.

   B. who wrote the text and what his or her credentials are.

   C. where to find information on a given subject within a book.

   D. why the author believes the main idea of a text is important.

5. On a chart, horizontal lines are called _____, whereas vertical lines are called _____.

   A. keys, rows

   B. legends, keys

   C. rows, columns

   D. columns, legends

6. A topic sentence always expresses:

   A. an opinion.

   B. the main idea.

   C. the conclusion.

   D. supporting details.

7. What is the main idea of a text?

   A. The most important idea in a text

   B. The most persuasive sentence in a text

   C. An example that supports the central point

   D. An opening sentence that grabs the attention

8. Supporting details must:

   A. relate to the main idea.

   B. follow the topic sentence.

   C. convey factual information.

   D. provide a counter-argument.

9. **When you follow instructions, one way to ensure understanding is to**

   A. follow the steps backwards once and forwards once.

   B. read the whole document thoroughly before following the steps.

   C. focus only on the main idea, ignoring the supporting details.

   D. pay more attention to graphic elements than written instructions.

CHAPTER 5 LITERARY ANALYSIS PRACTICE QUIZ 1 — ANSWER KEY

1. **C.** Graphic elements in a text present information visually in order to back up an argument, illustrate factual information or instructions, or present key facts and statistics. **See Lesson: Summarizing Text and Using Text Features.**

2. **C.** A summary may restate implicit ideas as long as they are clearly indicated in the original text. **See Lesson: Summarizing Text and Using Text Features.**

3. **A.** By convention, north on a map is up. Mapmakers include a compass if they break this convention for some reason. **See Lesson: Evaluating and Integrating Data.**

4. **C.** An index lists subtopics of a book along with page numbers where those topics will be covered. **See Lesson: Evaluating and Integrating Data.**

5. **C.** Horizontal lines on a chart are called rows, and vertical lines are called legends. Using this terminology, it is possible to describe the spaces on the chart (e.g. "What is the value in the fourth column of the second row?") **See Lesson: Evaluating and Integrating Data.**

6. **B.** A topic sentence expresses the main idea of the text. **See Lesson: Main Ideas, Topic Sentences, and Supporting Details.**

7. **A.** The main idea is the central idea of a text. It may or may not be intended to persuade the reader. **See Lesson: Main Ideas, Topic Sentences, and Supporting Details.**

8. **A.** Supporting details can develop the topic, contribute further information, or provide examples. No matter what, they must relate to the main idea. **See Lesson: Main Ideas, Topic Sentences, and Supporting Details.**

9. **B.** By reading a technical document thoroughly before following the steps, you can avoid pitfalls and make it easier to do work efficiently. **See Lesson: Summarizing Text and Using Text Features.**

CHAPTER 5 LITERARY ANALYSIS PRACTICE QUIZ 2

1. Which of the following characteristics is essential in an effective summary?

   A. Critical

   B. Objective

   C. Sequential

   D. Exaggerated

2. A _____ restates the main idea of a text in different words, attributing the ideas to the author.

   A. summary

   B. sequence

   C. topic sentence

   D. graphic element

3. Which of the following is not a formatting feature?

   A. Italics

   B. Charts

   C. Boldfacing

   D. Underlining

4. What is a text feature?

   A. A movie adaptation of a book

   B. An unwritten summary of a text

   C. A group of contiguous paragraphs

   D. An element that stands out from a text

5. What do footnotes do?

   A. Show the reader how ideas are organized

   B. Illustrate ideas that cannot clearly be stated in words

   C. Provide source information and peripheral information

   D. Provide nutrition facts about the contents of a package

Read the following sentence and answer questions 6-8.

Numerous robotic missions to Mars have revealed tantalizing evidence of a planet that may once have been capable of supporting life.

6. **Imagine this sentence is a *supporting detail* in a well-developed paragraph. Which of the following sentences would best function as a *topic sentence*?**

   A. Venus is an intensely hot planet surrounded by clouds full of drops of sulfuric acid.

   B. Of all the destinations within human reach, Mars is the planet most similar to Earth.

   C. Liquid water—a necessary ingredient of life—may once have flowed on the planet's surface.

   D. Space research is a costly, frivolous exercise that brings no clear benefit to people on Earth.

7. Imagine this sentence is the *topic sentence* of a well-developed paragraph. Which of the following sentences would best function as a *supporting detail*?

   A. Of all the destinations within human reach, Mars is the planet most similar to Earth.

   B. Venus is an intensely hot planet surrounded by clouds full of drops of sulfuric acid.

   C. Space research is a costly, frivolous exercise that brings no clear benefit to people on Earth.

   D. Liquid water—a necessary ingredient of life—may once have flowed on the planet's surface.

8. How could this sentence function as a *supporting detail* in a persuasive text arguing that space research is worth the expense and effort because it teaches us more about Earth and ourselves?

   A. By using statistics to back up an argument that needs support to be believed

   B. By showing how a space discovery could earn money for investors here on Earth

   C. By providing an example of a space discovery that enhances our understanding of life

   D. By developing the main idea that no space discovery can reveal information about Earth

Read the text below and answer question 9.

Before I came to America, I couldn't have known how difficult it would be. I knew I would miss my mother and my friends and my language, but I didn't know I would have to scrabble so desperately for so long to earn my place. Even when I had managed to make a living, I overworked myself with an animal terror. When I left home, I thought I was leaving poverty behind, but eventually I came to understand that I had escaped physical poverty by stepping into a poverty of the soul.

9. Which sequence accurately describes what happened first, second, and third in the passage?

   A. Arriving in America, overworking, escaping physical poverty.

   B. Coming to America, escaping physical poverty, stepping into a poverty of the soul.

   C. Knowing how difficult America would be, leaving home, stepping into a poverty of the soul.

   D. Expecting to miss friends, knowing how difficult America would be, arriving in America.

10. A source is considered credible if readers can _____ it.

   A. trust   C. analyze

   B. publish   D. decipher

CHAPTER 5 LITERARY ANALYSIS PRACTICE QUIZ 2 — ANSWER KEY

1. **B.** An effective summary must restate the main ideas of a text without exaggerating, distorting, or judging them. **See Lesson: Summarizing Text and Using Text Features.**

2. **A.** A summary restates another author's ideas in different ways. **See Lesson: Summarizing Text and Using Text Features.**

3. **B.** Formatting features make text stand out in a title or within a paragraph. Charts are graphic elements that present data or illustrate information. **See Lesson: Evaluating and Integrating Data.**

4. **D.** A text feature is any element that stands out from the text, such as a title, a boldfaced section, or a graphic element. **See Lesson: Evaluating and Integrating Data.**

5. **C.** Footnotes may provide information about source materials or give the reader interesting information that is not essential to the main point. **See Lesson: Evaluating and Integrating Data.**

6. **B.** The sentence above conveys factual information about Mars in an excited tone that suggests a positive interest in the subject. This makes it most likely to fit into an informational paragraph sharing facts about Mars. **See Lesson: Main Ideas, Topic Sentences, and Supporting Details..**

7. **D.** If the above sentence were a topic sentence, its supporting details would likely share information to develop the idea that Mars may have supported life in the past. **See Lesson: Main Ideas, Topic Sentences, and Supporting Details..**

8. **C.** The sentence above could act as an example to show how space discoveries teach us about Earth and ourselves. **See Lesson: Main Ideas, Topic Sentences, and Supporting Details..**

9. **B.** This paragraph discusses the past and future in a way that shifts constantly between the two. Some events are vague and may overlap with others. However, coming to America is a clear event that happened before the escape from physical poverty and the entrance into the poverty of the soul. **See Lesson: Summarizing Text and Using Text Features.**

10. **A.** The word *credible* means trustworthy. **See Lesson: Understanding Primary Sources, Making Inferences, and Drawing Conclusions.**

CHAPTER 6 MAKING INFERENCES & EVALUATING AN ARGUMENT

FACTS, OPINIONS, AND EVALUATING AN ARGUMENT

Nonfiction writing is based on facts and real events, but most nonfiction nevertheless expresses a point of view. Effective readers must evaluate the author's point of view and form their own conclusions about the points in the text.

Fact and Opinion

Many texts make an **argument.** In this context, the word *argument* has nothing to do with anger or fighting. It simply means the author is trying to convince readers of something.

Arguments are present in a wide variety of texts. Some relate to controversial issues, for instance by advocating support for a political candidate or change in laws. Others may defend a certain interpretation of facts or ideas. For example, a literature paper may argue that an author's story suggests a certain theme, or a science paper may argue for a certain interpretation of data. An argument may also present a plan of action such as a business strategy.

To evaluate an argument, readers must distinguish between **fact** and **opinion.** A fact is verifiably true. An opinion is someone's belief.

> **Fact:** Seattle gets an average of 37 inches of rain per year.

> **Opinion:** The dark, rainy, cloudy weather makes Seattle an unpleasant place to live in winter.

Meteorologists measure rainfall directly, so the above fact is verifiably true. The statement "it is unpleasant" clearly reflects a feeling, so the second sentence is an opinion.

The difference between fact and opinion is not always straightforward. For instance, a text may present a fact that contains an opinion within it:

> **Fact:** Nutritionist Fatima Antar questions the wisdom of extreme carbohydrate avoidance.

Assuming the writer can prove that this sentence genuinely reflects Fatima Antar's beliefs, it is a factual statement of her point of view. The reader may trust that Fatima Antar really holds this opinion, whether or not the reader is convinced by it.

If a text makes a judgment, it is not a fact:

> **Opinion:** The patient's seizure drug regimen caused horrendous side effects.

The above sentence uses language that different people would interpret in different ways. Because people have varying ideas about what they consider "horrendous," this sentence is an opinion as it is written, even though the actual side effects and the patient's opinion of them could both be verified.

COMPARE!

Small changes to the statement about seizure drugs could turn it into a factual statement:

Fact: The patient's seizure drug regiment caused side effects such as migraines, confusion, and dangerously high blood pressure.

The above statement can be verified because the patient and other witnesses could confirm the exact nature of her symptoms. This makes it a fact.

Fact: The patient reported that her seizure drug regimen caused horrendous side effects.

This statement can also be verified because the patient can verify that she considers the side effects horrendous. By framing the statement in this way, the writer leaves nothing up to interpretation and is clearly in the realm of fact.

The majority of all arguments contain both facts and opinions, and strong arguments may contain both fact and opinion elements. It is rare for an argument to be composed entirely of facts, but it can happen if the writer is attempting to convince readers to accept factual information that is little-known or widely questioned. Most arguments present an author's opinion and use facts, reasoning, and expert testimony to convince readers.

Evaluating an Argument

Effective readers must evaluate an argument and decide whether or not it is valid. To do this, readers must consider every claim the author presents, including both the main argument and any supporting statements. If an argument is based on poor reasoning or insufficient evidence, it is not valid—even if you agree with the main idea.

KEY POINT!

Most of us want to agree with arguments that reflect our own beliefs. But it is inadvisable to accept an argument that is not properly rooted in good reasoning. Consider the following statements about global climate change:

Poor Argument: It just snowed fifteen inches! How can anyone say the world is getting warmer?

Poor Argument: It's seventy degrees in the middle of February! How can anyone deny global warming?

Both of these arguments are based on insufficient evidence. Each relies on *one* weather event in *one* location to support an argument that the entire world's climate is or is not changing. There is not nearly enough information here to support an argument on either side.

Beware of any argument that presents opinion information as fact.

False Claim of Fact: I know vaccines cause autism because my niece began displaying autism symptoms after receiving her measles vaccine.

The statement above states a controversial idea as fact without adequate evidence to back it up. Specifically, it makes a false claim of cause and effect about an incident that has no clear causal relationship.

Any claim that is not supported by sufficient evidence is an example of **faulty reasoning**.

Type of Faulty Reasoning	Definition	Example	Explanation
Circular Reasoning	Restating the argument in different words instead of providing evidence	Baseball is the best game in the world because it is more fun than any other game.	Here, everything after the word *because* says approximately the same thing as everything before it. It looks like the author is providing a reason, but no evidence has actually been offered.
Either/Or Fallacy	Presenting an issue as if it involves only two choices when in fact it is not so simple	Women should focus on motherhood, not careers.	This statement assumes that women cannot do both. It also assumes that no woman needs a career in order to provide for her children.
Overgeneralizations	Making a broad claim based on too little evidence	All elderly people have negative stereotypes of teenagers.	This statement lumps a whole category of people into a group and claims the whole group shares the same belief—always an unlikely prospect.

Most texts about evaluating arguments focus on faulty reasoning and false statements of fact. But arguments that attempt to misrepresent facts as opinions are equally suspicious. A careful reader should be skeptical of any text that denies clear physical evidence or questions the truth of events that have been widely verified.

Assumptions and Biases

A well-reasoned argument should be supported by facts, logic, and clearly explained opinions. But most arguments are also based on **assumptions**, or unstated and unproven ideas about what is true. Consider the following argument:

Argument: To improve equality of opportunity for all children, schools in underprivileged areas should receive as much taxpayer funding as schools in wealthy districts.

This argument is based on several assumptions. First is the assumption that all children should have equal opportunities. Another is that taxpayer-funded public schools are the best way to provide these opportunities. Whether or not you disagree with either of these points, it is worth noting that the second idea in particular is not the only way to proceed. Readers who examine the assumptions behind an argument can sometimes find points of disagreement even if an author's claims and logic are otherwise sound.

Examining an author's assumptions can also reveal a writer's biases. A **bias** is a preconceived idea that makes a person more likely to show unfair favor for certain thoughts, people, or groups. Because every person has a different experience of the world, every person has a different set of biases. For example, a person who has traveled widely may feel differently about world political events than someone who has always lived in one place.

Virtually all writing is biased to some degree. However, effective writing attempts to avoid bias as much as possible. Writing that is highly biased may be based on poor assumptions that render the entire argument invalid.

Highly biased writing often includes overgeneralizations. Words like *all, always, never,* and so on may indicate that the writer is overstating a point. While these words can exist in true statements, unbiased writing is more likely to qualify ideas using words like *usually, often,* and *rarely.*

Another quality of biased writing is excessively emotional word choice. When writers insult people who disagree with them or engage the emotions in a way that feels manipulative, they are being biased.

> **Biased:** Power-hungry politicians don't care that their standardized testing requirements are producing a generation of overanxious, incurious, impractical kids.

> **Less biased:** Politicians need to recognize that current standardized testing requirements are causing severe anxiety and other negative effects in children.

Biased writing may also reflect stereotypical thinking. A **stereotype** is a particularly harmful type of bias that applies specifically to groups of people. Stereotypical thinking is behind racism, sexism, homophobia, and so on. Even people who do not consider themselves prejudiced can use language that reflects common stereotypes. For example, the negative use of the word *crazy* reflects a stereotype against people with mental illnesses.

Historically, writers in English have used male nouns and pronouns to indicate all people. Revising such language for more inclusivity is considered more effective in contemporary writing.

> **Biased:** The history of the human race proves that man is a violent creature.

> **Less biased:** The history of the human race proves that people are violent.

Let's Review!

- A text meant to convince someone of something is making an argument.
- Arguments may employ both facts and opinions.
- Effective arguments must use valid reasoning.
- Arguments are based on assumptions that may be reasonable or highly biased.
- Almost all writing is biased to some degree, but strong writing makes an effort to eliminate bias.

Understanding Primary Sources, Making Inferences, and Drawing Conclusions

Effective readers must understand the difference between types of sources and choose credible sources of information to support research. Readers must also consider the content of their reading materials and draw their own conclusions.

Primary Sources

When we read and research information, we must differentiate between different types of sources. Sources are often classified depending on how close they are to the original creation or discovery of the information they present.

Primary sources include firsthand witness accounts of events, research described by the people who conducted it, and any other original information. Contemporary researchers can often access mixed media versions of primary sources such as video and audio recordings, photographs of original work, and so on. Note that original content is still considered primary even if it is reproduced online or in a book.

> **Examples:** Diaries, scientific journal articles, witness testimony, academic conference presentations, business memos, speeches, letters, interviews, and original literature and artwork.

Secondary sources respond to, analyze, summarize, or comment on primary sources. They add value to a discussion of the topic by giving readers new ways to think about the content. However, they may also introduce errors or layers of bias. Secondary sources may be very good sources of information, but readers must evaluate them carefully.

> **Examples:** Biographies, books and articles that summarize research for wider audiences, analyses of original literature and artwork, histories, political commentary.

Tertiary sources compile information in a general, highly summarized, and sometimes simplified way. Their purpose is not to add anything to the information, but rather to present the information in an accessible manner, often for audiences who are only beginning to familiarize themselves with a topic.

> **Examples:** Encyclopedias, guidebooks, literature study guides.

Source Materials in Action

Primary sources are often considered most trustworthy because they are closest to the original material and least likely to contain errors. However, readers must take a common sense approach to evaluating trustworthiness. For example, a single letter written by one biased witness of a historical event may not provide as much insight into what really happened as a secondary account by a historian who has considered the points of view of a dozen firsthand witnesses.

Tertiary sources are useful for readers attempting to gain a quick overview of understanding about a subject. They are also a good starting point for readers looking for keywords and subtopics to use for further research of a subject. However, they are not sufficiently detailed or credible to support an article, academic paper, or other document intended to add valuable analysis and commentary on a subject.

Evaluating Credibility

Not everything you read is equally trustworthy. Many sources contain mistakes, faulty reasoning, or deliberate misinformation designed to manipulate you. Effective readers seek out information from **credible**, or trustworthy, sources.

There is no single formula for determining credibility. Readers must make judgment calls based on individual texts and their purpose.

FOR EXAMPLE

Most sources should attempt to be objective. But if you're reading an article that makes an argument, you do not need to demand perfect objectivity from the source. The purpose of a persuasive article is to defend a point of view. As long as the author does this openly and defends the point of view with facts, logic, and other good argumentative techniques, you may trust the source.

Other sources may seem highly objective but not be credible. For example, some scientific studies meet all the criteria for credibility below except the one about trustworthy publishers. If a study is funded or conducted by a company that stands to profit from it, you should treat the results with skepticism no matter how good the information looks otherwise.

Sources and References

Credible texts are primary sources or secondary sources that refer to other trustworthy sources. If the author consults experts, they should be named, and their credentials should be explained. Authors should not attempt to hide where they got their information. Vague statements like "studies show" are not as trustworthy as statements that identify who completed a study.

Objectivity

Credible texts usually make an effort to be objective. They use clear, logical reasoning. They back arguments up with facts, expert opinions, or clear explanations. The assumptions behind the arguments do not contain obvious stereotypes.

Emotional arguments are acceptable in some argumentative writing, but they should not be manipulative. For example, photos of starving children may be acceptable for raising awareness of a famine, but they need to be respectful of both the victims and the audience—not just there for shock value.

Date of Publication

Information changes quickly in some fields, especially the sciences and technology. When researching a fast-changing topic, look for sources published in the last ten years.

Author Information

If an author and/or a respected organization take public credit for information, it is more likely to be reliable. Information published anonymously on the Internet may be suspicious because nobody is clearly responsible for mistakes. Authors with strong credentials such as university professors in a given field are more trustworthy than authors with no clear resume.

Publisher Information

Information published by the government, a university, a major national news organization, or another respected organization is often more credible. On the Internet, addresses ending in .edu or .gov may be more trustworthy than .com addresses. Publishers who stand to profit or otherwise benefit from the content of a text are always questionable.

BE CAREFUL!
Strong credentials only make a source more trustworthy if the credentials are related to the topic. A Columbia University Professor of Archeology is a credible source on ancient history. But if she writes a parenting article, it's not necessarily more credible than a parenting article by someone without a flashy university title.

Professionalism

Credible sources usually look professional and present information free of grammatical errors or major factual errors.

Making Inferences and Drawing Conclusions

In reading—and in life—people regularly make educated guesses based on limited information. When we use the information we have to figure out something nobody has told us directly, we are making an **inference**. People make inferences every day.

> **Example:** You hear a loud thump. Then a pained voice says, "Honey, can you bring the first aid kit?"

From the information above, it is reasonable to infer that the speaker is hurt. The thumping noise, the pain in the speaker's voice, and the request for a first aid kit all suggest this conclusion.

When you make inferences from reading, you use clues presented in the text to help you draw logical conclusions about what the author means. Before you can make an inference, you must read the text carefully and understand the explicit, or overt, meaning. Next, you must look for clues to any implied, or suggested, meanings behind the text. Finally, consider the clues in light of your prior knowledge and the author's purpose, and draw a conclusion about the meaning.

As soon as Raizel entered the party, someone handed her a plate. She stared down at the hot dog unhappily.

"What?" asked an unfamiliar woman nearby with an edge to her voice. "You don't eat dead animal?"

From the passage above, it would be reasonable to infer that the unfamiliar woman has a poor opinion of vegetarians. Several pieces of information suggest this: her combative tone, the edge in her voice, and the mocking question at the end.

When you draw inferences from a text, make sure your conclusion is truly indicated by the clues provided.

> Author Glenda Davis had high hopes for her children's book *Basketball Days*. But when the novel was released with a picture of a girl on the cover, boys refused to pick it up. The author reported this to her publisher, and the paperback edition was released with a new cover—this time featuring a dog and a basketball hoop. After that, many boys read the book. And Davis never heard anyone complain that the main character was a girl.

BE CAREFUL!

Before you make a conclusion about a text, consider it in light of your prior knowledge and the clues presented.

After reading the paragraph above, you might suspect that Raizel is a vegetarian. But the text does not fully support that conclusion. There are many reasons why Raizel might not want to eat a hot dog.

Perhaps she is keeping kosher, or she has social anxiety that makes it difficult to eat at parties, or she simply isn't hungry. The above inference about the unfamiliar woman's dislike for vegetarians is strongly supported. But you'd need further evidence before you could safely conclude that Raizel is actually a vegetarian.

The text above implies that boys are reluctant to read books with a girl on the cover. A hasty reader might stop reading early and conclude that boys are reluctant to read about girls—but this inference is not suggested by the full text.

Let's Review!

- Effective readers must consider the credibility of their sources.
- Primary sources are usually considered the most trustworthy.
- Readers must often make inferences about ideas that are implied but not explicitly stated in a text.

TYPES OF PASSAGES, TEXT STRUCTURES, GENRE AND THEME

To read effectively, you must understand what kind of text you are reading and how it is structured. You must also be able to look behind the text to find its deeper meanings.

Types of Passages

There are many ways of breaking texts down into categories. To do this, you need to consider the author's **purpose**, or what the text exists to do. Most texts exist to inform, persuade, or entertain. You also need to consider what the text does—whether it tells a story, describes facts, or develops a point of view.

Type of Passage	Examples
Narrative writing tells a story. The story can be fictional, or it can describe real events. The primary purpose of narrative writing is to entertain.	• An autobiography • A memoir • A short story • A novel
Expository writing provides an explanation or a description. Many academic essays and informational nonfiction books are expository writing. Stylistically, expository writing is highly varied. Although the explanations can be dry and methodical, many writers use an artful or entertaining style. Expository writing is nonfiction. Its primary purpose is to inform.	• A book about a historical event • An essay describing the social impacts of a new technology • A description of changing gender roles in marriages • A philosophical document exploring the nature of truth. • Recipes
Technical writing explains a complex process or mechanism. Whereas expository writing is often academic, technical writing is used in practical settings such as businesses. The style of a technical document is almost always straightforward and impersonal. Technical writing is nonfiction, and its purpose is to inform.	• Instructions • User manuals • Process descriptions
Persuasive writing makes an argument. It asks readers to believe something or do something. Texts that make judgments, such as movie reviews, are persuasive because they are attempting to convince readers to accept a point of view. Texts that suggest a plan are also persuasive because they are trying to convince readers to take an action. As the name "persuasive writing" indicates, the author's primary purpose is to persuade.	• Op-ed newspaper articles • Book reviews • Project proposals • Advertisements • Persuasive essays

Text Structures

Authors rarely present ideas within a text in a random order. Instead, they organize their thoughts carefully. To read effectively, you must be able to recognize the **structure** of a text. That is, you need to identify the strategies authors use to organize their ideas. The five most common text structures are listed below.

Text Structure	Examples
In a **sequence** text, an author explains what happened first, second, third, and so on. In other words, a sequence text is arranged in **chronological order**, or time order. This type of text may describe events that have already happened or events that may happen in the future.	• A story about a birthday party. • A historical paper about World War II. • A list of instructions for baking a cake. • A series of proposed steps in a plan for business expansion.
A **compare/contrast** text explains the similarities and differences between two or more subjects. Authors may compare and contrast people, places, ideas, events, cultures, and so on.	• An essay describing the similarities and differences between women's experiences in medieval Europe and Asia. • A section in an op-ed newspaper article explaining the similarities and differences between two types of gun control.
A **cause/effect** text describes an event or action and its results. The causes and effects discussed can be actual or theoretical. That is, the author can describe the results of a historical event or predict the results of a possible future event.	• An explanation of ocean acidification and the coral bleaching that results. • A paper describing a proposed new law and its likely effects on the economy.
A **problem-solution** text presents a problem and outlines a solution. Sometimes it also predicts or analyzes the results of the solution. The solution can be something that already happened or a plan the author is proposing. Note that a problem can sometimes be expressed in terms of a wish or desire that the solution fulfills.	• An explanation of the problems smallpox caused and the strategies scientists used to eradicate it. • A business plan outlining a group of potential customers and the strategy a company should use to get their business.
A **description** text creates a mental picture for the reader by presenting concrete details in a coherent order. Description texts are usually arranged spatially. For instance, authors may describe the subject from top to bottom, or they may describe the inside first and then the outside, etc.	• An explanation of the appearance of a character in a story. • A paragraph in a field guide detailing the features of a bird. • A section on an instruction sheet describing how the final product should look.

KEEP IN MIND . . .

The text structures above do not always work in isolation. Authors often combine two or more structures within one text. For example, a business plan could be arranged in a problem-solution structure as the author describes what the business wants to achieve and how she proposes to achieve it. The "how" portion could also use a sequence structure as the author lists the steps to follow first, second, third, and so on.

CONNECTIONS

Different types of texts can use the same structures.

1. A story about a birthday party is a narrative, and its purpose is to entertain.
2. A historical paper about a war is an expository text meant to inform.
3. A list of instructions for baking a cake is a technical text meant to inform.
4. A series of proposed steps in a plan for business expansion is a persuasive text meant to persuade.

If all of these texts list ideas in chronological order, explaining what happened (or what may happen in the future) first, second, third, and so on, they are all using a sequence structure.

Genre and Theme

Literature can be organized into categories called **genres**. The two major genres of literature are fiction and nonfiction.

Fiction is made up. It can be broken down into many sub-genres, or sub-categories. The following are some of the common ones:

*   Short story – Short work of fiction.
*   Novel – Book-length work of fiction.
*   Science fiction – A story set in the future
*   Romance – A love story
*   Mystery – A story that answers a concrete question, often about who committed a crime
*   Mythology – A traditional story that reflects cultural traditions and beliefs but does not usually teach an explicit lesson
*   Legends – Traditional stories that are presented as histories, even though they often contain fantastical or magical elements
*   Fables – Traditional stories meant to teach an explicit lesson

---

COMPARE!

The differences between myths and fables are sometimes hard to discern.

Myths are often somewhat religious in nature. For instance, stories about Ancient Greek gods and goddesses are myths. These stories reflect cultural beliefs, for example by showing characters being punished for failing to please their gods. But the lesson is implicit. These stories do not usually end with a moral lesson that says to readers, "Do not displease the gods!"

Fables are often for children, and they usually end with a sentence stating an explicit moral. For example, there's a story called "The Tortoise and the Hare," in which a tortoise and a hare agree to have a race. The hare, being a fast animal, gets cocky and takes a lot of breaks while the tortoise plods slowly toward the finish line without stopping. Because the tortoise keeps going, it eventually wins. The story usually ends with the moral, "Slow and steady win the race."

Nonfiction is true. Like fiction, it can be broken down into many sub-genres. The following are some of the common ones:

- Autobiography and memoir – The author's own life story
- Biography – Someone else's life story (not the author's)
- Histories – True stories about real events from the past
- Criticism and reviews – A response or judgment on another piece of writing or art
- Essay – A short piece describing the author's outlook or point of view.

CONNECTIONS

Everything under "Fiction" and several items under "Nonfiction" above are examples of narrative writing. We use labels like "narrative" and "persuasive" largely when we discuss writing tasks or the author's purpose. We could use these labels here too, but at the moment we're more concerned with the words that are most commonly used in discussions about literature's deeper meanings.

Literature reflects the human experience. Texts from different genres often share similar **themes**, or deeper meanings. Texts from different cultures do too. For example, a biography of a famous civil rights activist may highlight the same qualities of heroism and interconnectedness that appear in a work of mythology from Ancient India. Other common themes in literature may relate to war, love, survival, justice, suffering, growing up, and other experiences that are accessible to virtually all human beings.

Many students confuse the term *theme* with the term *moral*. A **moral** is an explicit message contained in the text, like "Don't lie" or "Crime doesn't pay." Morals are a common feature of fables and other traditional stories meant to teach lessons to children. Themes, in contrast, are implicit. Readers must consider the clues in the story and figure out themes for themselves. Because of this, themes are debatable. For testing purposes, questions focus on themes that are clearly and consistently indicated by clues within the text.

Let's Review!

- Written texts can be organized into the following categories: narrative, expository, technical, and persuasive.
- Texts of all categories may use the following organizational schemes or structures: sequence, compare/contrast, cause/effect, problem-solution, description.
- Literature can be organized into genres including fiction, nonfiction, and many sub-genres.
- Literature across genres and cultures often reflects the same deeper meanings, or themes.

CHAPTER 6 MAKING INFERENCES & EVALUATING AN ARGUMENT PRACTICE QUIZ 1

1. **What is a bias?**

   A. A preconceived and sometimes unfair belief

   B. A person or group that often faces prejudice

   C. An unstated idea that underlies an argument

   D. A sweeping statement that may not always be true

2. **A particularly harmful kind of bias is called a(n):**

   A. opinion.

   B. stereotype.

   C. assumption.

   D. overgeneralization.

3. **Which statement, if true, is a fact?**

   A. The 1918 flu pandemic killed more people than World War I.

   B. The 1918 flu pandemic was more devastating than World War I.

   C. The 1918 flu pandemic was a terrifying display of nature's power.

   D. The 1918 flu pandemic caused greater social instability than the plague.

4. **What are the two basic genres that encompass all of literature?**

   A. Fable and myth

   B. Fiction and nonfiction

   C. Technical and expository

   D. Sequence and description

5. **Narrative writing:**

   A. tells a story.

   B. explains an idea.

   C. describes a process.

   D. makes an argument.

6. **Which of the following is an example of technical writing?**

   A. A user manual

   B. A history book

   C. An op-ed article

   D. An autobiography

7. **Which sources are usually considered most trustworthy?**

   A. Primary sources

   B. Secondary sources

   C. Tertiary sources

   D. Quaternary sources

8. **A source is not credible if:**

   A. its publisher is government funded.

   B. any of its sources are primary sources.

   C. any of its sources are secondary sources.

   D. its publisher is profiting from the information.

9. **Readers make inferences when they:**

    A. restate the main idea of a text in different words.

    B. differentiate between primary and secondary sources.

    C. determine that a text is not a credible source of information.

    D. use clues in the text to help them deduce implicit information.

CHAPTER 6 MAKING INFERENCES & EVALUATING AN ARGUMENT PRACTICE QUIZ 1 — ANSWER KEY

1. **A.** Biases may be stated or unstated, and they are not necessarily sweeping. They are preconceived and sometimes unfair ideas about the world. **See Lesson: Facts, Opinions, and Evaluating an Argument.**

2. **B.** A stereotype is a particularly harmful kind of bias against a group of people. **See Lesson: Facts, Opinions, and Evaluating an Argument.**

3. **A.** All of these statements contain beliefs or feelings that are subject to interpretation except the statement about the number of people killed in the 1918 flu pandemic compared to World War I. This is a verifiable piece of information, or a fact. **See Lesson: Facts, Opinions, and Evaluating an Argument.**

4. **B.** All of literature can be arranged into two basic categories, or genres: fiction and nonfiction. **See Lesson: Types of Passages, Text Structures, Genre and Theme.**

5. **A.** Narrative writing may be fiction or nonfiction as long as it tells a story. **See Lesson: Types of Passages, Text Structures, Genre and Theme.**

6. **A.** A user manual describes a complex mechanism and the processes for maintaining it, so it is a technical text. **See Lesson: Types of Passages, Text Structures, Genre and Theme.**

7. **A.** The authors of primary sources witnessed the original creation or discovery of the information they present. For this reason, they are considered the most trustworthy. **See Lesson: Understanding Primary Sources, Making Inferences, and Drawing Conclusions.**

8. **D.** A text is highly unlikely to be credible if its publisher is an organization that stands to benefit if people believe the information it contains. **See Lesson: Understanding Primary Sources, Making Inferences, and Drawing Conclusions.**

9. **D.** Readers make inferences when they deduce implicit information in a text. **See Lesson: Understanding Primary Sources, Making Inferences, and Drawing Conclusions.**

Chapter 6 Making Inferences & Evaluating an Argument Practice Quiz 2

1. **Which statement is an opinion?**

   A. Freshman Anita Jones states that excessive homework requirements cause her undue stress.

   B. Students reported symptoms such as headaches, anxiety attacks, and difficulty sleeping.

   C. Excessive homework requirements cause students undue stress and harm their quality of life.

   D. Students who do homework more than three hours per day show elevated cortisol levels compared to students who do no homework.

2. **An argument may be composed of:**

   A. facts only.

   B. opinions only.

   C. both facts and opinions.

   D. neither facts nor opinions.

3. **A statement that is probably true is a(n):**

   A. fact.   C. opinion.

   B. claim.   D. argument.

4. **In literature, a genre is a:**

   A. moral.   C. category.

   B. theme.   D. narrative.

5. **When we discuss the _____ of a text, we are talking about how it is organized.**

   A. genre   C. structure

   B. purpose   D. description

6. **The theme of a text is:**

   A. nonfiction but not narrative.

   B. narrative but not nonfiction.

   C. suggested but not stated outright.

   D. stated outright, not just suggested.

7. **_____ provide insight and commentary on the topic but may also introduce biases or errors.**

   A. Primary sources

   B. Secondary sources

   C. Tertiary sources

   D. Quaternary sources

8. **Which type of evidence would not be considered credible to back up arguments in a persuasive text?**

   A. Logic

   B. Statistics

   C. Scare tactics

   D. Firsthand accounts

Chapter 6 Making Inferences & Evaluating an Argument Practice Quiz 2 — Answer Key

1. C. Words like "excessive" and "undue" are subject to interpretation and reflect beliefs rather than verifiable facts. However, words like these may appear in factual statements about what people said they felt or believed. **See Lesson: Facts, Opinions, and Evaluating an Argument.**

2. C. An argument may include both verifiably true statements, or facts, and statements based on belief, or opinions. **See Lesson: Facts, Opinions, and Evaluating an Argument.**

3. A. Unlike an opinion, a fact is verifiably true. An argument or claim may express a fact, an opinion, or a mixture of the two. **See Lesson: Facts, Opinions, and Evaluating an Argument.**

4. C. The word *genre* is synonym of *category*. We use the word *genre* to discuss categories of literature. **See Lesson: Types of Passages, Text Structures, Genre and Theme.**

5. C. A genre is a category of a text, and the purpose it what it is meant to do. The structure is how it is organized. **See Lesson: Types of Passages, Text Structures, Genre and Theme.**

6. C. In contrast with a moral, which is explicitly stated, a theme is a suggested, or implicit, deeper meaning behind a text. **See Lesson: Types of Passages, Text Structures, Genre and Theme.**

7. B. Secondary sources add value to the discussion of a topic but are also removed from the original information. **See Lesson: Understanding Primary Sources, Making Inferences, and Drawing Conclusions.**

8. C. Emotional arguments may reasonably appear in a persuasive text, but not if they use manipulative strategies like scare tactics. **See Lesson: Understanding Primary Sources, Making Inferences, and Drawing Conclusions.**

CHAPTER 7 THE AUTHOR'S USE OF LANGUAGE

THE AUTHOR'S PURPOSE AND POINT OF VIEW

In order to understand, analyze, and evaluate a text, readers must know how to identify the author's purpose and point of view. Readers also need to attend to an author's language and rhetorical strategies.

Author's Purpose

When writers put words on paper, they do it for a reason. This reason is the author's **purpose**. Most writing exists for one of three purposes: to inform, to persuade, or to entertain.

> **TEST TIP**
>
> You may have learned about a fourth purpose for writing: conveying an emotional experience. Many poems as well as some works of fiction, personal essays, and memoirs are written to give the reader a sense of how an event or moment might feel. This type of text is rarely included on placement tests, and if it is, it tends to be lumped in with literature meant to entertain.

If a text is designed to share knowledge, its purpose is to **inform**. Informational texts include technical documents, cookbooks, expository essays, journalistic newspaper articles, and many nonfiction books. Informational texts are based on facts and logic, and they usually attempt an objective tone. The style may otherwise vary; some informational texts are quite dry, whereas others have an engaging style.

If a text argues a point, its purpose is to **persuade**. A persuasive text attempts to convince a reader to believe a certain point of view or take a certain action. Persuasive texts include op-ed newspaper articles, book and movie reviews, project proposals, and argumentative essays. Key signs of persuasive texts include judgments, words like *should,* and other signs that the author is sharing opinions.

If a text is primarily for fun, its purpose is to **entertain**. Entertaining texts usually tell stories or present descriptions. Entertaining texts include novels, short stories, memoirs, and some poems. Virtually all stories are lumped into this category, even if they describe unpleasant experiences.

> **CONNECTIONS**
>
> You may have read elsewhere that readers can break writing down into the following basic categories. These categories are often linked to the author's purpose.
>
> **Narrative** writing tells a story and is usually meant to entertain.
> **Expository** writing explains an idea and is usually meant to inform.
> **Technical** writing explains a mechanism or process and is usually meant to inform.
> **Persuasive** writing argues a point and, as the label suggests, is meant to persuade.

A text can have more than one purpose. For example, many traditional children's stories come with morals or lessons. These are meant both to entertain children and persuade them to behave in ways society considers appropriate. Also, commercial nonfiction texts like popular science books are often written in an engaging or humorous style. The purpose of such a text is to inform while also entertaining the reader.

Point of View

Every author has a general outlook or set of opinions about the subject. These make up the author's **point of view**.

To determine point of view, a reader must recognize implicit clues in the text and use them to develop educated guesses about the author's worldview. In persuasive texts, the biggest clue is the author's explicit argument. From considering this argument, a reader can usually make some inferences about point of view. For instance, if an author argues that parents should offer kids opportunities to exercise throughout the day, it would be reasonable to infer that the author has an overall interest in children's health, and that he or she is troubled by the idea of kids pursuing sedentary behaviors like TV watching.

It is more challenging to determine point of view in a text meant to inform. Because the writer does not present an explicit argument, readers must examine assumptions and word choice to determine the writer's point of view.

> **Example:** Models suggest that at the current rate of global warming, hurricanes in 2100 will move 9 percent slower and drop 24 percent more rain. Longer storm durations and rainfall rates will likely translate to increased economic damage and human suffering.

It is reasonable to infer that the writer of this passage has a general trust for science and scientists. This writer assumes that global warming is happening, so it is clear he or she is not a global warming denier. Although the writer does not suggest a plan to prevent future storm damage, the emphasis on negative effects and the use of negative words like "damage" and "suffering" suggest that the author is worried about global warming.

Texts meant to entertain also contain clues about the author's point of view. That point of view is usually evident from the themes and deeper meanings. For instance, a memoirist who writes an upbeat story about a troubled but loving family is likely to believe strongly in the power of love. Note, however, that in this type of work, it is not possible to determine point of view merely from one character's words or actions. For instance, if a character says, "Your mother's love doesn't matter much if she can't take care of you," the reader should *not* automatically assume the writer agrees with that statement. Narrative writers often present a wide range of characters with varying outlooks on life. A reader can only determine the author's point of view by considering the work as a whole. The attitudes that are most emphasized and the ones that win out in the end are likely to reflect the author's point of view.

Rhetorical Strategies

Rhetorical strategies are the techniques an author uses to support an argument or develop a main idea. Effective readers need to study the language of a text and determine how the author is supporting his or her points.

One strategy is to appeal to the reader's reason. This is the foundation of effective writing, and it simply means that the writer relies on factual information and the logical conclusions that follow from it. Even persuasive writing uses this strategy by presenting facts and reasons to back up the author's opinions.

Ineffective: Everyone knows *Sandra and the Lumps* is the best band of the new millennium.

Effective: The three most recent albums by *Sandra and the Lumps* are the first, second, and third most popular records released since the turn of the millennium.

Another strategy is to establish trust. A writer can do this by choosing credible sources and by presenting ideas in a clear and professional way. In persuasive writing, writers may show they are trustworthy by openly acknowledging that some people hold contradicting opinions and by responding fairly to those positions. Writers should never attack or misrepresent their opponents' position.

Ineffective: People who refuse to recycle are too lazy to protect their children's future.

Effective: According to the annual Throw It Out Questionnaire, many people dislike the onerous task of sorting garbage, and some doubt that their effort brings any real gain.

A final strategy is to appeal to the reader's emotions. For instance, a journalist reporting on the opioid epidemic could include a personal story about an addict's attempts to overcome substance abuse. Emotional content can add a human dimension to a story that would be missing if the writer only included statistics and expert opinions. But emotions are easily manipulated, so writers who use this strategy need to be careful. Emotions should never be used to distort the truth or scare readers into agreeing with the writer.

Ineffective: If you don't take action on gun control, you're basically killing children.

Effective: Julie was puzzling over the Pythagorean Theorem when she heard the first gunshot.

Let's Review!

- Every text has a purpose.
- Most texts are meant to inform, persuade, or entertain.
- Texts contain clues that imply an author's outlook or set of opinions about the subject.
- Authors use rhetorical strategies to appeal to reason, establish trust, or invoke emotions.

CONTEXT CLUES AND MULTIPLE MEANING WORDS

Sometimes when you read a text, you come across an unfamiliar word. Instead of skipping the word and reading on, it is important to figure out what that word means so you can better understand the text. There are different strategies you can use to determine the meaning of unfamiliar words. This lesson will cover (1) how to determine unfamiliar words by reading context clues, (2) multiple meaning words, and (3) using multiple meaning words properly in context.

Using Context Clues to Determine Meaning

When reading a text, it is common to come across unfamiliar words. One way to determine the meaning of unfamiliar words is by studying other context clues to help you better understand what the word means.

Context means the other words in the sentences around the unfamiliar word.

You can look at these other words to find **clues** or **hints** to help you figure out what the word means.

FOR EXAMPLE

Look at the following sentence:

Some of the kids in the cafeteria _ostracized_ Janice because she dressed differently; they never allowed her to sit at their lunch table, and they whispered behind her back.

If you did not know what the word _ostracized_ meant, you could look at the **other words** for **clues** to help you.

Here is what we know based on the clues in the sentence:

- Janice dressed differently
- Some kids did not allow her to sit at their table
- They whispered behind her back

We know that the kids **never allowed her to sit at their lunch** table and that they **whispered behind her back**. If you put all these clues together, you can conclude that the other students were **mistreating** Janice by **excluding** her.

Therefore, based on these context clues, _ostracized_ means "excluded from the group."

Here's another example:

> **EXAMPLE 2**
>
> Look at this next sentence:
>
> Louis's teacher was offended because after she called on him he gave a *flippant* response instead of a serious answer.
>
> If you did not know what the word *flippant* meant, you could look at the **other words** for **clues** to help you.
>
> Here is what we know based on the clues in the sentence:
>
> • Louis's teacher was offended
> • He gave a flippant response instead of a serious answer
>
> We know that Louis said something that **offended** his teacher. Another keyword in this sentence is the word **instead**. This means that **instead of a serious answer** Louis gave the **opposite** of a serious answer.
>
> Therefore, based on these context clues, *flippant* means "lacking respect or seriousness."

Multiple Meaning Words

Sometimes when we read words in a text, we encounter words that have **multiple meanings**.

Multiple meaning words are words that have **more than one definition** or meaning.

> **FOR EXAMPLE**
>
> The word **current** is a multiple meaning word. Here are the different definitions of *current:*
>
> CURRENT:
>
> 1. adj: happening or existing in the present time
>   Example: *It is important to keep up with* current *events so you know what's happening in the world.*
> 2. noun: the continuous movement of a body of water or air in a certain direction
>   Example: *The river's* current *was strong as we paddled down the rapids.*
> 3. noun: a flow of electricity
>   Example: *The electrical* current *was very weak in the house.*

Here are some other examples of words with multiple meanings:

Multiple Meaning Word	Definition #1	Definition #2	Definition #3
Buckle	noun: a metal or plastic device that connects one end of a belt to another	verb: to fasten or attach	verb: to bend or collapse from pressure or heat
Cabinet	noun: a piece of furniture used for storing things	noun: a group of people who give advice to a government leader	-
Channel	noun: a radio or television station	noun: a system used for sending something	noun: a long, narrow place where water flows
Doctor	noun: a person skilled in the science of medicine, dentistry, or one holding a PhD	verb: to change something in a way to trick or deceive	verb: to give medical treatment
Grave	noun: a hole in the ground for burying a dead body	adj: very serious	-
Hamper	noun: a large basket used for holding dirty clothes	verb: to slow the movement, action, or progress of	-
Plane	noun: a mode of transportation that has wings and an engine and can carry people and things in the air	noun: a flat or level surface that extends outward	noun: a level of though, development, or existence
Reservation	noun: an agreement to have something (such as a table, room, or seat) held for use at a later time	noun: a feeling of uncertainty or doubt	noun: an area of land kept separate for Native Americans to live an area of land set aside for animals to live for protection
Season	noun: one of the four periods in which a year is divided (winter, spring, summer, and fall)	noun: a particular period of time during the year	verb: to add spices to something to give it more flavor
Sentence	noun: a group words that expresses a statement, question, command, or wish	noun: the punishment given to someone by a court of law	verb: to officially state the punishment given by a court of law

From this chart you will notice that words with multiple meanings may have different **parts of speech**. A part of speech is a category of words that have the same grammatical properties. Some of the main parts of speech for words in the English language are: nouns, adjectives, verbs, and adverbs.

Part of Speech	Definition	Example
Noun	a person, place, thing, or idea	*Linda, New York City, toaster, happiness*
Adjective	a word that describes a noun or pronoun	*adventurous, young, red, intelligent*
Verb	an action or state of being	*run, is, sleep, become*
Adverb	a word that describes a verb, adjective, or other adverb	*quietly, extremely, carefully, well*

For example, in the chart above, *season* is can be a **noun** or a **verb**.

Using Multiple Meaning Words Properly in Context

When you come across a **multiple meaning word** in a text, it is important to discern which meaning of the word is being used so you do not get confused.

You can once again turn to the **context clues** to clarify which meaning of the word is being used.

Let's take a look at the word *coach*. This word has several definitions:

COACH:
1. noun: a person who teaches and trains an athlete or performer
2. noun: a large bus with comfortable seating used for long trips
3. noun: the section on an airplane with the least expensive seats
4. verb: to teach or train someone in a specific area
5. verb: to give someone instructions on what to do or say in a certain situation

Since *coach* has so many definitions, you need to look at the **context clues** to figure out which definition of the word is being used:

The man was not happy that he had to sit in coach on the 24-hour flight to Australia.

In this sentence, the context clues **sit in** and **24-hour flight** help you see that *coach* means the least expensive seat on an airplane.

Let's look at another sentence using the word *coach*:

The lawyer needed to coach her witness so he would answer all the questions properly.

In this sentence, the context clues **so he would answer all the questions properly** help you see that the lawyer was giving the witness instructions on what to say.

Let's Review!

- When you come across an unfamiliar word in a text you can use context clues to help you define it.
- Context clues can also help you determine which definition of a multiple meaning word to use.

Tone, Mood, and Transition Words

Authors use language to show their emotions and to make readers feel something too. They also use transition words to help guide the reader from one idea to the next.

Tone and Mood

The **tone** of a text is the author's or speaker's attitude toward the subject. The tone may reflect any feeling or attitude a person can express: happiness, excitement, anger, boredom, or arrogance.

Readers can identify tone primarily by analyzing word choice. The reader should be able to point to specific words and details that help to establish the tone.

Example: The train rolled past miles and miles of cornfields. The fields all looked the same. They swayed the same. They produced the same dull nausea in the pit of my stomach. I'd been sent out to see the world, and so I looked, obediently. What I saw was sameness.

Here, the author is expressing boredom and dissatisfaction. This is clear from the repetition of words like "same" and "sameness." There's also a sense of unpleasantness from phrases like "dull nausea" and passivity from words like "obediently."

Sometimes an author uses an ironic tone. Ironic texts often mean the opposite of what they actually say. To identify irony, you need to rely on your prior experience and common sense to help you identify texts with words and ideas that do not quite match.

Example: With that, the senator dismissed the petty little problem of mass shootings and returned to the really important issue: his approval ratings.

> **BE CAREFUL!**
>
> When you're asked to identify the tone of a text, be sure to keep track of *whose* tone you're supposed to identify, and which part of the text the question is referencing. The author's tone can be different from that of the characters in fiction or the people quoted in nonfiction.
>
> **Example:** The reporter walked quickly, panting to catch up to the senator's entourage. "Senator Biltong," she said. "Are you going to take action on mass shootings?"
>
> "Sure, sure. Soon," the senator said vaguely. Then he turned to greet a newcomer. "Ah ha! Here's the man who can fix my approval ratings!" And with that, he returned to the really important issue: his popularity.
>
> *
>
> In the example above, the author's tone is ironic and angry. But the tone of the senator's dialogue is different. The line beginning with the words "Sure, sure" has a distracted tone. The line beginning with "Ah ha!" has a pleased tone.

Here the author flips around the words most people would usually use to discuss mass murder and popularity. By calling a horrific issue "petty" and a trivial issue "important," the author highlights what she sees as a politician's backwards priorities. Except for the phrase "mass shootings," the words here are light and airy—but the tone is ironic and angry.

A concept related to tone is **mood**, or the feelings an author produces in the reader. To determine the mood of a text, a reader can consider setting and theme as well as word choice and tone. For example, a story set in a haunted house may produce an unsettled or frightened feeling in a reader.

Tone and mood are often confused. This is because they are sometimes the same. For instance, in an op-ed article that describes children starving while food aid lies rotting, the author may use an outraged tone and simultaneously arouse an outraged mood in the reader.

However, tone and mood can be different. When they are, it's useful to have different words to distinguish between the author's attitude and the reader's emotional reaction.

> **Example:** I had to fly out of town at 4 a.m. for my trip to the Bahamas, and my wife didn't even get out of bed to make me a cup of coffee. I told her to, but she refused just because she'd been up five times with our newborn. I'm only going on vacation for one week, and she's been off work for a month! She should show me a little consideration.

Here, the tone is indignant. The mood will vary depending on the reader, but it is likely to be unsympathetic.

Transitions

Authors use connecting words and phrases, or **transitions**, to link ideas and help readers follow the flow of their thoughts. The number of possible ways to transition between ideas is almost limitless.

Below are a few common transition words, categorized by the way they link ideas.

Transitions	Examples
Time and sequence transitions orient the reader within a text. They can also help show when events happened in time.	*First, second, next, now, then, at this point, after, afterward, before this, previously, formerly, thereafter, finally, in conclusion*
Addition or emphasis transitions let readers know the author is building on an established line of thought. Many place extra stress on an important idea.	*Moreover, also, likewise, furthermore, above all, indeed, in fact*
Example transitions introduce ideas that illustrate a point.	*For example, for instance, to illustrate, to demonstrate*
Causation transitions indicate a cause-and-effect relationship.	*As a result, consequently, thus*
Contrast transitions indicate a difference between ideas.	*Nevertheless, despite, in contrast, however*

Transitions may look different depending on their function within the text. Within a paragraph, writers often choose short words or expressions to provide transitions and smooth the flow. Between paragraphs or larger sections of text, transitions are usually longer. They may use some of the key words or ideas above, but the author often goes into detail restating larger concepts and explaining their relationships more thoroughly.

> **Between Sentences:** Students who cheat do not learn what they need to know. *As a result,* they get farther behind and face greater temptation to cheat in the future.

Between Paragraphs: *As a result of the cheating behaviors described above,* students find themselves in a vicious cycle.

Longer transitions like the latter example may be useful for keeping the reader clued in to the author's focus in an extended text. But long transitions should have clear content and function. Some long transitions, such as the very wordy "due to the fact that" take up space without adding more meaning and are considered poor style.

Let's Review!

- Tone is the author's or speaker's attitude toward the subject.
- Mood is the feeling a text creates in the reader.
- Transitions are connecting words and phrases that help readers follow the flow of a writer's thoughts.

CHAPTER 7 THE AUTHOR'S USE OF LANGUAGE PRACTICE QUIZ 1

1. **Select the word from the following sentence that has more than one meaning.**

   Cassandra's voice has a much different pitch than her brother's, so they sound great when they sing together.

   A. Voice
   B. Different
   C. Pitch
   D. Sing

2. **Select the word from the following sentence that has more than one meaning.**

   They need to prune the bushes every year or else they will lose their shape.

   A. Need
   B. Prune
   C. Lose
   D. Shape

3. **Select the word from the following sentence that has more than one meaning.**

   Javier was overjoyed when he finally finished his application for college.

   A. Overjoyed
   B. Finally
   C. Application
   D. College

4. **Read the sentences below.**

   My tame wolf is not a danger to humans. <u>Despite</u> her size and alarming appearance, she is basically a big, warm hearted puppy.

   What is the function of the <u>underlined</u> transition word in sentence two?

   A. To express a contrast
   B. To provide an example
   C. To add emphasis to a point
   D. To indicate time or sequence

5. **Read the sentences below.**

   However you look at the problem, it's a thorny one. It's also going to be a pleasure to solve.

   Which word functions as a transition?

   A. However
   B. One
   C. Also
   D. Going

6. **Read the sentences below.**

   Shaniqua shows clearly that she is driven to succeed as a student. _____ I have often noticed her waiting outside the library before it opens at 6:00 a.m. _____ her teachers report that she frequently asks for help outside of class.

   Which words or phrases should be inserted into the blanks to provide clear transitions between these ideas?

   A. In conclusion; Thus
   B. First; Consequently
   C. Although; In contrast
   D. For instance; Furthermore

7. **Which phrase describes the set of techniques an author uses to support an argument or develop a main idea?**

   A. Points of view
   B. Logical fallacies
   C. Statistical analyses
   D. Rhetorical strategies

8. The author's _____ is the reason for writing.

   A. purpose

   B. rhetoric

   C. main idea

   D. point of view

9. What is the most likely purpose of a popular science book describing recent advances in genetics?

   A. To decide

   B. To inform

   C. To persuade

   D. To entertain

CHAPTER 7 THE AUTHOR'S USE OF LANGUAGE PRACTICE QUIZ 1 — ANSWER KEY

1. **C.** The word "pitch" has more than one meaning. **See Lesson: Context Clues and Multiple Meaning Words.**

2. **B.** The word "prune" has more than one meaning. **See Lesson: Context Clues and Multiple Meaning Words.**

3. **C.** The word "application" has more than one meaning. **See Lesson: Context Clues and Multiple Meaning Words.**

4. **A.** Transition words like "despite" express a contrast between ideas. **See Lesson: Tone and Mood, Transition Words.**

5. **C.** The transition is the word that links the two ideas: *also*. The word *however* here is not a transition word indicating contrast; it's an adverb meaning "in whichever way." **See Lesson: Tone and Mood, Transition Words.**

6. **D.** The sentences above would be best served with an example transition and an addition transition. **See Lesson: Tone and Mood, Transition Words.**

7. **D.** The techniques an author uses to support an argument or develop a main idea are called rhetorical strategies. **See Lesson: Understanding the Author's Purpose, Point of View, and Rhetorical Strategies.**

8. **A.** The main idea of a text is its key point, and the point of view is the author's outlook on the subject. The purpose is the reason for writing. **See Lesson: Understanding the Author's Purpose, Point of View, and Rhetorical Strategies.**

9. **B.** If a book is describing information, its purpose is to inform. **See Lesson: Understanding the Author's Purpose, Point of View, and Rhetorical Strategies.**

CHAPTER 7 THE AUTHOR'S USE OF LANGUAGE PRACTICE QUIZ 2

1. Select the word from the following sentence that has more than one meaning.

   It was a grave situation, and many people had given up hope.

   A. Hope   C. People

   B. Grave   D. Situation

2. Select the word from the following sentence that has more than one meaning.

   The teacher was content with the quality of her students' work on their math exam.

   A. Teacher   C. Quality

   B. Content   D. Math

3. Select the word from the following sentence that has more than one meaning.

   Only an animal with a strong constitution will be able to survive the Arctic's climate.

   A. Strong   C. Survive

   B. Constitution D. Climate

4. Which of the following is *not* a common function of transitions?

   A. Introducing an example

   B. Orienting the reader in time

   C. Telling the reader the mood

   D. Creating a sense of emphasis

5. Read the sentences below.

   Durham played professional football in his twenties. He became a commentator thereafter.

   Which word functions as a transition?

   A. Twenties   C. Became

   B. He   D. Thereafter

6. Read the sentences below.

   Mary's college career had a rocky start. She is determined to graduate with honors.

   Which word or phrase, if inserted at the beginning of sentence two, would effectively transition between these two ideas?

   A. Likewise   C. Previously

   B. However   D. For example

7. An author's point of view is a(n):

   A. lack of purpose.

   C. rhetorical strategy.

   B. general outlook.

   D. appeal to the emotions.

8. What is the most likely purpose of a science fiction book about genetic mutants waging war against human beings?

   A. To decide   C. To persuade

   B. To inform   D. To entertain

9. What is the most likely purpose of an article that claims some genetic research is immoral?

   A. To decide   C. To persuade

   B. To inform   D. To entertain

Chapter 7 The Author's Use of Language Practice Quiz 2 — Answer Key

1. **B.** The word "grave" has more than one meaning. **See Lesson: Context Clues and Multiple Meaning Words.**

2. **B.** The word "content" has more than one meaning. **See Lesson: Context Clues and Multiple Meaning Words.**

3. **B.** The word "constitution" has more than one meaning. **See Lesson: Context Clues and Multiple Meaning Words.**

4. **C.** Transitions are not meant to tell the reader the mood of a text (and since mood is the reader's emotional reaction, it's not something that can be dictated to the reader anyway.) **See Lesson: Tone and Mood, Transition Words.**

5. **D.** The transition is the word that links the two ideas: *thereafter*. This word doesn't appear between the two sentences, but it does show how the two sentences are related in time. **See Lesson: Tone and Mood, Transition Words.**

6. **B.** A transition between these two sentences would likely suggest contrast. Good choices would be words like *however* or *nevertheless*. **See Lesson: Tone and Mood, Transition Words.**

7. **B.** An author's point of view is a general outlook on the subject. **See Lesson: Understanding the Author's Purpose, Point of View, and Rhetorical Strategies.**

8. **D.** Narrative works like science fiction novels are usually meant to entertain. **See Lesson: Understanding the Author's Purpose, Point of View, and Rhetorical Strategies.**

9. **C.** An article that takes a moral position is meant to persuade. **See Lesson: Understanding the Author's Purpose, Point of View, and Rhetorical Strategies.**

SECTION III
WRITING

Grammar: 20 questions, untimed

Areas assessed: The Mechanics of Writing, Parts of Speech, and Sentence Structure & Logic

GRAMMAR TIPS

- Rules of Language Arts and Grammar may be explicitly asked.
- Know the eight parts of a basic sentence: nouns, pronouns, verbs, adjectives, adverbs, conjunctions, prepositions, and interjections.
- Understand dependent and independent clauses of a complex sentence. Know how to join two independent clauses.
- Know subject-verb agreement.
- Study grammar terms. Know what they are and how they work; i.e., coordinate conjunctions, subject verb agreement.
- Review basic rules of punctuation; i.e., semi-colon and dash usage.

CHAPTER 8 THE MECHANICS OF WRITING

SPELLING

Spelling correctly is important to accurately convey thoughts to an audience. This lesson will cover (1) vowels and consonants, (2) suffixes and plurals, (3) homophones and homographs.

Vowels and Consonants

Vowels and **consonants** are different speech sounds in English.

The letters A, E, I, O, U and sometimes Y are **vowels** and can create a variety of sounds. The most common are short sounds and long sounds. Long **vowel** sounds sound like the name of the letter such as the *a* in late. Short **vowel** sounds have a unique sound such as the *a* in cat. A rule for **vowels** is that when two vowels are walking, the first does the talking as in pain and meat.

Consonants include the other twenty-one letters in the alphabet. **Consonants** are weak letters and only make sounds when paired with **vowels**. That is why words always must have a **vowel**. This also means that **consonants** need to be doubled to make a stronger sound like sitting, grabbed, progress. Understanding general trends and patterns for **vowels** and **consonants** will help with spelling. The table below represents the difference between short and long **vowels** and gives examples for each.

	Symbol	Example Words
Short a	a	Cat, mat, hat, pat
Long a	ā	Late, pain, pay, they, weight, straight
Short e	e	Met, said, bread
Long e	ē	Breeze, cheap, dean, equal
Short i	i	Bit, myth, kiss, rip
Long i	ī	Cry, pie, high

	Symbol	Example Words
Short o	o	Dog, hot, pop
Long o	ō	Snow, nose, elbow
Short u	u	Run, cut, club, gum
Long u	ū	Duty, rule, new, food
Short oo	oo	Book, foot, cookie
Long oo	ōō	Mood, bloom, shoot

Suffixes and Plurals

A **suffix** is a word part that is added to the ending of a root word. A **suffix** changes the meaning and spelling of words. There are some general patterns to follow with **suffixes**.

- Adding -er, -ist, or -or changes the root to mean *doer* or *performer*

  - Paint → Painter
  - Abolition → Abolitionist
  - Act → Actor

- Adding -ation or -ment changes the root to mean *an action* or *a process*

  - Ador(e) → Adoration
  - Develop → Development

- Adding -ism changes the root to mean *a theory or ideology*

  - Real → Realism

- Adding -ity, -ness, -ship, or -tude changes the root to mean *a condition, quality, or state*

  - Real → Reality
  - Sad → Sadness
  - Relation → Relationship
  - Soli(tary) → Solitude

- **Plurals** are similar to suffixes as letters are added to the end of the word to signify more than one person, place, thing, or idea. There are also general patterns to follow when creating **plurals**.

- If a word ends in -s,-ss,-z,-zz,-ch, or -sh, add -es.

  - Bus → Buses

- If a word ends in a -y, drop the -y and add -ies.

  - Pony → Ponies

- If a word ends in an -f, change the f to a v and add -es.

  - Knife → Knives

- For all other words, add an -s.

  - Dog → Dogs

Homophones and Homographs

A **homophone** is a word that has the same sound as another word, but does not have the same meaning or spelling.

- To, too, and two
- There, their, and they're
- See and sea

A **homograph** is a word that has the same spelling as another word, but does not have the same sound or meaning.

- Lead (to go in front of) and lead (a metal)
- Bass (deep sound) and bass (a fish)

Let's Review!

- Vowels include the letters A, E, I, O, U and sometimes Y and have both short and long sounds.
- Consonants are the other twenty-one letters and have weak sounds. They are often doubled to make stronger sounds.
- Suffixes are word parts added to the root of a word and change the meaning and spelling.
- To make a word plural, add -es, -ies, -ves, or -s to the end of a word.
- Homophones are words that have the same sound, but not the same meaning or spelling.
- Homographs are words that have the same spelling, but not the same meaning or sound.

CAPITALIZATION

Correct capitalization helps readers understand when a new sentence begins and the importance of specific words. This lesson will cover the capitalization rules of (1) geographic locations and event names, (2) organizations and publication titles, (3) individual names and professional titles, and (4) months, days, and holidays.

Geographic Locations and Event Names

North, east, south, and west are not **capitalized** unless they relate to a **definite region**.

- Go north on I-5 for 200 miles.
- The West Coast has nice weather.

Words like northern, southern, eastern, and western are also not **capitalized** unless they describe **people or the cultural and political activities of people**.

- There is nothing interesting to see in eastern Colorado.
- Midwesterners are known for being extremely nice.
- The Western states almost always vote Democratic.

These words are not **capitalized** when placed before a name or region unless it is part of the **official name**.

- She lives in southern California.
- I loved visiting Northern Ireland.

Continents, countries, states, cities, and **towns** need to be **capitalized**.

- Australia has a lot of scary animals.
- Not many people live in Antarctica.
- Albany is the capital of New York.

Historical events should be **capitalized** to separate the specific from the general.

- The bubonic plague in the Middle Ages killed a large portion of the population in Europe.
- The Great Depression took place in the early 1930s.
- We are living in the twenty-first century.

Organizations and Publication Titles

The **names of national organizations** need to be **capitalized**. Short prepositions, articles, and conjunctions within the title are not **capitalized** unless they are the first word.

- The National American Woman Suffrage Association was essential in passing the Nineteenth Amendment.
- The House of Representatives is one part of Congress.
- The National Football League consists of thirty-two teams.

The **titles of books, chapters, articles, poems, newspapers, and other publications** should be capitalized.

- Her favorite book is *A Wrinkle in Time*.
- I do the crossword in *The New York Times* every Sunday.
- *The Jabberwocky* by Lewis Carroll has many silly sounding words.

Individual Names and Professional Titles

People's names as well as their **familial relationship title** need to be **capitalized**.

- Barack Obama was our first African American president.
- Uncle Joe brought the steaks for our Memorial Day grill.
- Aunt Sarah lives in California, but my other aunt lives in Florida.

Professional titles need to be **capitalized** when they precede a name, or as a direct address. If it is after a name or is used generally, titles do not need to be **capitalized**.

- Governor Cuomo is trying to modernize the subway system in New York.
- Andrew Cuomo is the governor of New York.
- A governor runs the state. A president runs the country.
- Thank you for the recommendation, Mr. President.
- I need to see Doctor Smith.
- I need to see a doctor.

Capitalize the **title of high-ranking government officials** when an individual is referred to.

- The Secretary of State travels all over the world.
- The Vice President joined the meeting.

With **compound titles**, the prefixes or suffixes do not need to be **capitalized**.

- George W. Bush is the ex-President of the United States.

Months, Days, and Holidays

Capitalize all months of the year (January, February, March, April, May, June, July, August, September, October, November, December) and **days of the week** (Sunday, Monday, Tuesday, Wednesday, Thursday, Friday, Saturday).

- Her birthday is in November.
- People graduate from college in May or June.
- Saturdays and Sundays are supposed to be fun and relaxing.

Holidays are also **capitalized**.

- Most kid's favorite holiday is Christmas.
- The new school year usually starts after Labor Day.
- It is nice to go to the beach over Memorial Day weekend.

The **seasons** are not **capitalized**.

- It gets too hot in the summer and too cold in the winter.
- The flowers and trees bloom so beautifully in the spring.

Let's Review!

- Only capitalize directional words like north, south, east, and, west when they describe a definite region, people, and their political and cultural activities, or when it is part of the official name.
- Historical periods and events are capitalized to represent their importance and specificity.
- Every word except short prepositions, conjunctions, and articles in the names of national organizations are capitalized.
- The titles of publications follow the same rules as organizations.
- The names of individual people need to be capitalized.
- Professional titles are capitalized if they precede a name or are used as a direct address.
- All months of the year, days of the week, and holidays are capitalized.
- Seasons are not capitalized.

PUNCTUATION

Punctuation is important in writing to accurately represent ideas. Without correct punctuation, the meaning of a sentence is difficult to understand. This lesson will cover (1) periods, question marks, and exclamation points, (2) commas, semicolons, and colons, and (3) apostrophes, hyphens, and quotation marks.

Terminal Punctuation Marks: Periods, Question Marks, and Exclamation Points

Terminal punctuation are used at the end of a sentence. Periods, question marks, and exclamation points are the three types of terminal punctuation.

Periods (.) mark the end of a declarative sentence, one that states a fact, or an imperative sentence, one that states a command or request). Periods can also be used in abbreviations.

- Doctors save lives.
- She has a B.A. in Psychology.

Question Marks (?) signify the end of a sentence that is a question. Where, when, who, whom, what, why, and how are common words that begin question sentences.

- Who is he?
- Why is the sky blue?
- Where is the restaurant?

Exclamation Points (!) indicate strong feelings, shouting, or emphasize a feeling.

- Watch out!
- I hate you!
- That is incredible!

Internal Punctuation: Commas, Semicolons, and Colons

Internal punctuation is used within a sentence to help keep words, phrases, and clauses in order. These punctuation marks can be used to indicate elements such as direct quotations and definitions in a sentence.

A **comma** (,) signifies a small break within a sentence and separates words, clauses, or ideas.

Commas are used before conjunctions that connect two independent clauses.

- I ate some cookies, and I drank some milk.

Commas are also used to set off an introductory phrase.

- After the test, she grabbed dinner with a friend.

Short phrases that emphasis thoughts or emotions are enclosed by **commas**.

- The school year, thankfully, ends in a week.

Commas set off the words yes and no.

- Yes, I am available this weekend.
- No, she has not finished her homework.

Commas set off a question tag.

- It is beautiful outside, isn't it?

Commas are used to indicate direct address.

- Are you ready, Jack?
- Mom, what is for dinner?

Commas separate items in a series.

- We ate eggs, potatoes, and toast for breakfast.
- I need to grab coffee, go to the store, and put gas in my car.

Semicolons (;) are used to connect two independent clauses without a coordinating conjunction like *and* or *but*. A **s**emicolon creates a bond between two sentences that are related. Do not capitalize the first word after the **semicolon** unless it is a word that is normally capitalized.

- The ice cream man drove down my street; I bought a popsicle.
- My mom cooked dinner; the chicken was delicious.
- It is cloudy today; it will probably rain.

Colons (:) introduce a list.

- She teaches three subjects: English, history, and geography.

At the end of a sentence, **colons** can create emphasis of a word or phrase.

- She had one goal: pay the bills.

More Internal Punctuation: Apostrophes, Hyphens, and Quotation Marks

Apostrophes (') are used to indicate possession or to create a contraction.

- Bob has a car - Bob's car is blue.
- Steve's cat is beautiful.

For plurals that are also possessive, put the **apostrophe** after the s.

- Soldiers' uniforms are impressive.

Make contractions by combining two words.

- I do not have a dog - I don't have a dog
- I can't swim.

Its and it's do not follow the normal possessive rules. Its is possessive while it's means it is.

- It's a beautiful day to be at the park.
- The dog has many toys, but its favorite is the rope.

Hyphens (-) are mainly used to create compound words.

- The documentary was a real eye-opener for me.
- We have to check-in to the hotel before midnight.
- The graduate is a twenty-two-year-old woman.

Quotation Marks (") are used when directly using another person's words in your own writing. Commas and periods, sometimes question marks and exclamation points, are placed within **quotation marks**. Colons and semicolons are placed outside of the **quotation marks**, unless they are part of the quoted material. If quoting an entire sentence, capitalize the first word. If it is a fragment, do not capitalize the first word.

- Ernest Hemingway once claimed, "There is nothing noble in being superior to your fellow man; true nobility is being superior to your former self."
- Steve said, "I will be there at noon."

An indirect quote which paraphrases what someone else said does not need **quotation marks**.

- Steve said he would be there at noon.

Quotation marks are also used for the titles of short works such as poems, articles, and chapters. They are not italicized.

- Robert Frost wrote "The Road Not Taken."

Let's Review!

- **Periods (.)** signify the end of a sentence or are used in abbreviations.
- **Question Marks (?)** are also used at the end of a sentence and distinguish the sentence as a question.
- **Exclamation Points (!)** indicate strong feelings, shouting, or emphasis and are usually at the end of the sentence.
- **Commas (,)** are small breaks within a sentence that separate clauses, ideas, or words. They are used to set off introductory phrases, the words yes and no, question tags, indicate direct address, and separate items in a series.
- **Semicolons (;)** connect two similar sentences without a coordinating conjunctions such as and or but.
- **Colons (:)** are used to introduce a list or emphasize a word or phrase.
- **Apostrophes (')** indicate possession or a contraction of two words.
- **Hyphens (-)** are used to create compound words.
- **Quotation Marks (")** are used when directly quoting someone else's words and to indicate the title of poems, chapters, and articles.

Chapter 8 The Mechanics of Writing Practice Quiz 1

1. **Which of the following is correct?**

   A. May

   B. Spring

   C. easter

   D. sunday

2. **Fill in the blank with the correctly capitalized form.**

   My favorite book in the Harry Potter series is _____.

   A. *harry potter and the prisoner of azkaban*

   B. *Harry Potter and the prisoner of azkaban*

   C. *Harry Potter And The Prisoner Of Azkaban*

   D. *Harry Potter and the Prisoner of Azkaban*

3. **Which word(s) in the following sentence should be capitalized?**

   My friend's birthday is december 25. she does not like that her birthday is on christmas.

   A. christmas

   B. december

   C. december and christmas

   D. december, she, and christmas

4. **What is the sentence with the correct use of punctuation?**

   A. Offcampus apartments are nicer.

   B. Off campus apartments are nicer.

   C. Off-campus apartments are nicer.

   D. Off-campus-apartments are nicer.

5. **What is the mistake in the following sentence?**

   The highestranking officer can choose his own work, including his own hours.

   A. Highestranking needs a hyphen.

   B. There should be a comma after *officer*.

   C. There should be no comma after *work*.

   D. There should be a semicolon after *work*.

6. **What is missing from the following sentence?**

   Classical music helps with studying, I always listen to it before a test.

   A. There needs to be a colon after studying.

   B. There needs to be a semicolon after studying.

   C. There should be an exclamation point at the end.

   D. Nothing is missing.

7. **Which of the following spellings is correct?**

   A. Busines

   B. Business

   C. Buseness

   D. Bussiness

8. **On Earth, ____ are seven continents.**

   A. their

   B. there

   C. theer

   D. they're

9. **What is the correct plural of bush?**

   A. bush

   B. bushs

   C. bushes

   D. bushies

CHAPTER 8 THE MECHANICS OF WRITING PRACTICE QUIZ 1 – ANSWER KEY

1. **A.** May. Months, days, and holidays need to be capitalized, and seasons do not need to be. **See Lesson: Capitalization.**

2. **D.** Harry Potter and the Prisoner of Azkaban. Short prepositions, conjunctions, and articles are not capitalized in publication titles. **See Lesson: Capitalization.**

3. **D.** *december, she, and christmas.* All months and holidays are capitalized. She is the beginning of a sentence and needs to be capitalized. **See Lesson: Capitalization.**

4. **C.** *Off-campus apartments are nicer.* Hyphens are often used for compound words that are placed before the noun to help with understanding. **See Lesson: Punctuation.**

5. **A.** *Highestranking needs a hyphen.* Hyphens are used for compound words that describe a person or object. **See Lesson: Punctuation.**

6. **B.** *There needs to be a semicolon after studying.* A semicolon is used to connect two related sentences. **See Lesson: Punctuation.**

7. **B.** *Business* is the only correct spelling. **See Lesson: Spelling.**

8. **B.** *There* describes a place or position and is correctly spelled. **See Lesson: Spelling.**

9. **C.** With a word ending in -sh, add -es. **See Lesson: Spelling.**

CHAPTER 8 THE MECHANICS OF WRITING PRACTICE QUIZ 2

1. **Which of the following is correct?**

    A. *Gone With The Wind*

    B. *Gone With the Wind*

    C. *Gone with the Wind*

    D. *Gone with the wind*

2. **Fill in the blank with the correctly capitalized form.**

    Everyone wants to live in ___ ____, because it has nice weather and beaches.

    A. southern California

    B. Southern California

    C. Southern california

    D. southern california

3. **Choose the correct sentence.**

    A. Arnold Schwarzenegger was the governor of California.

    B. Arnold Schwarzenegger was the Governor of California.

    C. Arnold Schwarzenegger was the governor of california.

    D. arnold schwarzenegger was the governor of california.

4. **Which sentence is correct?**

    A. What is wrong.

    B. Honesty is the best policy.

    C. You dont need an umbrella.

    D. A band needs a guitarist singer and drummer.

5. **What is the mistake in the following sentence?**

    Albert Einstein claimed "Imagination is more important than knowledge."

    A. *Albert Einstein* needs an apostrophe.

    B. There should be a colon after *claimed*.

    C. There should be a comma before *than*.

    D. There needs to be a comma after *claimed*.

6. **What is the correct use of a period in the following sentence?**

    A. She had a bad day

    B. She had a bad day.

    C. She had. a bad day.

    D. She. had. a. bad. day.

7. **Which of the following spellings is correct?**

    A. Argument   C. Arguement

    B. Arguemint   D. Arguemant

8. **What is the correct plural of morning?**

    A. Morning   C. Morninges

    B. Mornings   D. Morningies

9. **Subjects ___ to their king to show respect.**

    A. bow   C. baw

    B. bou   D. beau

CHAPTER 8 THE MECHANICS OF WRITING
PRACTICE QUIZ 2 — ANSWER KEY

1. **C.** *Gone with the Wind.* Publication titles are capitalized. Shorter prepositions, articles, and conjunctions within titles are not capitalized. **See Lesson: Capitalization.**

2. **A.** *southern California.* Words such as southern are not capitalized unless they are a part of the official name. States are always capitalized. **See Lesson: Capitalization.**

3. **A.** Arnold Schwarzenegger was the governor of California. Individual names and states are always capitalized. Professional titles are capitalized when they precede a name or are part of a direct address. **See Lesson: Capitalization.**

4. **B.** *Honesty is the best policy.* All the other sentences are missing some punctuation. **See Lesson: Punctuation.**

5. **D.** *There needs to be a comma after claimed.* Commas are needed for introductory phrases and before the quoted material. **See Lesson: Punctuation.**

6. **B.** *She had a bad day.* A period is only used at the end of a sentence, and not anywhere in between. **See Lesson: Punctuation.**

7. **A.** *Argument* is the only correct spelling. **See Lesson: Spelling.**

8. **B.** For most words ending in consonants, just add -s. **See Lesson: Spelling.**

9. **A.** People *bow*, or bend down, to show respect. **See Lesson: Spelling.**

CHAPTER 9 PARTS OF SPEECH

Nouns

In this lesson, you will learn about nouns. A noun is a word that names a person, place, thing, or idea. This lesson will cover (1) the role of nouns in sentences and (2) different types of nouns.

Nouns and Their Role in Sentences

A **noun** names a person, place, thing, or idea.

Some examples of nouns are:

- Gandhi
- New Hampshire
- garden
- happiness

A noun's role in a sentence is as **subject** or **object**. A subject is the part of the sentence that does something, whereas the object is the thing that something is done to. In simple terms, the subject acts, and the object is acted upon.

Look for the nouns in these sentences.

1. The Louvre is stunning. (subject noun: The Louvre)
2. Marco ate dinner with Sara and Petra. (subject noun: Marco; object nouns: dinner, Sara, Petra)
3. Honesty is the best policy. (subject noun: honesty; object noun: policy)
4. After the election, we celebrated our new governor. (object nouns: governor, election)
5. I slept. (0 nouns)

KEEP IN MIND . . .
The subjects *I* and *we* in the two sentences to the left are pronouns, not nouns.

Look for the nouns in these sentences.

1. Mrs. Garcia makes a great pumpkin pie. (subject noun: Mrs. Garcia; object noun: pie)
2. We really need to water the garden. (object noun: garden)
3. Love is sweet. (subject noun: love)
4. Sam loves New York in the springtime. (subject noun: Sam; object nouns: New York, springtime)
5. Lin and her mother and father ate soup, fish, potatoes, and fruit for dinner. (subject nouns: Lin, mother, father; object nouns: soup, fish, potatoes, fruit, dinner)

Why isn't the word *pumpkin* a noun in the first sentence? *Pumpkin* is often a noun, but here it is used as an adjective that describes what kind of *pie*.

Why isn't the word *water* a noun in the second sentence? Here, *water* is an **action verb**. To *water the garden* is something we do.

How is the word *love* a noun in the third sentence and not in the fourth sentence? *Love* is a noun (thing) in sentence 3 and a verb (action) in the sentence 4.

How many nouns can a sentence contain? As long as the sentence remains grammatically correct, it can contain an unlimited number of nouns.

> **BE CAREFUL!**
> Words can change to serve different roles in different sentences. A word that is usually a noun can sometimes be used as an adjective or a verb. Determine a word's function in a sentence to be sure of its part of speech.

Types of Nouns

A. Singular and Plural Nouns

Nouns can be **singular** or **plural**. A noun is singular when there is only one. A noun is plural when there are two or more.

- The book has 650 pages.

Book is a singular noun. *Pages* is a plural noun.

Often, to make a noun plural, we add *-s* at the end of the word: *cat/cats*. This is a **regular** plural noun. Sometimes we make a word plural in another way: *child/children*. This is an **irregular** plural noun. Some plurals follow rules, while others do not. The most common rules are listed here:

> **KEEP IN MIND . . .**
> **Some nouns are countable,** and others are not. For example, we eat *three blueberries*, but we **do not** drink *three milks*. Instead, we drink *three glasses of milk* or *some milk*.

Singular noun	Plural noun	Rule for making plural
star	stars	for most words, add *-s*
box	boxes	for words that end in *-j, -s, -x, -z, -ch* or *-sh*, add *-es*
baby	babies	for words that end in *-y*, change *-y* to *-i* and add *-es*
woman	women	irregular
foot	feet	irregular

B. Common and Proper Nouns

Common nouns are general words, and they are written in lowercase. **Proper nouns** are specific names, and they begin with an uppercase letter.

Examples:

Common noun	Proper noun
ocean	Baltic Sea
dentist	Dr. Marx
company	Honda
park	Yosemite National Park

C. Concrete and Abstract Nouns

Concrete nouns are people, places, or things that physically exist. We can use our senses to see or hear them. *Turtle, spreadsheet,* and *Australia* are concrete nouns.

Abstract nouns are ideas, qualities, or feelings that we cannot see and that might be harder to describe. *Beauty, childhood, energy, envy, generosity, happiness, patience, pride, trust, truth,* and *victory* are abstract nouns.

Some words can be either concrete or abstract nouns. For example, the concept of *art* is abstract, but *art* that we see and touch is concrete.

- We talked about *art*. (abstract)
- She showed me the *art* she had created in class. (concrete)

Let's Review!

- A noun is a person, place, thing, or idea.
- A noun's function in a sentence is as subject or object.
- Common nouns are general words, while proper nouns are specific names.
- Nouns can be concrete or abstract.

PRONOUNS

A pronoun is a word that takes the place of or refers to a specific noun. This lesson will cover (1) the role of pronouns in sentences and (2) the purpose of pronouns.

Pronouns and Their Role in Sentences

A **pronoun** takes the place of a noun or refers to a specific noun.

Subject, Object, and Possessive Pronouns

A pronoun's role in a sentence is as **subject, object,** or **possessive.**

Subject Pronouns	Object Pronouns	Possessive Pronouns
I	me	my, mine
you	you	your, yours
he	her	his
she	him	her, hers
it	it	its
we	us	ours
they	them	their, theirs

In simple sentences, subject pronouns come before the verb, object pronouns come after the verb, and possessive pronouns show ownership.

Look at the pronouns in these examples:

BE CAREFUL!
It is easy to make a mistake when you have multiple words in the role of subject or object.

- <u>She</u> forgot <u>her</u> coat. (subject: she; possessive: her)
- <u>I</u> lent <u>her</u> <u>mine</u>. (subject: I; object: her; possessive: mine)
- <u>She</u> left <u>it</u> at school. (subject: she; object: it)
- <u>I</u> had to go and get <u>it</u> the next day. (subject: I; object: it)
- <u>I</u> will never lend <u>her</u> something of <u>mine</u> again! (subject: I; object: her; possessive: mine)

Correct	Incorrect	Why?
John and I went out.	*John and me* went out.	*John and I* is a subject. *I* is a subject pronoun; *me* is not.
Johan took *Sam and me* to the show.	Johan took *Sam and I* to the show.	*Sam and me* is an object. *Me* is an object pronoun; *I* is not.

Relative Pronouns

Relative pronouns connect a clause to a noun or pronoun.

These are some relative pronouns:

who, whom, whoever, whose, that, which

- Steve Jobs, *who founded Apple*, changed the way people use technology.

The pronoun *who* introduces a clause that gives more information about Steve Jobs.

- This is the movie *that Emily told us to see.*

The pronoun *that* introduces a clause that gives more information about the movie.

Other Pronouns

Some other pronouns are:

this, that, what, anyone, everything, something

DID YOU KNOW?
Pronouns can sometimes refer to general or unspecified things.

Look for the pronouns in these sentences.

- What is that?
- There is something over there!
- Does anyone have a pen?

Pronouns and Their Purpose

The purpose of a pronoun is to replace a noun. Note the use of the pronoun *their* in the heading of this section. If we did not have pronouns, we would have to call this section *Pronouns and Pronouns' Purpose.*

What Is an Antecedent?

A pronoun in a sentence refers to a specific noun, and this noun called the **antecedent**.

- John Hancock signed the Declaration of Independence. <u>He</u> signed <u>it</u> in 1776.

The antecedent for *he* is John Hancock. The antecedent for *it* is the Declaration of Independence.

Find the pronouns in the following sentence. Then identify the antecedent for each pronoun.

BE CAREFUL!
Look out for unclear antecedents, such as in this sentence:

- Take the furniture out of the room and paint *it*.

What needs to be painted, the furniture or the room?

Erin had an idea *that she* suggested to Antonio: "*I'*ll help *you* with *your* math homework if *you* help *me* with *my* writing assignment."

Pronoun	Antecedent
that	idea
she	Erin
I	Erin
you	Antonio
your	Antonio's
you	Antonio
me	Erin
my	Erin's

What Is Antecedent Agreement?

A pronoun must agree in **gender** and **number** with the antecedent it refers to. For example:

- Singular pronouns *I, you, he, she,* and *it* replace singular nouns.
- Plural pronouns *you, we,* and *they* replace plural nouns.
- Pronouns *he, she,* and *it* replace masculine, feminine, or neutral nouns.

Correct	Incorrect	Why?
<u>Students</u> should do <u>their</u> homework every night.	<u>A student</u> should do <u>their</u> homework every night.	The pronoun *their* is plural, so it must refer to a plural noun such as *students.*
When <u>an employee</u> is sick, <u>he or she</u> should call the office.	When <u>an employee</u> is sick, <u>they</u> should call the office.	The pronoun *they* is plural, so it must refer to a plural noun. *Employee* is not a plural noun.

Let's Review!

- A pronoun takes the place of or refers to a noun.
- The role of pronouns in sentences is as subject, object, or possessive.
- A pronoun must agree in number and gender with the noun it refers to.

ADJECTIVES AND ADVERBS

An **adjective** is a word that describes a noun or a pronoun. An **adverb** is a word that describes a verb, an adjective, or another adverb.

Adjectives

An **adjective** describes, modifies, or tells us more about a **noun** or a **pronoun**. Colors, numbers, and descriptive words such as *healthy*, *good*, and *sharp* are adjectives.

> **KEEP IN MIND . . .**
>
> Adjectives typically come **before the noun** in English. However, with **linking verbs** (non-action verbs such as *be, seem, look*), the adjective may come **after the verb** instead. Think of it like this: a linking verb **links** the adjective to the noun or pronoun.

Look for the adjectives in the following sentences:

	Adjective	Noun or pronoun it describes
I rode the blue bike.	blue	bike
It was a long trip.	long	trip
Bring two pencils for the exam.	two	pencils
The box is brown.	brown	box
She looked beautiful.	beautiful	she
That's great!	great	that

Multiple adjectives can be used in a sentence, as can multiple nouns. Look at these examples:

	Adjectives	Noun or pronoun it describes
The six girls were happy, healthy, and rested after their long beach vacation.	six, happy, healthy, rested; long, beach	girls; vacation
Leo has a good job, but he is applying for a better one.	good; better	job; one

> **KEEP IN MIND . . .**
>
> Note comparative and superlative forms of adjectives, such as:
>
> fast, faster, fastest
>
> far, farther, farthest
>
> good, better, best
>
> bad, worse, worst

Articles: *A, An, The*

Articles are a unique part of speech, but they work like adjectives. An article tells more about a noun. *A* and *an* are **indefinite** articles. Use *a* before a singular **general** noun. Use *an* before a singular general noun that begins with a vowel.

The is a **definite** article. Use *the* before a singular or plural **specific** noun.

Look at how articles are used in the following sentences:

- I need *a* pencil to take *the* exam. (any pencil; specific exam)

- Is there *a* zoo in town? (any zoo)
- Let's go to *the* zoo today. (specific zoo)
- Can you get me *a* glass of milk? (any glass)
- Would you bring me *the* glass that's over there? (specific glass)

Adverbs

An **adverb** describes, modifies, or tells us more about a **verb**, an **adjective**, or another **adverb**. Many adverbs end in -*ly*. Often, adverbs tell when, where, or how something happened. Words such as *slowly, very,* and *yesterday* are adverbs.

Adverbs that Describe Verbs

Adverbs that describe verbs tell something more about the action.

Look for the adverbs in these sentences:

	Adverb	Verb it describes
They walked quickly.	quickly	walked
She disapproved somewhat of his actions, but she completely understood them.	somewhat; completely	disapproved; understood
The boys will go inside if it rains heavily.	inside; heavily	go; rains

Adverbs that Describe Adjectives

Adverbs that describe adjectives often add intensity to the adjective. Words like *quite, more,* and *always* are adverbs.

Look for the adverbs in these sentences:

	Adverb	Adjective it describes
The giraffe is very tall.	very	tall
Do you think that you are more intelligent than them?	more	intelligent
If it's really loud, we can make the volume slightly lower.	really; slightly	loud; lower

Adverbs that Describe Other Adverbs

Adverbs that describe adverbs often add intensity to the adverb.

Look for the adverbs in these sentences:

	Adverb	Adverb it describes
The mouse moved too quickly for us to catch it.	too	quickly
This store is almost never open.	almost	never
Those women are quite fashionably dressed.	quite	fashionably

Adjectives vs. Adverbs

Not sure whether a word is an adjective or an adverb? Look at these examples.

	Adjective	Adverb	Explanation
fast	You're a *fast* driver.	You drove *fast*.	The adjective *fast* describes *driver* (noun); the adverb *fast* describes *drove* (verb).
early	I don't like *early* mornings!	Try to arrive *early*.	The adjective *early* describes *mornings* (noun); the adverb *early* describes *arrive* (verb).
good/well	They did *good* work together.	They worked *well* together.	The adjective *good* describes *work* (noun); the adverb *well* describes *worked* (verb).
bad/badly	The dog is *bad*.	The dog behaves *badly*.	The adjective *bad* describes *dog* (noun); the adverb *badly* describes *behaves* (verb).

Let's Review!

- An **adjective** describes, modifies, or tells us more about a **noun** or a **pronoun**.
- An **adverb** describes, modifies, or tells us more about a **verb**, an **adjective**, or another **adverb**.

BE CAREFUL!

When an adverb ends in *-ly*, add *more* or *most* to make comparisons.

Correct: The car moved *more slowly*.

Incorrect: The car moved *slower*.

CONJUNCTIONS AND PREPOSITIONS

A **conjunction** is a connector word; it connects words, phrases, or clauses in a sentence. A **preposition** is a relationship word; it shows the relationship between two nearby words.

Conjunctions

A **conjunction** connects words, phrases, or clauses.

And, so, and *or* are conjunctions.

Types of Conjunctions

> **KEEP IN MIND . . .**
>
> A clause is a phrase that has a subject and a verb.
>
> Some clauses are **independent**. An independent clause can stand alone.
>
> Some clauses are **dependent**. A dependent clause relies on another clause in order to make sense.

- **Coordinating** conjunctions connect two words, phrases, or independent clauses. The full list of coordinating conjunctions is: *and, or, but, so, for, nor, yet.*
- **Subordinating** conjunctions connect a main (independent) clause and a dependent clause. The conjunction may show a relationship or time order for the two clauses. Some subordinating conjunctions are: *after, as soon as, once, if, even though, unless.*
- **Correlative** conjunctions are pairs of conjunctions that work together to connect two words or phrases. Some correlative conjunctions are: *either/or, neither/nor, as/as.*

Example	Conjunction	What it is connecting
Verdi, Mozart, **and** *Wagner* are famous opera composers.	and	three nouns
Would you like *angel food cake, chocolate lava cake,* **or** *banana cream pie* for dessert?	or	three noun phrases
I took the bus to work, **but** *I walked home.*	but	two independent clauses
It was noisy at home, **so** *we went to the library.*	so	two independent clauses
They have to clean the house **before** *the realtor shows it.*	before	a main clause and a dependent clause
Use **either** hers **or** mine.	either/or	two pronouns
After everyone leaves, make sure you lock up.	after	a main clause and a dependent clause
I'd **rather** *fly* **than** *take the train.*	rather/than	two verb phrases
As soon as they announced the winning number, she looked at her ticket and shouted, "Whoopee!"	as soon as	a main clause and a dependent clause

> **DID YOU KNOW?**
>
> In the last example above, "*Whoopee!*" is an interjection. An **interjection** is a short phrase or clause that communicates emotion.
>
> Some other interjections are:
>
> - *Way to go!*
> - *Yuck.*
> - *Hooray!*
> - *Holy cow!*
> - *Oops!*

Prepositions

A **preposition** shows the relationship between two nearby words. Prepositions help to tell information such as direction, location, and time. *To, for,* and *with* are prepositions.

KEEP IN MIND . . .

Some prepositions are more than one word. *On top of* and *instead of* are prepositions.

Example	Preposition	What it tells us
The desk is in the classroom.	in	location
We'll meet you at 6:00.	at	time
We'll meet you at the museum.	at	place
The book is on top of the desk.	on top of	location

Prepositional Phrases

A preposition must be followed by an **object of the preposition**. This can be a noun or something that serves as a noun, such as a pronoun or a gerund.

DID YOU KNOW?

A gerund is the *-ing* form a verb that serves as a noun. *Hiking* is a gerund in this sentence:

I wear these shoes for *hiking*.

A **prepositional phrase** is a preposition plus the object that follows it.

Look for the prepositional phrases in the following examples. Note that a sentence can have more than one prepositional phrase.

Example	Preposition	Object of the preposition
The tiny country won the war *against all odds*.	against	all odds
Look *at us*!	at	us
Why don't we go swimming *instead of sweating in this heat?*	instead of; in	sweating; this heat
Aunt Tea kept the trophy *on a shelf of the cabinet between the sofas in the living room.*	on; of; between; in	a shelf; the cabinet; the sofas; the living room

BE CAREFUL!

Sometimes a word looks like a preposition but is actually part of the verb. In this case, the verb is called a phrasal verb, and the preposition-like word is called a particle. Here is an example:

- *Turn on* the light. (*Turn on* has a meaning of its own; it is a phrasal verb. *On* is a particle here, rather than a preposition.)
- *Turn on that street.* (*On that street* shows location; it is a prepositional phrase. *On* is a preposition here.)

Let's Review!

- A **conjunction** connects words, phrases, or clauses. *And, so,* and *or* are conjunctions.
- A **preposition** shows the relationship between two nearby words. *To, for,* and *with* are prepositions.
- A **prepositional phrase** includes a preposition plus the object of the preposition.

VERBS AND VERB TENSES

A **verb** is a word that describes a **physical or mental action** or a **state of being**. This lesson will cover the role of verbs in sentences, verb forms and tenses, and helping verbs.

The Role of Verbs in Sentences

A verb describes an action or a state of being. A complete sentence must have at least one verb.

Verbs have different tenses, which show time.

Verb Forms

Each verb has three primary forms. The **base form** is used for simple present tense, and the **past form** is used for simple past tense. The **participle form** is used for more complicated time situations. Participle form verbs are accompanied by a helping verb.

Base Form	Past Form	Participle Form
end	ended	ended
jump	jumped	jumped
explain	explained	explained
eat	ate	eaten
take	took	taken
go	went	gone
come	came	come

Some verbs are **regular**. To make the **past** or **participle** form of a regular verb, we just add *-ed*. However, many verbs that we commonly use are **irregular**. We need to memorize the forms for these verbs.

In the chart above, *end, jump,* and *explain* are regular verbs. *Eat, take, go,* and *come* are irregular.

Using Verbs

A simple sentence has a **subject** and a **verb**. The subject tells us who or what, and the verb tells us the action or state.

Example	Subject	Verb	*Explanation/Time*
They ate breakfast together yesterday.	They	ate	*happened yesterday*
I walk to school.	I	walk	*happens regularly*
We went to California last year.	We	went	*happened last year*
She seems really tired.	She	seems	*how she seems right now*
The teacher is sad.	teacher	is	*her state right now*

You can see from the examples in this chart that **past tense verbs** are used for a time in the past, and **present tense verbs** are used for something that happens regularly or for a state or condition right now.

Often a sentence has more than one verb. If it has a connector word or more than one subject, it can have more than one verb.

- The two cousins <u>live</u>, <u>work</u>, and <u>vacation</u> together. (3 verbs)
- The girls <u>planned</u> by phone, and then they <u>met</u> at the movies. (2 verbs)

> **BE CAREFUL!**
> When you have more than one verb in a sentence, make sure both verb tenses are correct.

Helping Verbs and Progressive and Perfect Tenses

Helping Verbs

A **helping verb** is a supporting verb that accompanies a main verb.

Questions, negative sentences, and certain time situations require helping verbs.

forms of helping verb "to be"	forms of helping verb "to have"	forms of helping verb "to do"	some modals (used like helping verbs)
am, are, is, was, were, be, being, been	have, has, had, having	do, does, did, doing	will, would, can, could, must, might, should

Here are examples of helping verbs in questions and negatives.

- Where *is* he *going*?
- *Did* they *win*?
- I *do*n't *want* that.
- The boys *can*'t go.

Progressive and Perfect Tenses

Helping verbs accompany main verbs in certain time situations, such as when an action is or was ongoing, or when two actions overlap in time. To form these tenses, we use a **helping verb** with the **base form plus -*ing*** or with the **participle form** of the main verb.

The **progressive tense** is used for an action that is or was ongoing. It takes base form of the main verb plus -*ing*.

Example sentence	Tense	Explanation/Time
I <u>am taking</u> French this semester.	Present progressive	*happening now, over a continuous period of time*
I <u>was working</u> when you stopped by.	Past progressive	*happened over a continuous period of time in the past*

The **perfect tense** is used to cover two time periods. It takes the *participle* form of the main verb.

Example sentence	Tense	Explanation/Time
I <u>have lived</u> here for three years.	Present perfect	*started in the past and continues to present*
I <u>had finished</u> half of my homework when my computer stopped working.	Past perfect	*started and finished in the past, overlapping in time with another action*

Sometimes we use both the **progressive** and **perfect** tenses together.

Example sentence	Tense	Explanation/Time
I <u>have been walking</u> for hours!	Present perfect progressive	*started in the past, took place for a period of time, and continues to present*
She <u>had been asking</u> for a raise for months before she finally received one.	Past perfect progressive	*started in the past, took place for a period of time, and ended*

Let's Review!

- A verb describes an action or state of being.
- Each verb has three primary forms: base form, past form, and participle form.
- Verbs have different tenses, which are used to show time.
- Helping verbs are used in questions, negative sentences, and to form progressive and perfect tenses.

CHAPTER 9 PARTS OF SPEECH PRACTICE QUIZ 1

1. Select the correct word to complete the following sentence.

   It was a treacherous route, and they traveled more ___ when they had a guide.

   A. safe
   B. safer
   C. safest
   D. safely

2. Select the part of speech of the underlined word in the following sentence.

   She did <u>quite</u> well on the exam.

   A. Noun
   B. Adverb
   C. Adjective
   D. Preposition

3. Select the noun that the underlined adjectives describe.

   Two weeks after his surgery, Henry felt <u>strong</u> and <u>healthy</u>.

   A. weeks
   B. his
   C. surgery
   D. Henry

4. Which word is <u>not</u> a conjunction?

   A. Or
   B. The
   C. So
   D. But

5. What part of speech are the underlined words in the following sentence?

   Twelve students passed the exam, <u>but</u> seven did not, <u>so</u> the teacher is letting them retake it.

   A. Adjective
   B. Preposition
   C. Conjunction
   D. Adverb

6. What is the object of the underlined preposition?

   I found our cat <u>under</u> the table by the window next to the TV.

   A. our cat
   B. the table
   C. the window
   D. the TV

7. Which of the following nouns can be made plural by simply adding -*s*?

   A. Fox
   B. Frog
   C. Cherry
   D. Potato

8. How many nouns in the following sentence have incorrect capitalization?

   The Patel Family moved to the United States, and now they live in the Boston Area.

   A. 0
   B. 1
   C. 2
   D. 3

9. What part of speech is the underlined word in the following sentence?

   Douglas served on the <u>Supreme Court</u> for 36 years.

   A. Noun
   B. Pronoun
   C. Adjective
   D. Preposition

10. Which word in the following sentence is a pronoun?

    To whom should the applicant address the letter?

    A. To
    B. the
    C. whom
    D. should

11. Which pronoun correctly completes the following sentence?

Nigel introduced Van and ___ to the new administrator.

A. I

B. me

C. she

D. they

12. Select the noun to which the underlined pronoun refers.

Greta Garbo, <u>who</u> performed in both silent and talking pictures, is my favorite actress.

A. actress

B. pictures

C. performed

D. Greta Garbo

13. How many verbs are in the following sentence?

They toured the art museum and saw the conservatory.

A. 0

B. 1

C. 2

D. 3

14. Which word in the following sentence is a helping verb?

They did not ask for our help.

A. did

B. ask

C. for

D. our

15. Select the correct verb form to complete the following sentence.

William didn't think he would enjoy the musical, but he ___.

A. do

B. did

C. liked

D. would

CHAPTER 9 PARTS OF SPEECH PRACTICE QUIZ 1 — ANSWER KEY

1. **D.** *Safely* is an adverb that describes the verb *traveled*. **See Lesson: Adjectives and Adverbs.**

2. **B.** *Quite* is an adverb that describes the adverb *well*. **See Lesson: Adjectives and Adverbs.**

3. **D.** These adjectives describe *Henry*. **See Lesson: Adjectives and Adverbs**

4. **B.** *The* is an article, not a conjunction. **See Lesson: Conjunctions and Prepositions.**

5. **C.** *But* and *so* are coordinating conjunctions. These two conjunctions connect three independent clauses in this sentence. **See Lesson: Conjunctions and Prepositions.**

6. **B.** *The table* is the object of the preposition *under*. **See Lesson: Conjunctions and Prepositions.**

7. **B.** To make the word *frog* plural, simply add *-s*. **See Lesson: Nouns.**

8. **C.** *Family* and *area* are common nouns and should not be capitalized. **See Lesson: Nouns.**

9. **A.** *Supreme Court* is a noun. **See Lesson: Nouns.**

10. **C.** *Whom* is a pronoun. **See Lesson: Pronouns.**

11. **B.** An object pronoun must be used here. **See Lesson: Pronouns.**

12. **D.** *Who* is a relative pronoun that refers to the subject *Greta Garbo*. **See Lesson: Pronouns.**

13. **C.** *Toured* and *saw* are verbs. **See Lesson: Verbs and Verb Tenses.**

14. **A.** *Did* is a helping verb; *ask* is the main verb. **See Lesson: Verbs and Verb Tenses.**

15. **B.** *Did* can be used here, for a shortened form of *did enjoy it*. **See Lesson: Verbs and Verb Tenses.**

CHAPTER 9 PARTS OF SPEECH PRACTICE QUIZ 2

1. **Which word is an adverb that describes the underlined verb?**

   The man <u>spoke</u> to us wisely.

   A. man   C. us

   B. to   D. wisely

2. **Which word in the following sentence is an adjective?**

   After they signed the mortgage on their first house, they went out to celebrate.

   A. they   C. mortgage

   B. signed   D. first

3. **How many adjectives are in the following sentence?**

   The new building is tall and modern.

   A. 1   C. 3

   B. 2   D. 4

4. **Which word in the following sentence is a conjunction?**

   Margot can speak English, Russian, and Polish fluently.

   A. can   C. and

   B. speak   D. fluently

5. **Identify the conjunction in the following sentence.**

   He is sick, yet he came to work.

   A. is   C. came

   B. yet   D. to

6. **Which is <u>not</u> a prepositional phrase?**

   Keep me informed about the status of the problem throughout the day.

   A. Keep me informed

   B. about the status

   C. of the problem

   D. throughout the day

7. **Select the correct nouns for the blanks in the following sentence.**

   We can use these ____ to cut these fillets of ____.

   A. knives, salmon

   B. knifes, salmon

   C. knifes, salmons

   D. knives, salmons

8. **Identify the nouns in the following sentence.**

   Marie Curie won the Nobel Prize in 1911.

   A. won, in, 1911

   B. won, Nobel Prize, 1911

   C. Marie Curie, won, Nobel Prize

   D. Marie Curie, Nobel Prize, 1911

9. **Choose the correct plural noun to complete the following sentence.**

   It was surprising to suddenly see some ____ as we drove along the deserted road.

   A. mooses   C. cactuses

   B. churchs   D. passersby

10. Which word in the following sentence is a pronoun?

The driver checked her side mirror.

A. The
C. side
B. her
D. driver

11. Select the pronoun that could be used in the following sentence.

Mrs. Sato, ___ lives down the street, is 99 years old.

A. she
C. which
B. who
D. whom

12. What is the role of the pronoun *him* in a sentence?

A. Object
C. Possessive
B. Subject
D. Any of these

13. Select the response that correctly describes both of the underlined verbs.

When a buyer <u>offered</u> 5% below our asking price, our realtor <u>advised</u> us to accept the offer.

A. Helping verbs
B. Past tense verbs
C. Present tense verbs
D. Progressive tense verbs

14. Why is the following <u>not</u> a correct sentence?

The clown sad.

A. It does not have a verb.
B. It does not have a noun.
C. The verb tense is incorrect.
D. The words are in the wrong order.

15. Select the verb that best completes the following sentence.

Katharina didn't ___ her job as an accountant, so she decided to change careers.

A. like
C. liken
B. likes
D. liked

CHAPTER 9 PARTS OF SPEECH PRACTICE QUIZ 2 – ANSWER KEY

1. D. *Wisely* is an adverb that describes the verb *spoke*. **See Lesson: Adjectives and Adverbs**

2. D. *First* is an adjective that describes the noun *house*. **See Lesson: Adjectives and Adverbs**

3. C. The adjectives *new, tall,* and *modern* describe the noun *building*. **See Lesson: Adjectives and Adverbs**

4. C. *And* is a conjunction. **See Lesson: Conjunctions and Prepositions.**

5. B. *Yet* is a conjunction. **See Lesson: Conjunctions and Prepositions.**

6. A. *Keep me informed* does not contain a preposition. *About, of,* and *throughout* are prepositions. **See Lesson: Conjunctions and Prepositions.**

7. A. *Knives* is the plural form of knife. *Salmon* is a non-count noun, so it does not have a plural form. **See Lesson: Nouns.**

8. D. *Marie Curie, Nobel Prize,* and *1911* are nouns. **See Lesson: Nouns.**

9. D. *Passersby* is the only correct plural form offered. It is the plural of the noun *passerby*. **See Lesson: Nouns.**

10. B. *Her* is a possessive pronoun. **See Lesson: Pronouns.**

11. B. The relative pronoun *who* introduces a clause that gives more information about the noun *Mrs. Sato*. **Pronouns.**

12. A. *Him* is an object pronoun. **Pronouns.**

13. B. *Offered* and *advised* are simple past tense verb forms. **See Lesson: Verbs and Verb Tenses.**

14. A. A complete sentence must have a verb. **See Lesson: Verbs and Verb Tenses.**

15. A. This is a past tense negative, so it takes the helping verb *did* with the base form *like*. **See Lesson: Verbs and Verb Tenses.**

CHAPTER 10 SENTENCE STRUCTURE & LOGIC

TYPES OF SENTENCES

Sentences are a combination of words that communicate a complete thought. Sentences can be written in many ways to signal different relationships among ideas. This lesson will cover (1) simple sentences (2) compound sentences (3) complex sentences (4) parallel structure.

Simple Sentences

A **simple sentence** is a group of words that make up a **complete thought**. To be a complete thought, simple sentences must have one **independent clause**. An independent clause contains a single **subject** (who or what the sentence is about) and a **predicate** (a **verb** and something about the subject.)

Let's take a look at some simple sentences:

Simple Sentence	Subject	Predicate	Complete Thought?
The car was fast.	car	was fast (verb = was)	Yes
Sally waited for the bus.	Sally	waited for the bus (verb = waited)	Yes
The pizza smells delicious.	pizza	smells delicious (verb = smells)	Yes
Anton loves cycling.	Anton	loves cycling (verb = loves)	Yes

It is important to be able to recognize what a simple sentence is in order to avoid **run-ons** and **fragments**, two common grammatical errors.

A **run-on** is when two or more independent clauses are combined without proper punctuation:

FOR EXAMPLE

Gregory is a very talented actor he was the lead in the school play.

If you take a look at this sentence, you can see that it is made up of 2 independent clauses or simple sentences:

1. *Gregory is a very talented actor*
2. *he was the lead in the school play*

You <u>cannot</u> have two independent clauses running into each other without proper punctuation.

You can fix this run-on in the following way:

Gregory is a very talented actor. He was the lead in the school play.

A **fragment** is a group of words that looks like a sentence. It starts with a capital letter and has end punctuation, but when you examine it closely you will see it is not a complete thought.

Let's put this information all together to determine whether a group of words is a simple sentence, a run-on, or a fragment:

Group of Words	Category
Mondays are the worst they are a drag.	Run-On: These are two independent clauses running into one another without proper punctuation. FIX: *Mondays are the worst. They are a drag.*
Because I wanted soda.	Fragment: This is a dependent clause and needs more information to make it a complete thought. FIX: *I went to the store because I wanted soda.*
Ereni is from Greece.	Simple Sentence: YES! This is a simple sentence with a subject (*Ereni*) and a predicate (*is from Greece*), so it is a complete thought.
While I was apple picking.	Fragment: This is a dependent clause and needs more information to make it a complete thought. FIX: *While I was apple picking, I spotted a bunny.*
New York City is magical it is my favorite place.	Run-On: These are two independent clauses running into one another without proper punctuation. FIX: *New York City is magical. It is my favorite place.*

Compound Sentences

A **compound sentence** is a sentence made up of two independent clauses connected with a **coordinating conjunction**.

Let's take a look at the following sentence:

Joe waited for the bus, but it never arrived.

If you take a close look at this compound sentence, you will see that it is made up of two independent clauses:

1. *Joe waited for the bus*
2. *it never arrived*

The word *but* is the coordinating conjunction that connects these two sentences. Notice that the coordinating conjunction has a comma right before it. This is the proper way to punctuate compound sentences.

Here are other examples of compound sentences:

> **FOR EXAMPLE**
>
> *I want to try out for the baseball team, and I also want to try out for track.*
>
> *Sally can play the clarinet in the band, **or** she can play the violin in the orchestra.*
>
> *Mr. Henry is going to run the half marathon, **so** he has a lot of training to do.*
>
> All these sentences are compound sentences since they each have two independent clauses joined by a comma and a coordinating conjunction.

The following is a list of **coordinating conjunctions** that can be used in compound sentences. You can use the mnemonic device "FANBOYS" to help you remember them:

For

And

Nor

But

Or

Yet

So

Think back to Section 1: Simple Sentences. You learned about run-ons. Another way to fix run-ons is by turning the group of words into a compound sentence:

RUN-ON: *Gregory is a very talented actor he was the lead in the school play.*

FIX: *Gregory is a very talented actor,* **so** *he was the lead in the school play.*

Complex Sentences

A **complex** sentence is a sentence that is made up of an independent clause and one or more dependent clauses connected to it.

Think back to Section 1 when you learned about fragments. You learned about a **dependent clause**, the part of a sentence that cannot stand by itself. These clauses need other information to make them complete.

You can recognize a dependent clause because they always begin with a **subordinating conjunction**. These words are a key ingredient in complex sentences.

Here is a list of **subordinating conjunctions**:

after	although	as	because	before
despite	even if	even though	if	in order
that	once	provided that	rather than	since
so that	than	that	though	unless
until	when	whenever	where	whereas
wherever	while	why		

Let's take a look at a few complex sentences:

FOR EXAMPLE

Since the alarm clock didn't go off, I was late for class.

This is an example of a complex sentence because it contains:

A dependent clause: *Since the alarm clock didn't go off*
An independent clause: *I was late for class*
A subordinating conjunction: *since*

Sarah studied all night for the exam even though she did not receive an A.

This is an example of a complex sentence because it contains:

A dependent clause: *even though she did not receive an A*
An independent clause: *Sarah studied all night*
A subordinating conjunction: *even though*

NOTE: To make a complex sentence, you can either start with the dependent clause or the independent clause. When beginning with the dependent clause, you need a comma after it. When beginning with an independent clause, you do not need a comma after it.*

Parallel Structure

Parallel structure is the repetition of a grammatical form within a sentence to make the sentence sound more harmonious. Parallel structure comes into play when you are making a list of items. Stylistically, you want all the items in the list to line up with each other to make them sound better.

Let's take a look at when to use parallel structure:

1. Use parallel structure with verb forms:

    In a sentence listing different verbs, you want all the verbs to use the same form:

    Manuel likes hiking, biking, and mountain climbing.

    In this example, the words *hiking, biking* and *climbing* are all gerunds (having an -ing ending), so the sentence is balanced since the words are all using the gerund form of the verb.

    Manuel likes to hike, bike, and mountain climb.

    In this example, the words *hike, bike* and *climb* are all infinitives (using the basic form of the verb), so the sentence balanced.

    You do not want to mix them up:

    Manuel likes, hiking, biking, and to mountain climb.

    This sentence **does not** use parallel structure since *hiking* and *biking* use the gerund form of the verb and *to mountain climb* uses the infinitive form.

2. Use parallel structure with active and passive voice:

In a sentence written in the **active voice**, the subject performs the action:

Sally kicked the ball.

Sally, the subject, is the one doing the action, kicking the ball.

In a sentence written in the **passive voice**, the subject is acted on by the verb.

The ball was kicked by Sally.

When using parallel structure, you want to make sure your items in a list are either all in **active voice**:

Raymond baked, frosted, and decorated the cake.

Or all in **passive voice**:

The cake was baked, frosted, and decorated by Raymond.

You do not want to mix them up:

The cake was baked, frosted, and Raymond decorated it.

This sentence **does not** use parallel structure because it starts off with passive voice and then switches to active voice.

3. Use parallel structure with the length of terms within a list:

When making a list, you should either have all short individual terms or all long phrases.

Keep these consistent by either choosing short, individual terms:

Cassandra is bold, courageous, and strong.

Or longer phrases:

Cassandra is brave in the face of danger, willing to take risks, and a force to be reckoned with.

You do not want to mix them up:

Cassandra is bold, courageous, and a force to be reckoned with.

This sentence **does not** use parallel structure because the first two terms are short, and the last one is a longer phrase.

Let's Review!

- A simple sentence consists of a clause, which has a single subject and a predicate.
- A compound sentence is made up of two independent clauses connected by a coordinating conjunction.
- A complex sentence is made up of a subordinating conjunction, an independent clause and one or more dependent clauses connected to it.
- Parallel structure is the repetition of a grammatical form within a sentence to make the sentence sound more harmonious.

TYPES OF CLAUSES

There are four types of clauses that are used to create sentences. Sentences with several clauses, and different types of clauses, are considered complex. This lesson will cover (1) independent clauses, (2) dependent clauses and subordinate clauses, and (3) coordinate clauses.

Independent Clause

An **independent clause** is a simple sentence. It has a subject, a verb, and expresses a complete thought.

- Steve went to the store.
- She will cook dinner tonight.
- The class was very boring.
- The author argues that listening to music helps productivity.

Two **independent clauses** can be connected by a semicolon. There are some common words that indicate the beginning of an **independent clause** such as: moreover, also, nevertheless, however, furthermore, consequently.

- I wanted to go to dinner; however, I had to work late tonight.
- She had a job interview; therefore, she dressed nicely.

Dependent and Subordinate Clauses

A **dependent clause** is not a complete sentence. It has a subject and a verb but does not express a complete thought. **Dependent clauses** are also called **subordinate clauses**, because they depend on the **independent or main clause** to complete the thought. A sentence that has both at least one **independent clause** and one **subordinate clause** are considered complex.

Subordinate clauses can be placed before or after the **independent clause**. When the **subordinate clause** begins the sentence, there should be a comma before the **main clause**. If the **subordinate clause** ends the sentence, there is no need for a comma.

Dependent clauses also have common indicator words. These are often called **subordinating conjunctions** because they connect a **dependent clause** to an **independent clause**. Some of these include: although, after, as, because, before, if, once, since, unless, until, when, whether, and while. Relative pronouns also signify the beginning of a **subordinate clause**. These include: that, which, who, whom, whichever, whoever, whomever, and whose.

- When I went to school...
- Since she joined the team...
- After we saw the play...
- *Because she studied hard*, she received an A on her exam.
- *Although the professor was late*, the class was very informative.
- I can't join you unless I finish my homework.

Coordinate Clause

A **coordinate clause** is a sentence or phrase that combines clauses of equal grammatical rank (verbs, nouns, adjectives, phrases, or independent clauses) by using a coordinating conjunction (and, but, for, nor, or so, yet). **Coordinating conjunctions** cannot connect a **dependent or subordinate clause** and an **independent clause.**

- She woke up, and he went to bed.
- We did not have cheese, so I went to the store to get some.
- Ice cream and candy taste great, but they are not good for you.
- Do you want to study, or do you want to go to Disneyland?

Let's Review!

- An **independent clause** is a simple sentence that has a noun, a verb, and a complete thought. Two **independent clauses** can be connected by a semicolon.
- A **dependent or subordinate clause** depends on the main clause to complete a thought. A **dependent or subordinate clause** can go before or after the **independent clause** and there are indicator words that signify the beginning of the **dependent or subordinate clause.**
- A **coordinate clause** connects two verbs, nouns, adjectives, phrases, or **independent clauses** using a **coordinating conjunction** (and, but, for, nor, or, so, yet).

SUBJECT AND VERB AGREEMENT

Every sentence must include a **subject** and a **verb**. The subject tells **who or what**, and the verb describes an **action or condition**. Subject and verb agree in number and person.

Roles of Subject and Verb

A complete sentence includes a **subject** and a **verb**. The verb is in the part of the sentence called the **predicate**. A predicate can be thought of as a verb phrase.

Simple Sentences

A sentence can be very simple, with just one or two words as **subject** and one or two words as **predicate**.

Sometimes, in a command, a subject is "understood," rather than written or spoken.

> **BE CAREFUL!**
> **It's** is a contraction of *it is*.
> **Its** (without an apostrophe) is the possessive of the pronoun *it*.

Look at these examples of short sentences:

Sentence	Subject	Predicate, with main verb(s) underlined
I ate.	I	ate
They ran away.	They	ran away
It's OK.	It	is OK
Go and find the cat!	(You)	go and find the cat

More Complex Sentences

Sometimes a subject or predicate is a long phrase or clause.

Some sentences have more than one subject or predicate, or even a predicate within a predicate.

Sentence	Subject(s)	Predicate(s), with main verb(s) underlined
My friend from work had a bad car accident.	My friend from work	had a bad car accident
John, his sister, and I plan to ride our bikes across the country this summer.	John, his sister, and I	plan to ride our bikes across the country this summer
I did so much for them, and they didn't even thank me.*	I; they	did so much for them; didn't even thank me
She wrote a letter that explained the problem.**	She	wrote a letter that explained the problem

*This sentence consists of two clauses, and each clause has its own subject and its own predicate.

**In this sentence, *that explained the problem* is part of the predicate, and it is also a relative clause with own subject and predicate.

Subject and Verb Agreement

Subjects and verbs must agree in **number** and **person**. This means that different subjects take different forms of a verb.

With **regular** verbs, simply add *-s* to the singular third person verb, as shown below:

	Singular		Plural	
	Subject	**Verb**	**Subject**	**Verb**
(first person)	I	play	we	play
(second person)	you	play	you	play
(third person)	he/she/it	plays	they	play

Some verbs are **irregular**, so simply adding *-s* doesn't work. For example:

verb	form for third person singular subject
have	has
do	does
fix	fixes

Look for subject-verb agreement in the following sentences:

- *I* usually <u>eat</u> a banana for breakfast.
- *Marcy* <u>does</u> well in school.
- The *cat* <u>licks</u> its fur.

Subject-Verb Agreement for the Verb *Be*

Present		Past	
I am	we are	I was	we were
you are	you are	you were	you were
he/she/it is	they are	they were	they were

Things to Look Out For

Subject-verb agreement can be tricky. Be careful of these situations:

- **Sentences with more than one subject:** If two subjects are connected by *and,* the subject is **plural**. When two singular subjects are connected by *neither/nor,* the subject is **singular**.

  Sandra and Luiz <u>shop</u>. (plural)
  Neither Sandra nor Luiz <u>has</u> money. (singular)

- **Collective nouns:** Sometimes a noun stands for a group of people or things. If the subject is **one group**, it is considered **singular**.

Those students are still on chapter three. (plural)
That class <u>is</u> still on chapter three. (singular)

- ***There is*** **and** ***there are***: With pronouns such as *there, what,* and *where*, the verb agrees with the noun or pronoun that follows it.

  There'<u>s</u> a rabbit! (singular)
  Where <u>are</u> my shoes? (plural)

- **Indefinite pronouns:** Subjects such as *everybody, someone,* and *nobody* are **singular**. Subjects such as *all, none,* and *any* can be either **singular or plural**.

  Everyone in the band <u>plays</u> well. (singular)
  All of the students <u>are</u> there. (plural)
  All <u>is</u> well. (singular)

Let's Review!

- Every sentence has a subject and a verb.
- The predicate is the part of the sentence that contains the verb.
- The subject and verb must agree in number and person.
- The third person singular subject takes a different verb form.

MODIFIERS

A modifier is a word, phrase, or clause that adds detail or changes (modifies) another word in the sentence. Descriptive words such as adjectives and adverbs are examples of modifiers.

The Role of Modifiers in a Sentence

Modifiers make a sentence more descriptive and interesting.

Look at these simple sentences. Notice how much more interesting they are with modifiers added.

Simple sentence	With modifiers added
I drove.	I drove my family along snowy roads to my grandmother's house.
They ate.	They ate a fruit salad of blueberries, strawberries, peaches, and apples.
The boy looked.	The boy in pajamas looked out the window at the birds eating from the feeder.
He climbed.	He climbed the ladder to fix the roof.

Look at the modifiers in bold type in the following sentences. Notice how these words add description to the basic idea in the sentence.

	Modifier	Word it Modifies	Type
The hungry man ate **quickly**.	1. the; 2. hungry; 3. quickly	1. man 2. man; 3. ate	1. article 2. adjective; 3. adverb
The small child, **who had scraped his knee**, cried **quietly**.	1. the; 2. small; 3. who had scraped his knee; 4. quietly	1. child; 2. child; 3. child; 4. cried	1. article; 2. adjective; 3. adjective clause; 4. adverb
The horse **standing near the fence** is **beautiful**.	1. the; 2. standing near the fence; 3. beautiful	1. horse; 2. horse; 3. horse	1. article; 2. participle phrase; 3. adjective
Hana and Mario stood **by the lake** and watched **a gorgeous** sunset.	1. by the lake; 2. a; 3. gorgeous	1. stood; 2. sunset; 3. sunset	1. prepositional phrase; 2. article; 3. adjective
They tried **to duck out of the way as the large spider dangled from the ceiling**.	1. to duck out of the way; 2. as the large spider dangled; 3. from the ceiling	1. tried; 2. duck; 3. dangled	1. infinitive phrase; 2. adverb clause; 3. prepositional phrase

DID YOU KNOW?

Adjectives and adverbs are not the only modifiers. With a participle phrase, **an -ing verb** can act as a modifier. For example, *eating from the feeder* modifies *the birds*. With an infinitive, ***to* plus the main form of a verb** can act as a modifier. For example, *to fix the roof* modifies *climbed*.

Misplaced and Dangling Modifiers

A **misplaced modifier** is a modifier that is placed incorrectly in a sentence, so that it modifies the wrong word.

A **dangling modifier** is a modifier that modifies a word that should be included in the sentence but is not.

Look at these examples.

- First, notice the modifier, in bold.
- Next, look for the word it modifies.

> **BE CAREFUL!**
> Sometimes there is a modifier within a modifier. For example, in the clause *as the large spider dangled,* the and *large* are words that modify *spider.*

Incorrect	Problem	How to fix it	Correct
Sam wore his new shirt to school, **which was too big for him.**	Misplaced modifier. Notice the placement of the modifier **which was too big for him**. It is placed after the word *school*, which makes it seem like *school* is the word it describes. However, this was not the writer's intention. The writer intended for **which was too big for him** to describe the word *shirt*.	The modifier needs to be placed after the word *shirt*, rather than after the word *school*.	Sam wore his new shirt, **which was too big for him**, to school.
Running down the hallway, Maria's bag of groceries fell.	Dangling modifier. The modifier **running down the hallway** is placed before the phrase *Maria's bag of groceries*, which makes it seem this is what it describes. However, this was not the writer's intention; the *bag of groceries* cannot run! The correct reference would be the noun *Maria*, which was omitted from the sentence completely.	The modifier must reference *Maria*, rather than *Maria's bag of groceries*. This can be fixed by adding the noun *Maria* as a subject.	**Running down the hallway,** Maria dropped her bag of groceries.
With a leash on, my sister walked the dog.	Misplaced modifier. The modifier **with a leash on** is placed before *my sister*, which makes it seem like she is wearing a leash.	Move the modifier so that it is next to *the dog*, rather than *my sister*.	My sister walked the dog, **who had a leash on**.

Let's Review!

- A modifier is a word, phrase, or clause that adds detail by describing or modifying another word in the sentence.
- Adverbs, adjectives, articles, and prepositional phrases are some examples of modifiers.
- Misplaced and dangling modifiers have unclear references, leading to confusion about the meaning of a sentence.

> **BE CAREFUL!**
> A modifier should be placed next to the word it modifies. Misplaced and dangling modifiers lead to confusion about the meaning of a sentence.

Chapter 10 Sentence Structure & Logic Practice Quiz 1

1. **Which modifier, if any, modifies the underlined word in the following sentence?**

   We always visit the <u>bakery</u> on the corner when we are in town.

   A. always

   B. on the corner

   C. when we are in town

   D. No modifier describes it.

2. **Identify the dangling or misplaced modifier, if there is one.**

   Having been repaired, we can drive the car again.

   A. Having been repaired

   B. we can drive

   C. the car again

   D. There is no dangling or misplaced modifier.

3. **Which word does the underlined modifier describe?**

   I looked up to Marvin, <u>who was a year older</u>.

   A. I   C. up

   B. looked   D. Marvin

4. **Which part of the following sentence is the predicate?**

   Mai and her friend Oksana love to ride roller coasters.

   A. Mai and her friend Oksana

   B. and her friend Oksana

   C. love to ride roller coasters

   D. roller coasters

5. **Select the "understood" subject with which the underlined verb must agree.**

   <u>Watch</u> out!

   A. You   C. I

   B. He   D. Out

6. **How many verbs must agree with the underlined subject in the following sentence?**

   <u>Kareem Abdul-Jabbar</u>, my favorite basketball player, dribbles, shoots, and scores to win the game!

   A. 0   C. 2

   B. 1   D. 3

7. **Identify the dependent clause in the following sentence.**

   Joe always did his homework before he went to bed.

   A. Went to bed

   B. Before he went to bed

   C. Joe always did his homework

   D. Did his homework

8. **Fill in the blank with the correct subordinating conjunction.**

   You cannot go to the movies with your friends ____ you finish your homework.

   A. If   C. Since

   B. Once   D. Unless

9. Identify the independent clause in the following sentence.

Although most people understand the benefits of exercise, people do not exercise as much as they should.

A. Although most people understand

B. The benefits of exercise

C. People do not exercise as much as they should

D. People do not exercise

10. The house at the top of the hill

_____.

Which of the following options would complete the above sentence to make it a simple sentence?

A. is very old.

B. it is very old

C. is very old despite having a modern feel.

D. is very old, and it has a very modern feel.

11. Which of the following is an example of a simple sentence?

A. Tamara's sporting goods store.

B. Tamara has a sporting good store in town.

C. Tamara has a sporting goods store it is in town.

D. Tamara's sporting goods store is in town, and she is the owner.

12. During the movie.

Which of the following options correctly fixes the above fragment?

A. During the movie I spilled my popcorn.

B. During the movie, I spilled my popcorn.

C. During the movie. I spilled my popcorn.

D. During the movie, and I spilled my popcorn.

CHAPTER 10 SENTENCE STRUCTURE & LOGIC PRACTICE QUIZ 1 – ANSWER KEY

1. B. *On the corner* modifies *bakery*. **See Lesson: Modifiers.**

2. A. *Having been repaired* is placed where it references *we*, but it should reference *the car.* **See Lesson: Modifiers.**

3. D. *Who was a year older* describes *Marvin.* **See Lesson: Modifiers.**

4. C. The subject is *Mai and her friend Oksana*, and the predicate is *love to ride roller coasters.* **See Lesson: Subject and Verb Agreement.**

5. A. In a command like this one, the "understood" subject is *you.* **See Lesson: Subject and Verb Agreement.**

6. D. The verbs *dribbles, shoots,* and *scores* must agree with the subject *Kareem Abdul-Jabbar.* **See Lesson: Subject and Verb Agreement.**

7. B. Before he went to bed. It is dependent because it does not express a complete thought and relies on the independent clause. The word "before" also signifies the beginning of a dependent clause. **See Lesson: Types of Clauses.**

8. D. Unless. The word "unless" signifies the beginning of a dependent clause and is the only conjunction that makes sense in the sentence. **See Lesson: Types of Clauses.**

9. C. People do not exercise as much as they should. It is independent because it has a subject, verb, and expresses a complete thought. **See Lesson: Types of Clauses.**

10. A. This option would make the sentence a complete thought with a subject and a predicate. **See Lesson: Types of Sentences.**

11. B. This is a simple sentence since it contains one independent clause consisting of a simple subject and a predicate. **See Lesson: Types of Sentences.**

12. B. This sentence correctly fixes the fragment. **See Lesson: Types of Sentences.**

CHAPTER 10 SENTENCE STRUCTURE & LOGIC PRACTICE QUIZ 2

1. Which word is a modifier in the following sentence?

   I am following the news story closely.

   A. I
   B. am
   C. following
   D. closely

2. Identify the dangling modifier in the following sentence.

   After reading the book, the movie that just came out must be pretty bad.

   A. After reading the book
   B. the movie
   C. that just came out
   D. must be really bad

3. Identify the likely misplaced modifier in the following sentence.

   Earlier this week, the young fishermen caught twenty fish, who were out all day.

   A. Earlier this week
   B. young
   C. twenty
   D. who were out all day

4. Select the subject that would be incorrect in the following sentence.

   ___ are excited about the upcoming election.

   A. He
   B. We
   C. You
   D. They

5. Select the correct verb to complete the following sentence.

   Our family ___ staying home for the holidays this year.

   A. is
   B. be
   C. am
   D. are

6. Select the part of speech that is always in the predicate.

   A. Noun
   B. Pronoun
   C. Adjective
   D. Verb

7. Identify the dependent clause in the following sentence.

   We decided to take our dog to the park although it was hot outside.

   A. We decided to take our dog
   B. to the park
   C. although it was hot outside
   D. to take our dog

8. Fill in the blank with the correct subordinating conjunction.

   I had a bad stomach flu but started to regain my appetite, ___ is good news.

   A. so
   B. that
   C. which
   D. whereas

9. Identify the independent clause in the following sentence.

You need to call your mother as soon as you get home.

A. You need to call your mother

B. As soon as you get home

C. You get home

D. You need to call

10. You can see the wonders of our country
_____.

Which of the following options would complete the above sentence to make it a simple sentence?

A. on a road trip

B. take a road trip.

C. and, on a road trip.

D. rather than taking a road trip.

11. Eating salmon once a week
_____.

Which of the following options would complete the above sentence to make it a simple sentence?

A. is a healthy choice.

B. is good, and it is healthy.

C. is healthy it is a good choice.

D. is healthy while still being good.

12. Which of the following is an example of a simple sentence?

A. Calcium for bones.

B. Calcium makes bones strong.

C. Calcium is necessary it makes bones strong.

D. Calcium is good for bones, so people need it.

CHAPTER 10 SENTENCE STRUCTURE & LOGIC PRACTICE QUIZ 2 – ANSWER KEY

1. **D.** *Closely* is a modifier; it is an adverb that describes *following*. **See Lesson: Modifiers.**

2. **A.** *After reading the book* is a modifier that, by its placement, is incorrectly referenced to *the movie*. The modifier is dangling because there is no noun or pronoun that references the person who read the book. **See Lesson: Modifiers.**

3. **D.** *Who were out all day* most likely refers to *fishermen*, so it should be placed after that word, not after *fish*. **See Lesson: Modifiers.**

4. **A.** The subject *he* takes the verb form *is*, not *are*. **See Lesson: Subject and Verb Agreement.**

5. **A.** The subject *family* is singular and takes the verb *is*. **See Lesson: Subject and Verb Agreement.**

6. **D.** The predicate is the part of the sentence that contains the verb. **See Lesson: Subject and Verb Agreement.**

7. **C.** Although it was hot outside. It is dependent because it does not express a complete thought and relies on the independent clause. The word "although" also signifies the beginning of a dependent clause. **See Lesson: Types of Clauses.**

8. **C.** Which. The word "which" signifies the beginning of a dependent clause and is the only conjunction that makes sense in the sentence. **See Lesson: Types of Clauses.**

9. **A.** You need to call your mother. It is independent because it has a subject, verb, and expresses a complete thought. **See Lesson: Types of Clauses.**

10. **A.** This option would make the sentence a simple sentence. **See Lesson: Types of Sentences.**

11. **A.** This option would make the sentence a simple sentence. **See Lesson: Types of Sentences.**

12. **B.** This is a simple sentence since it contains one independent clause consisting of a simple subject and a predicate. **See Lesson: Types of Sentences.**

SECTION IV

THE ESSAY

The Essay: 1 essay prompt, untimed

Area assessed: Persuasive Essay Writing

ESSAY WRITING TIPS

- Know the steps of the Writing Process; use scrap paper provided to jot down ideas and plan your rough draft.
- Read the essay prompt carefully and slowly. Identify the objective of the prompt and be sure to answer the question provided.
- Use essay revision strategies to ensure that you have written a clear main idea with specific details and examples to support your position.
- Remember to use transition words to move from one paragraph to the next.
- Re-read your final draft to check your spelling, punctuation, and other conventions of English.

CHAPTER 11 ESSAY WRITING

THE WRITING PROCESS

Effective writers break the writing task down into steps to tackle one at a time. They allow a certain amount of room for messiness and mistakes in the early stages of writing but attempt to create a polished finished product in the end.

KEEP IN MIND . . .

If your writing process varies from the steps outlined below, that's okay—as long as you can produce a polished, organized text in the end. Some writers like to write part or all of the first draft before they go back to outline and organize. Others make a plan in the prewriting phase, only to change the plan when they're drafting. It is not uncommon for writers to compose the body of an essay before the introduction, or to change the thesis statement at the end to make it fit the essay they wrote rather than the one they intended to write.

The point of teaching the writing process is not to force you to follow all the steps in order every time. The point is to give you a sense of the mental tasks involved in creating a well-written text. If you are drafting and something is not working, you will know you can bounce back to the prewriting stage and change your plan. If you are outlining and you end up fleshing out one of your points in complete sentences, you will realize you still need to go back to finish the rest of the plan before you continue drafting.

In other words, it is fine to change the order of steps from the writing process,*or to jump around between them. Published writers do it all the time, and you can too.

*But almost everyone really does benefit from saving the editing until the end.

The Writing Process

A writer goes through several discrete steps to transform an idea into a polished text. This series of steps is called the **writing process**. Individual writers' processes may vary somewhat, but most writers roughly follow the steps below.

Prewriting is making a plan for writing. Prewriting may include brainstorming, free writing, outlining, or mind mapping. The prewriting process can be messy and include errors. Note that if a writing task requires research, the prewriting process is longer because you need to find, read, and organize source materials.

Drafting is getting the bulk of the text down on the page in complete sentences. Although most writers find drafting difficult, two things can make it easier: 1) prewriting to make a clear plan, and 2) avoiding perfectionism. Drafting is about moving ideas from the mind to the page, even if they do not sound right or the writer is not sure how to spell a word. For writing tasks that involve research, drafting also involves making notes about where the information came from.

Revising is making improvements to the content and structure of a draft. Revising may involve moving ideas around, adding information to flesh out a point, removing chunks of text that are redundant or off-topic, and strengthening the thesis statement. Revising may also mean improving readability by altering sentence structure, smoothing transitions, and improving word choice.

Editing is fixing errors in spelling, grammar, and punctuation. Many writers feel the urge to do this throughout the writing process, but it saves time to wait until the end. There is no point perfecting the grammar and spelling in a sentence that is going to get cut later.

For research projects, you also need to craft **citations,** or notes that tell readers where you got your information. If you noted this information while working on your prewriting and first draft, all you need to do now is format it correctly. (If you did not make notes as you worked, you will have to search laboriously through all your research materials again.) If you are using MLA or APA styles, citations are included in parentheses at the ends of sentences. If you are using Chicago style, citations appear in footnotes or endnotes.

Prewriting Techniques

Prewriting encompasses a wide variety of tasks that happen before you start writing. Many new writers skip or skimp on this step, perhaps because a writer's prewriting efforts are not clearly visible in the final product. But writers who spend time gathering and organizing information tend to produce more polished work.

Thinking silently is a valid form of prewriting. So is telling someone about what you are planning to write. For very short pieces based on your prior knowledge, it may be enough to use these—but most long writing tasks go better if you also use some or all of the strategies below.

Gathering Information

- **Conducting research** involves looking for information in books, articles, websites, and other sources. Internet research is almost always necessary, but do not overlook the benefits of a trip to a library, where you can find in-depth printed sources and also get help from research librarians.
- **Brainstorming** is making a list of short phrases or sentences related to the topic. Brainstorming works best if you literally write down every idea that comes to mind, whether or not you think you can use it. This frees up your mind to find unconscious associations and insights.
- **Free writing** is writing whatever comes to mind about your topic in sentences and paragraphs. Free writing goes fast and works best if you avoid judging your ideas as you go.

Organizing information

- **Mind mapping** arranges ideas into an associative structure. Write your topic, main idea, or argument in a circle in the middle of the page. Then draw lines and make additional circles for supporting points and details. You can combine this step with brainstorming to make a big mess of ideas, some of which you later cross out if you decide not to use them. Or you can do this after brainstorming, using the ideas from your brainstormed list to fill in the bubbles.

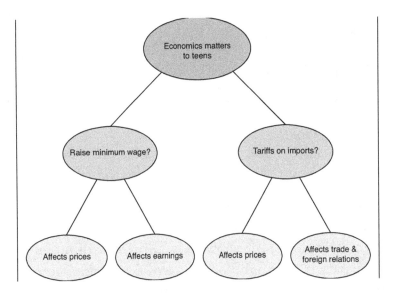

- **Outlining** arranges ideas into a linear structure. It starts with an introduction, includes supporting points and details to back them up, and ends with a conclusion. Traditionally, an outline uses Roman numerals for main ideas and letters for minor ideas.

  Example:
  I.   Introduction - Economics should be a required subject in high school because it affects political and social issues that matter to students.
  II. Domestic Issues - Minimum wage
       a. How do people decide if the minimum wage should be raised?
       b. They need to know how changes to the minimum wage affect workers, businesses, and prices.
  III. Foreign Issues - Tariffs
       a. How do people decide if they favor taxes on imports?
       b. They need to know how tariffs affect prices and trade.
  IV. Conclusion – These issues affect how much money high school graduates can earn and what they can afford to buy.

Paragraph Organization

Paragraphs need to have a clear, coherent organization. Whether you are providing information, arguing a point, or entertaining the reader, the ultimate goal is to make it easy for people to follow your thoughts.

Introductions

The opening of a text must hook the reader's interest, provide necessary background information on the topic, and state the main point. In an academic essay, all of this typically happens in a single paragraph. For instance, an analytical paper on the theme of unrequited love in a novel might start with a stark statement about love, a few sentences identifying the title and author of the work under discussion, and a thesis statement about the author's apparently bleak outlook on love.

Body Paragraphs

In informational and persuasive writing, body paragraphs should typically do three things:

1. Make a point.
2. Illustrate the point with facts, quotations, or examples.
3. Explain how this evidence relates to the point.

Body paragraphs need to stay on topic. That is, the point needs to relate clearly to the thesis statement or main idea. For example, in an analytical paper about unrequited love in a novel, each body paragraph should say something different about the author's bleak outlook on love. Each paragraph might focus on a different character's struggles with love, presenting evidence in the form of an example or quotation from the story and explaining what it suggests about the author's outlook. When you present evidence like this, you must introduce it clearly, stating where it came from in the book. Don't assume readers understand exactly what it has to do with your main point; spell it out for them with a clear explanation.

The structure above is useful in most academic writing situations, but sometimes you need to use other structures:

Chronological – Describe how events happen in order.

Sequential – Present a series of steps.

Descriptive – Describe a topic in a coherent spatial order, e.g. from top to bottom.

Cause/Effect – Present an action and its results.

Compare/Contrast – Describe the similarities and differences between two or more topics.

Conclusions

Like introductions, conclusions have a unique structure. A conclusion restates the thesis and main points in different words and, ideally, adds a bit more. For instance, it may take a broader outlook on the topic, giving readers a sense of why it matters or how the main point affects the world. A text should end with a sentence or two that brings the ideas together and makes the piece feel finished. This can be a question, a quotation, a philosophical statement, an intense image, or a request that readers take action.

Let's Review!

- The writing process includes prewriting, drafting, revision, and editing.
- For projects that involve research, writers must include the creation of citations within the writing process.
- Effective writers spend time gathering and organizing information during the prewriting stage.
- Writers must organize paragraphs coherently so that readers can follow their thoughts.

Essay Revisions and Transitions

A well-written essay should be easy to follow and convincing. The words should be well-chosen, and the transitions should be smooth.

Content, Organization, and Coherence

To revise an essay effectively, you must read through your own work with a critical eye. As you read, consider the content, organization, and flow of ideas.

Content

Every time you write, you are setting out to communicate something. Check to make sure you have clearly and succinctly stated an argument or main point, usually in a one-sentence thesis statement at the end of the first paragraph. Does your essay follow through on this point? By the end, you should have defended or developed it completely without leaving any holes or veering off onto other subjects. If you have not done this, add or delete information.

Organization

The ideas in your essay need to appear in an order that makes sense and avoids repetition. As you revise, check to make sure your ideas flow in a logical order, and move sentences around if they do not. Some topics lend themselves naturally to a particular type of organization. For instance, sometimes you will use chronological order, or you will outline causes first and effects second.

However, many analytical and persuasive papers do not fall into one natural organization. In this case, just choose an order that makes sense to you. In an argumentative paper, for instance, you could place your strongest arguments first and last, with the less impactful ones in the middle. No matter what, be sure each paragraph makes a point that is clearly distinguishable from the points in the other paragraphs. Do not just repeat the same idea in different words.

Coherence

When the ideas in an essay flow in a logical and consistent way that readers can easily follow, we say the writing has **coherence**. A well-written essay makes it possible for readers to follow the writer's thoughts. Make sure you have clear topic sentences in each paragraph to link back to the main idea. Do not bounce off onto new subtopics without explaining how they relate. Within paragraphs, explain your points and evidence explicitly. Do not leave gaps or make readers guess how one point relates to another.

Rhetorical Effectiveness and Use of Evidence

When you revise a persuasive essay, you must evaluate your work for **rhetorical effectiveness**. In other words, you need to make sure it is convincing. The cornerstones of rhetorically effective writing are reason, trust, and emotions.

Every good argument is grounded in logic and reasoning. When you offer opinions, you should present facts and logic to back them up. For example, if you are arguing that young children should not be required to do hours of homework every night, you could cite a study showing that kids under twelve did not learn more when they spent additional time doing homework outside of class.

Good arguments must also inspire trust. One of the primary ways to do this is to use credible sources and identify them clearly. The evidence above would generally be considered trustworthy if the study was conducted by a Harvard professor with a doctorate in education. It is a good idea to share information like this in an essay. It is not a good idea to use evidence if it comes from a source that is not credible.

It is also appropriate to engage the emotions in persuasive writing. In an essay opposing homework, you could call on readers' nostalgia and sense of fun by briefly describing the enjoyable activities kids could do instead of homework. But be careful. Good writing never uses personal attacks or scare tactics. In other words, it would be inappropriate to call people who believe in homework "fun killers" or to make an exaggerated suggestion that kids forced to do too much homework will suffer deep psychological damage.

Using Evidence

There are several rules of thumb for using evidence to back up your ideas.

- It must genuinely back up your thesis. Imagine you are arguing that kids under 12 should not do homework at all, and you find a study that says elementary school kids who did three hours of homework per night did not learn any more than kids who did only one hour. The study supports limited homework; it does not clearly support your thesis.
- If evidence comes from an outside source, it must be introduced and cited correctly. In general, you should name and share the credentials of your source the first time you introduce it. Afterward, you may refer to the same source by last name only.
- You need to explain how the evidence fits the argument. Readers may not understand what you are thinking about the evidence you present unless you spell it out for them.
- You need the right amount of evidence—not too much, not too little. Back up every opinion. One to three pieces of evidence per point should suffice. Do not continue piling on additional evidence to support a point you have already defended.

Word Choice

After you have revised for major issues like content, organization, and evidence, it is time to consider your word choice. This means you should attempt to use the right word at the right time. Below are several thoughts to consider as you hone your word choice.

Simplicity

The first goal of writing is to be understood. Many students try to use the biggest words they can, but it is usually a better style choice to choose an ordinary word. Do not use fancy vocabulary unless you have a good reason.

Precision

Sometimes the need for precision is a good reason for choosing a fancier word. There are times when it is best to say you hurt your knee, and there are times when it is best to say you injured your anterior cruciate ligament. Consider what your readers need to know and why. An audience of doctors might need or appreciate the medical terminology, whereas a general audience would likely be better served by the simpler language.

Tone

You can establish a clear tone by considering and manipulating the connotations of the words you use. Many words have a positive or negative connotation, whereas others are more neutral. *Cheap* has a negative tone, whereas *economical* is positive and *inexpensive* is neutral. If you are writing about making a purchase, choosing one or another of these words can subtly convey your attitude about what you bought.

Formality

Our language contains many levels of formality. Academic writing usually calls for slightly more formal language than daily speech. In academic writing, you should avoid slang, contractions, and abbreviations like *idk* or *tfw* that are commonly used in text messages and on the Internet. Depending on the writing task, you may also choose more formal words like *purchase* rather than less formal words like *buy*.

Inclusivity

Aim to use language that includes everyone, not language that plays into stereotypes and gender biases. Avoid referring to the entire human race as *man* or *mankind*. Use gender-neutral words like *firefighter* over gender-specific words like *fireman*. Do not assume people are male or female just because they belong to a certain profession. For example, do not automatically refer to a doctor as *he* or a preschool teacher as *she*. Note that using plurals can make it possible to write around gendered pronouns entirely. That is, if you refer to doctors or preschool teachers in the plural, you can refer back to them neutrally as *they*.

Transitions

At the very end of your revision process, read your work and make sure that your ideas flow smoothly from one to the next. Use connecting words and phrases, or **transitions**, to link ideas and help readers follow the flow of your thoughts. The number of possible ways to transition between ideas is almost limitless. Below are a few common transition words, categorized by the way they link ideas.

Type of Transition	Example
Time and sequence transitions help show when events happened in time.	First, second, next, now, then, at this point, after, afterward, before this, previously, formerly, thereafter, finally, in conclusion
Addition or emphasis transitions let readers know when you are building on an established line of thought or stressing an important idea.	Moreover, also, likewise, furthermore, above all, indeed, in fact
Example transitions introduce ideas that illustrate a point.	For example, for instance, to illustrate, to demonstrate
Causation transitions indicate a cause-and-effect relationship.	As a result, consequently, thus, therefore
Contrast transitions indicate a difference between ideas.	Nevertheless, despite, in contrast, however

Different types of transitions are necessary in different parts of an essay. Within a paragraph, you should use short transitions of one or two words to show how the information in one sentence is linked to the information preceding it. But when you are starting a new paragraph or making another major shift in thought, you may take time to explain relationships more thoroughly.

> **Between Sentences:** Clara was in a minor car accident last week. *Afterward*, she experienced headaches and dizziness that worsened over time.

> **Between Paragraphs:** *Because of her worsening headaches and dizziness*, Clara has found it increasingly difficult to work at her computer.

Note that longer transitions are long because they have content to explain how ideas relate. Some long transitions, such as the very wordy "due to the fact that" take up space without adding more meaning than simpler words like "because." Very long-winded transitions are considered poor style.

Let's Review!

- When you revise an essay, consider content, organization, and coherence first.
- Rhetorically effective writing appeals to the reader's reason and inspires trust and emotions appropriately.
- Use clear evidence to back up every opinion in your writing.
- Aim to use exactly the right words for the writing task at hand.
- Use appropriate transitions to create a smooth flow of ideas.

THE ESSAY SECTION

For the Essay Section of the TSI, you will be asked to write a five paragraph persuasive essay (350-500 words) on a controversial issue or current events topic.

You will be assessed on your ability to clearly state a main idea, provide specific examples and details to back up your main idea, and follow the conventions of standard English. You will not be allowed to outside resources, such as a dictionary, but you may use plain scratch paper (provided at the testing center) to plan your essay and write your rough draft(s).

How to Write a Persuasive Essay

The purpose of a persuasive essay is **to convince the reader** to think or act in a particular way.

A successful persuasive essay should:

- Clearly state the issue and your position on it in the introduction
- Use language appropriate to the audience you are trying to convince
- Support your position with facts, statistics, and reasons
- Answer possible objections to your position
- Show clear reasoning
- Conclude with a summary of your position or a call to action

A persuasive essay follows the traditional 5-paragraph essay structure and should contain an introductory paragraph, body paragraphs, and a concluding paragraph.

Paragraph 1:

The first goal of your **introductory paragraph** is to introduce your topic. The introduction should contain a strong opening sentence that hooks the reader. If your goal is to urge the reader to act a certain way, you must capture their interest and make them want to read your position. Start off with an anecdote, and unusual detail related to your subject, a quotation, a question, or some other strong statement that will grab the reader's attention.

The second goal of your introductory paragraph is to express your opinion about the topic. Your thesis statement should clearly state your position, or an opinion, about the subject. Your position statement should be clear and direct so the reader understands what you are trying to accomplish with your essay.

Paragraphs 2, 3, and 4:

The **body paragraphs** are where you will develop your position about your subject. This is where you state any facts, examples, and explanations that support your main ideas. Each body paragraph should contain one well-developed example. Your examples can come from just about anywhere: business, current events, entertainment, history, politics, pop culture, science, even your own personal experience.

Your goals for each body paragraph are to: introduce an example, describe the example, explain how the example fully supports your thesis. Be sure to use transition words at the beginning of each body paragraph to introduce your next example.

Paragraph 5:

The ultimate goal of your persuasive paper is to convince your audience to act or think about your given subject in a particular way. In your **concluding paragraph**, you should introduce the opposing side to your argument. Then refute their position by reinforcing the validity of your thesis. Use a strong ending sentence to emphasize the main point of your essay.

Sample Essay Prompts

Before you sit for your exam, practice writing sample essays to become familiar with the process and comfortable with the format. Below are three sample essay prompts. Choose at least 2 topics and write a practice essay.

Try to follow the paragraph organization as outlined above. Then, once you have written your draft, review the rules of grammar and conventions of English (spelling, punctuation, capitalization) in the Reading and Writing sections of this study guide to help you fine-tune your writing. If the opportunity permits, ask a teacher, relative, or friend read your essay and offer feedback on your work.

Essay Prompts:

1. **Is society too dependent on technology?** Text messaging has become a valuable way of communicating in today's society. However, some people spend too much time sending messages by phone instead of interacting with others face to face. Addressing an audience of your peers, explain why you agree or disagree with this observation.

2. **Should the minimum wage be increased?** Many business owners argue that raising the minimum wage would result in hardship and cause them to raise their prices. But many workers argue raising the minimum wage is necessary to help low-income workers dig out of poverty.

3. **Are security cameras an invasion of privacy?** While security cameras are in place to protect both businesses and the general public, some argue cameras have gone too far and actually invade privacy because people are constantly under surveillance.

SECTION V
FULL-LENGTH PRACTICE EXAMS

TSI PRACTICE EXAM 1

Section I. Math

1. A circle has an area of 12 square feet. Find the diameter to the nearest tenth of a foot. Use 3.14 for π.

    A. 1.0   C. 3.0

    B. 2.0   D. 4.0

2. Half of a circular garden with a radius of 11.5 feet needs weeding. Find the area in square feet that needs weeding. Round to the nearest hundredth. Use 3.14 for π.

    A. 207.64   C. 519.08

    B. 415.27   D. 726.73

3. What is the number of symmetry lines for a regular hexagon?

    A. 2   C. 6

    B. 4   D. 8

4. Which decimal is the least?

    A. 5.2304   C. 5.2403

    B. 5.3204   D. 5.3024

5. Change 2.5 to a fraction. Simplify completely.

    A. $2\frac{1}{8}$ C. $2\frac{1}{3}$

    B. $2\frac{1}{4}$ D. $2\frac{1}{2}$

6. Solve the equation for the unknown, $3x-8 + 5 + 2x = 4x-x + 6$.

    A. $-\frac{9}{2}$ C. $\frac{2}{9}$

    B. $-\frac{2}{9}$ D. $\frac{9}{2}$

7. Solve the system of equations,
    $x = -3y + 10$
    $x = 3y-8$.

    A. (-1, 3)   C. (1, 3)

    B. (-3, 1)   D. (3, 1)

8. Solve the system of equations by graphing, $\begin{aligned} 3x + 4y &= -5 \\ -2x + 2y &= 8 \end{aligned}$.

A.

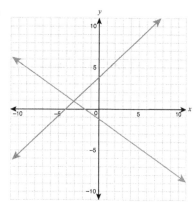

B.

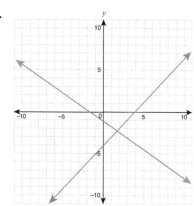

C.

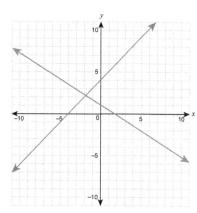

D.

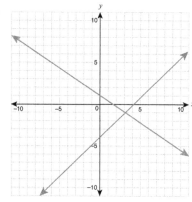

9. The bar chart shows the number of boys and girls who participate in sports. What year had the most participants?

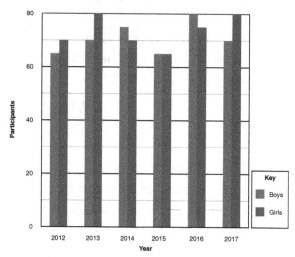

A. 2013   C. 2016

B. 2014   D. 2017

10. A basketball has a diameter of 10 inches. What is the volume in cubic inches inside the ball? Use 3.14 for π.

A. 261.67   C. 1,046.67

B. 523.33   D. 2,093.33

11. Multiply $\frac{2}{3} \times \frac{4}{15}$.

A. $\frac{3}{20}$ C. $\frac{8}{45}$

B. $\frac{1}{6}$ D. $\frac{1}{3}$

12. Perform the operation, $(8x^2 - 6x - 3) - (4x^2 - 5x + 4)$.

A. $4x^2 - 11x - 7$ C. $4x^2 - x - 7$

B. $4x^2 - 11x + 1$ D. $4x^2 - x + 1$

13. Simplify $(4x^3)^2$.

A. $8x^5$ C. $16x^5$

B. $8x^6$ D. $16x^6$

14. If the ratio of women to men in a certain industry is 5:4, how many people are in that industry?

    A. 9   C. 900

    B. 20   D. Not enough information

15. Which number satisfies the proportion $\frac{378}{?} = \frac{18}{7}$?

    A. 18   C. 972

    B. 147   D. 2,646

16. Given the coordinates for a rectangle $(-4, -1), (-9, -1), (-9, -8)(-4, -8)$, find the length of each side of the rectangle.

    A. 2 units and 3 units   C. 5 units and 3 units

    B. 2 units and 7 units   D. 5 units and 7 units

17. Solve the equation by any method, $x^2 + 16x + 33 = 0$.

    A. $-8 \pm \sqrt{31}$ C. $-8 \pm \sqrt{33}$

    B. $8 \pm \sqrt{31}$ D. $8 \pm \sqrt{33}$

18. A school wants to know the daily attendance of all classes. What data would be good for a census?

    A. Attendance on Fridays

    B. Attendance every day

    C. Attendance for math classes

    D. Attendance after holiday breaks

19. A car repair shop wants to create a survey about the performance of car batteries. Which is an example of a survey?

    A. Testing all car batteries

    B. Testing car batteries for sale

    C. Testing random car batteries

    D. Testing car batteries returned by customers

20. A bag contains 10 red marbles, 8 black marbles, and 7 white marbles. What is the probability of selecting a white marble twice in a row without replacement?

    A. $\frac{49}{625}$

    B. $\frac{49}{600}$

    C. $\frac{14}{25}$

    D. $\frac{343}{600}$

SECTION II. READING

1. **Select the context clue from the following sentence that helps you define the multiple meaning word <u>hatch</u>.**

   The group met each month to hatch a plan to overthrow the government.

   A. "group"   C. "plan"

   B. "met"   D. "overthrow"

2. **Select the meaning of the underlined word in the sentence based on the context clues.**

   When visiting the desert, the temperature tends to <u>fluctuate</u>, so you need to bring a variety of clothing.

   A. Rise   C. Change

   B. Drop   D. Stabilize

Read the following passage and answer questions 3-6.

Every time I visit the bookstore, I find a new science fiction title about post-apocalyptic survivors taking refuge in New York City's subway tunnels. Some of these survival stories are fun to read, but they have a pesky plausibility problem: if society collapses, those subway tunnels won't be there anymore—at least not for long. On a typical day in a functioning New York City, a crew of engineers works around the clock to pump about 13 million gallons of water out of the subway system, and a major rain event pushes that number up fast. What happens if you take the engineers—and the electricity to work the sump pumps—out of the equation? The first big storm will flood those tunnels, probably for good. At that point, any survivors left underground will have to grow gills or head for the surface.

3. **Which of the following is the best title for this passage?**

   A. A Visit to a Bookstore

   B. The Science of Growing Gills

   C. A Refuge in Fiction, But Not in Fact

   D. The Best Science Fiction of the Year

4. **Which graphic element would most clearly illustrate the author's point?**

   A. A schematic showing the depth and volume of all of New York City's subway tunnels

   B. A graph comparing the ridership of New York City's subways with those of other major American cities

   C. A table showing how much water runs through the New York City subway system in varying conditions

   D. A New York City subway map showing emergency exits and detailing procedures for exiting the system during a flood

5. **Which information would belong in a sidebar alongside this text?**

   A. An illustration showing how a family of people might look if they all had gills behind their ears

   B. A description of a subway's electrified third rail and an explanation of how it works to power the train

   C. A list of science fiction novels about people living in subway tunnels in a post-apocalyptic world

   D. A description of the job qualifications of a subway engineer who works the pumps to keep the tunnels functional

6. **Consider the following sentence from the passage:**

Mothers involved in prison nursery programs also reported better mental health and greater confidence in their own parenting skills.

Is this statement a fact or an opinion? Why?

A. An opinion because it shares information about confidence, which is an emotion

B. A fact because it states verifiable information about how women reported they felt

C. A fact because it focuses on information from medical records rather than faulty memories

D. An opinion because it relies on human input rather than objective sources like computer records

7. **Which statement expresses an opinion?**

A. A study of preschool age children showed that anxiety and depression are common among young children who are separated from their mothers at birth and reunited late

B. The idea of raising children in prison is controversial, but well-run prison nursery programs can actually be beneficial

C. Mothers involved in prison nursery programs also reported better mental health and greater confidence in their own parenting skills

D. Women who were allowed to remain with their infants during prison sentences were less likely to be convicted of another crime and less likely to use drugs after release

Please read the text below and answer questions 8-12.

A global temperature change of a few degrees is more significant than it may seem at first glance. This is not merely a change in weather in any one location. Rather, it is an average change in temperatures around the entire surface of the planet. It takes a vast amount of heat energy to warm every part of our world—including oceans, air, and land—by even a tiny measurable amount. Moreover, relatively small changes in the earth's surface temperatures have historically caused enormous changes in climate. In the last ice age 20,000 years ago, when much of the northern hemisphere was buried under huge sheets of ice, mean global temperatures were only about five degrees Celsius lower than they are now. Scientists predict a temperature rise of two to six degrees Celsius by 2100. What if this causes similarly drastic changes to the world we call home?

8. **Which sentence is the topic sentence?**

   A. What if this causes similarly drastic changes to the world we call home?

   B. A global temperature change of a few degrees is more significant than it may seem at first glance.

   C. It takes a vast amount of heat energy to warm every part of our world—including oceans, air, and land—by even a tiny measurable amount.

   D. In the last ice age 20,000 years ago, when much of the northern hemisphere was buried under huge sheets of ice, mean global temperatures were only about five degrees Celsius lower than they are now.

9. **In the paragraph above, global temperature change is:**

   A. the topic.

   B. the main idea.

   C. a supporting detail.

   D. the topic sentence.

10. **Which sentence summarizes the main idea of the paragraph?**

    A. A small change in weather at any one location is a serious problem.

    B. The author is manipulating facts to make global warming sound scary.

    C. People should be concerned by even minor global temperature change.

    D. It takes an enormous amount of energy to warm the earth even a little.

11. **What function does the information about temperature differences in the last ice age play in the paragraph?**

    A. Topic

    B. Opinion

    C. Main idea

    D. Supporting detail

12. **Which sentence would *best* function as a supporting detail in this paragraph?**

    A. Electricity and heat production create one quarter of all carbon emissions globally.

    B. The world was only about one degree cooler during the Little Ice Age from 1700 to 1850.

    C. China has surpassed the United States as the single largest producer of carbon emissions.

    D. Methane emissions are, in some ways, more concerning than carbon dioxide emissions.

The bar graph below provides information about book sales for a book called *The Comings*, which is the first book in a trilogy. Study the image and answer questions 13-14.

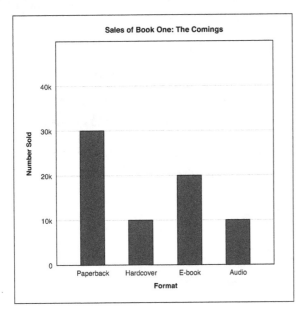

13. Which type of book has sold the most copies?

    A. E-book   C. Paperback

    B. Hardcover   D. Audio book

14. The marketing director for *The Comings* wants to use a different strategy for publishing book two in the series. Which argument does the bar graph *best* support?

    A. The first book in the trilogy has only sold 10,000 copies.

    B. The second book in the trilogy should not be released in hardcover.

    C. The second book in the trilogy should only be released as an e-book.

    D. The second and third books in the trilogy should be combined into one.

Read the passage below and answer questions 15-16.

The train was the most amazing thing ever even though it didn't go "choo choo." The toddler pounded on the railing of the bridge and supplied the sound herself. "Choo choo! Choo choooooo!" she shouted as the train cars whizzed along below.

In the excitement, she dropped her favorite binky.

Later, when she noticed the binky missing, all the joy went out of the world. The wailing could be heard three houses down. The toddler's usual favorite activities were garbage—even waving to Hank the garbage man, which she refused to do, so that Hank went away looking mildly hurt. It was clear the little girl would never, ever, ever recover from her loss.

Afterward, she played at the park.

15. The author of the passage first establishes the ironic tone by:
   A. describing the child's trip to play at the park.
   B. calling the train "the most amazing thing ever."
   C. pretending that the child can make the sounds "choo chooooo!"
   D. claiming inaccurately that the lost binky was the child's "favorite."

16. Which adjectives best describe the tone of the passage?
   A. Ironic, angry
   B. Earnest, angry
   C. Ironic, humorous
   D. Earnest, humorous

Read the following passage and answer questions 17-19.

There is inherent risk associated with the use of Rip Gym facilities. Although all Rip Gym customers sign a Risk Acknowledgment and Consent Form before gaining access to our grounds and equipment, litigation remains a possibility if customers suffer injuries due to negligence. Negligence complaints may include either staff mistakes or avoidable problems with equipment and facilities. It is therefore imperative that all Rip Gym employees follow the Safety Protocol in the event of a customer complaint.

Reports of Unsafe Equipment and Environs

Rip Gym employees must always respond promptly and seriously to any customer report of a hazard in our equipment or facilities, even if the employee judges the complaint frivolous. **Customers may not use rooms or equipment that have been reported unsafe until the following steps have been taken, in order, to confirm and/or resolve the problem.**

1. Place "Warning," "Out of Order," or "Off Limits" signs in the affected area or on the affected equipment, as appropriate. **Always follow this step first, before handling paperwork or attempting to resolve the reported problem.**

2. Fill out a Hazard Complaint Form. Include the name of the customer making the complaint and the exact wording of the problems being reported.

3. Visually check the area or equipment in question to verify the problem.

a) If the report appears to be **accurate** and a resolution is necessary, proceed to step 4.

b) If the report appears to be **inaccurate**, consult the manager on duty.

4. Determine whether you are qualified to correct the problem. Problems **all** employees are qualified to correct are listed on page 12 of the Employee Handbook.

a) Employees who have **not** undergone training for equipment repair and maintenance must....

17. This passage is best described as a(n):

A. narrative text.

B. technical text.

C. expository text.

D. persuasive text.

18. Which term best describes the structure of the opening paragraph?

A. Sequence

B. Description

C. Problem-solution

D. Compare/Contrast

19. Which term best describes the structure of the section under the subheading "Reports of Unsafe Equipment and Environs"?

A. Sequence

B. Description

C. Cause/effect

D. Compare/contrast

20. Which of the following sources should be treated with skepticism even though it is primary?

A. An original work of art that has been celebrated and imitated

B. The research notes of a technician studying infectious diseases

C. An opinion article by a person who witnessed a famine firsthand

D. A 1910 article on how to treat measles by an experienced doctor

21. Which of the following is a secondary source?

A. The diary of Anne Frank

B. A biography of Anne Frank

C. A study guide on the diary of Anne Frank

D. An encyclopedia article about Anne Frank

Read the passages below and answer questions 22-24.

Electroconvulsive therapy was pioneered in the 1930s as a method for combatting severe psychiatric symptoms such as intractable depression and paranoid schizophrenia. This procedure, which involves delivering a deliberate electrical shock to the brain, was controversial from the beginning because it caused pain and short-term memory loss. It fell strongly out of public favor after the 1962 publication of Ken Kesey's novel *One Flew Over the Cuckoo's Nest*, which featured an unprincipled nurse using electroconvulsive therapy as a means of control over her patients. Paradoxically, medical advances at the time of the novel's publication made electroconvulsive therapy significantly safer and more humane.

Although the public is still generally opposed to electroconvulsive therapy, it remains a genuine option for psychiatric patients whose symptoms do not improve with medication. Medical professionals who offer this option should be especially careful to make clear distinctions between myth and reality. On this topic, unfortunately, many patients tend to rely on fiction rather than fact.

*

We were led into a stark exam room, where three doctors positioned themselves so Mama and I had no direct path to the door. The one in charge cleared his throat and told me my mother needed electroshock. My brain buzzed—almost as if it was hooked up to some crackpot brainwashing machine— as Big Doctor droned on about his sadistic intentions. I didn't hear any of it.

All I could think was that these people wanted to tie my mother down and stick wires in her ears.

When Big Doctor was finished, he flipped through the papers on his clipboard and asked if I had questions. I mumbled something noncommittal. Then, when he and his silent escort left, I grabbed Mama and beat it out of that wacko ward as fast as I could make her go.

22. **What is the primary purpose of Passage 2?**

   A. To inform   C. To persuade

   B. To distract   D. To entertain

23. **What is the purpose of the second paragraph of Passage 1?**

   A. To inform   C. To persuade

   B. To distract   D. To entertain

24. **What is the purpose of the first paragraph of Passage 1?**

   A. To inform

   B. To distract

   C. To persuade

   D. To entertain

Section III. Writing

1. **Which word in the following sentence is an adjective?**

   Mrs. Washington loves red roses.

   A. Mrs. Washington

   B. loves

   C. red

   D. roses

2. **Fill in the blank with the correctly capitalized form.**

   Every week, they get together to watch _____.

   A. the bachelor

   B. The Bachelor

   C. The bachelor

   D. the Bachelor

3. **How many prepositions are in the following sentence?**

   The athletes traveled from Boston to Dallas for the competition.

   A. 0

   B. 1

   C. 2

   D. 3

4. **Select the pair of correlative conjunctions that would not be correct in the following sentence.**

   They went to _____ Tahiti _____ Bora Bora.

   A. either/or

   B. rather/than

   C. both/and

   D. not only/but also

5. **When you're considering which of two words to use in an essay and you have no strong reason to do otherwise, you should choose the:**

   A. simplest one.

   B. prettiest one.

   C. most positive one.

   D. most complicated one.

6. **Which word or phrase in the following sentence is not a modifier?**

   The woman found her lost earring yesterday.

   A. found

   B. her

   C. lost

   D. yesterday

7. **Which ending does not create a sentence with a dangling modifier?**

   Trying to earn some extra money, _____.

   A. the new position paid more.

   B. he got a second job.

   C. the job was difficult.

   D. it was an extra shift.

8. **Which words in the following sentence are proper nouns?**

   Matthew had a meeting with his supervisor on Tuesday.

   A. Matthew, meeting

   B. Matthew, Tuesday

   C. meeting, supervisor

   D. supervisor, Tuesday

9. **How many plural nouns are in the following sentence?**

   Marie's father's appendix was taken out.

   A. 0

   B. 1

   C. 2

   D. 3

10. Which word in the following sentence is a pronoun?

Alexi's grandfather was a well-known lawyer who won many cases.

A. was

C. who

B. won

D. Alexi's

11. Which of the following sentences is correct?

A. Ashley cant ride a bike.

B. Ashleys parents never taught her.

C. Its an impossible task for her.

D. Ashley's determined to learn.

12. What is the correct plural of half?

A. Half

C. Halfes

B. Halfs

D. Halves

13. Which of the following spellings is correct?

A. Prununciation

B. Pronuncietion

C. Pronunciation

D. Pronounciation

14. Select the correct verbs to complete the following sentence.

My dentist, who I ___ visited for years, ___ suddenly disappeared.

A. has, has

C. has, have

B. have, has

D. have, have

15. How would you connect the following clauses?

He ate a lot on vacation.
He did not gain any weight.

A. He ate a lot on vacation if he did not gain any weight.

B. He ate a lot on vacation, but he did not gain any weight.

C. He ate a lot on vacation since he did not gain any weight.

D. He ate a lot on vacation because he did not gain any weight.

16. Which of the following is an example of a compound sentence?

A. The Jankowskis typically go out for Italian food, tonight they tried Thai.

B. The Jankowskis typically go out for Italian food and tonight they tried Thai.

C. The Jankowskis typically go out for Italian food, but tonight they tried Thai.

D. The Jankowskis typically go out for Italian food even though tonight they tried Thai.

17. Timothy has a lot of goals in life like: getting his Masters in Education, volunteering his time to help others, and _____.

Which of the following options would give this sentence a parallel structure?

A. published his own book

B. publishing his own book

C. will publish his own book

D. would publish his own book

18. **Which word <u>cannot</u> be used to complete the following sentence?**

___ Stephanie and her brother take classes at the university?

A. Do

B. Will

C. Can

D. Are

PRACTICE EXAM 1
ANSWER EXPLANATIONS

Section I. Math

1. **D.** The correct solution is 4.0 because $A = \pi r^2$; $12 = 3.14\, r^2$; $3.82 = r^2$; $r \approx 2.0$. The diameter is twice the radius, or about 4.0 feet. **See Lesson: Circles.**

2. **A.** The correct solution is 207.64 because $A = \frac{1}{2}\pi r^2 \approx \frac{1}{2}(3.14)(11.5)^2 \approx \frac{1}{2}(3.14)(132.25) \approx 207.64$ square feet. **See Lesson: Circles.**

3. **C.** The correct solution is six lines of symmetry. There are three lines of symmetry through opposite vertices and three lines through the midpoints of opposite segments. **See Lesson: Congruence.**

4. **A.** The correct solution is 5.2304 because 5.2304 contains the smallest values in the tenths and the hundredths places. **See Lesson: Decimals and Fractions.**

5. **D.** The correct solution is $2\frac{1}{2}$ because $2\frac{0.5}{1} = 2\frac{5}{10} = 2\frac{1}{2}$. **See Lesson: Decimals and Fractions.**

6. **D.** The correct solution is $\frac{9}{2}$.

$5x{-}3 = 3x + 6$	Combine like terms on the left and right sides of the equation.
$2x{-}3 = 6$	Subtract $3x$ from both sides of the equation.
$2x = 9$	Add 3 to both sides of the equation.
$x = \frac{9}{2}$	Divide both sides of the equation by 2.

See Lesson: Equations with One Variable.

7. **C.** The correct solution is (1, 3).

The first equation is already solved for x.

$-3y + 10 = 3y{-}8$	Substitute $-3y + 10$ in for x in the second equation.
$-6y + 10 = -8$	Subtract $3y$ from both sides of the equation.
$-6y = -18$	Subtract 10 from both sides of the equation.
$y = 3$	Divide both sides of the equation by -6.
$x = -3(3) + 10$	Substitute 3 in the first equation for y.
$x = -9 + 10 = 1$	Simplify using order of operations.

See Lesson: Equations with Two Variables.

8. **A.** The correct graph has the two lines intersect at (-3, 1). **See Lesson: Equations with Two Variables.**

9. C. The correct solution is 2016 because there were 155 total participants. **See Lesson: Interpreting Graphics.**

10. B. The correct solution is 523.33 cubic inches. The radius is 5 inches. Substitute the values into the formula and simplify using the order of operations, $V = \frac{4}{3}\pi r^3 = \frac{4}{3}(3.14) 5^3 = \frac{4}{3}(3.14)(125) = 523.33$ cubic inches. **See Lesson: Measurement and Dimension.**

11. C. The correct solution is $\frac{8}{45}$ because $\frac{2}{3} \times \frac{4}{15} = \frac{8}{45}$. **See Lesson: Multiplication and Division of Fractions.**

12. C. The correct solution is $4x^2-x-7$.

$$(8x^2-6x-3)-(4x^2-5x+4) = (8x^2-6x-3) + (-4x^2 + 5x-4) = (8x^2-4x^2) + (-6x + 5x) + (-3-4) = 4x^2-x-7$$

See Lesson: Polynomials.

13. D. The correct solution is $16x^6$ because $(4x^3)^2 = 4^2 x^{3\times2} = 4^2 x^6 = 16x^6$. **See Lesson: Powers, Exponents, Roots, and Radicals.**

14. D. The ratio 5:4 is the industry's relative number of women to men. But the industry could have 10 women and 8 men, 100 women and 80 men, or any other breakdown whose ratio is 5:4. Therefore, the question provides too little information to answer. Had it provided the total number of people in the industry, it would have been possible to determine how many women and how many men are in the industry. **See Lesson: Ratios, Proportions, and Percentages.**

15. B. The number 147 satisfies the proportion. First, divide 378 by 18 to get 21. Then, multiply 21 by 7 to get 147. Check your answer by dividing 147 by 7: the quotient is also 21, so 147 satisfies the proportion. **See Lesson: Ratios, Proportions, and Percentages.**

16. D. The correct solution is 5 units and 7 units. The difference between the x-coordinates is $-4-(-9) = 5$ units, and the difference between the y-coordinates is $-1-(-8) = 7$ units. **See Lesson: Similarity, Right Triangles, and Trigonometry.**

17. A. The correct solutions are $-8 \pm \sqrt{31}$. The equation can be solved by completing the square.

$x^2 + 16x = -33$	Subtract 33 from both sides of the equation.
$x^2 + 16x + 64 = -33 + 64$	Complete the square, $(\frac{16}{2})^2 = 8^2 = 64$.
	Add 64 to both sides of the equation.
$x^2 + 16x + 64 = 31$	Simplify the right side of the equation.
$(x + 8)^2 = 31$	Factor the left side of the equation.
$x + 8 = \pm\sqrt{31}$	Apply the square root to both sides of the equation.
$x = -8 \pm \sqrt{31}$	Subtract 8 from both sides of the equation.

See Lesson: Solving Quadratic Equations.

18. B. The correct solution is attendance every day because data is collected from every class every day. **See Lesson: Statistical Measures.**

19. C. The correct solution is testing random car batteries because this is a sample of the population and demonstrates the performance of the population. **See Lesson: Statistical Measures.**

20. A. The correct solution is $\frac{49}{625}$. There are 7 white marbles out of 25 in the bag. The probability of the event is $\frac{7}{25} \times \frac{7}{25} = \frac{49}{625}$. **See Lesson: Statistics & Probability: The Rules of Probability.**

Section II. Reading

1. C. The meaning of hatch in this context is "to create or produce an idea in a secret way." The word "plan" helps you figure out which meaning of hatch is being used. **See Lesson: Context Clues and Multiple Meaning Words.**

2. C. The meaning of fluctuate in the context of this sentence is "change." **See Lesson: Context Clues and Multiple Meaning Words.**

3. C. The main point of this paragraph is that science fiction often depicts a particular kind of post-apocalyptic survival scenario that would not work in fact. The title of the passage should reflect this idea. **See Lesson: Evaluating and Integrating Data.**

4. C. The author argues that the New York City subway system would not be a good place to take refuge after a major weather event if nobody were working to pump the water out. Information about the water would help illustrate that point. **See Lesson: Evaluating and Integrating Data.**

5. C. Sidebar information should be peripheral to the text. That means it's clearly related and interesting to the same audience. Here, the list of sci-fi novels would be the best option. **See Lesson: Evaluating and Integrating Data.**

6. B. The statement makes a factual statement about how people said they felt. This makes it a fact even though it contains opinion information. **See Lesson: Facts, Opinions, and Evaluating an Argument.**

7. B. The argument that prison nursery programs can be beneficial is an opinion statement because it makes a judgment. **See Lesson: Facts, Opinions, and Evaluating an Argument.**

8. B. The first sentence of this paragraph expresses the main idea that people should be concerned by even a small amount of climate change. This makes it the topic sentence. **See Lesson: Main Ideas, Topic Sentences, and Supporting Details..**

9. A. The topic of a sentence is a word or phrase that describes what the text is about. **See Lesson: Main Ideas, Topic Sentences, and Supporting Details..**

10. C. This paragraph argues that a small change in global temperatures could have a major result. This idea is expressed in a topic sentence at the beginning of the paragraph. **See Lesson: Main Ideas, Topic Sentences, and Supporting Details..**

11. D. The information about temperature differences in the last ice age supports the main idea that people should be concerned by global climate change. This makes it a supporting detail. **See Lesson: Main Ideas, Topic Sentences, and Supporting Details..**

12. B. All of the above sentences relate to the topic of global climate change, but only the sentence about the Little Ice Age relates directly to the main idea that a small amount of climate fluctuation is cause for concern. **See Lesson: Main Ideas, Topic Sentences, and Supporting Details..**

13. C. Larger bars in a bar graph indicate higher numbers. This book has sold more paperback copies than any other. **See Lesson: Summarizing Text and Using Text Features.**

14. B. The bar graph shows fewer hardcover sales than any other kind. This could help support an argument that later books should only be released in electronic and paperback forms. **See Lesson: Summarizing Text and Using Text Features.**

15. B. This passage establishes irony in the opening sentence by applying the superlative phrase "the most amazing thing ever" to an ordinary occurrence. **See Lesson: Tone and Mood, Transition Words.**

16. C. This passage ironically is a humorous description of a toddler's emotions, written by an adult who has enough experience to know that a toddler's huge emotions will pass. **See Lesson: Tone and Mood, Transition Words.**

17. B. This is a technical text written to inform the reader about a complex process. **See Lesson: Types of Passages, Text Structures, Genre and Theme..**

18. C. The opening paragraph has a problem-solution structure. The problem it describes involves risks of injury and litigation, and the solution is that employees follow a process designed to minimize those risks. **See Lesson: Types of Passages, Text Structures, Genre and Theme..**

19. A. The step-by-step instructions under the subheading follow a sequential structure. Note key words and phrases such as "first" and "in order." **See Lesson: Types of Passages, Text Structures, Genre and Theme..**

20. D. A 1910 article on medicine is highly outdated. Even if the writer is an experienced doctor, the advice presented would likely not be worth following. **See Lesson: Understanding Primary Sources, Making Inferences, and Drawing Conclusions.**

21. B. A biography of Anne Frank would be a historical or analytical account that added insight on the topic. This makes it a secondary source. **See Lesson: Understanding Primary Sources, Making Inferences, and Drawing Conclusions.**

22. D. Passage 2 tells a story, which is meant to entertain. **See Lesson: Understanding the Author's Purpose, Point of View, and Rhetorical Strategies.**

23. C. The second paragraph of passage 1 makes opinion statements about what doctors should do. This is a sign of persuasive writing. **See Lesson: Understanding the Author's Purpose, Point of View, and Rhetorical Strategies.**

24. A. Passage 1 is intended to inform readers about electroconvulsive therapy. **See Lesson: Understanding the Author's Purpose, Point of View, and Rhetorical Strategies.**

Section III. Writing

1. C. *Red* is an adjective that describes the noun *roses*. **See Lesson: Adjectives and Adverbs**

2. B. *The Bachelor*. The names of TV shows are capitalized. The is capitalized here because it is the first word in the name. **See Lesson: Capitalization.**

3. D. *From, to,* and *for* are prepositions. **See Lesson: Conjunctions and Prepositions.**

4. B. Here, the correlative conjunction pair is connecting two nouns (place names). *Rather/than* would be better used to connect two verbs, such as *rather run than walk*. **See Lesson: Conjunctions and Prepositions.**

5. A. The first goal of writing is to be understood. Choose the simplest word unless you have a strong reason to do otherwise. **See Lesson: Essay Revision and Transitions.**

6. A. *Found* is the main verb in this sentence; it is not a modifier. **See Lesson: Modifiers.**

7. B. Of these choices, *trying to earn some extra money* can only reference *he*. **See Lesson: Modifiers.**

8. B. *Matthew* and *Tuesday* are proper nouns. **See Lesson: Nouns.**

9. A. *Marie's* and *father's* are possessive; neither is plural. *Appendix* is a singular noun. **See Lesson: Nouns.**

10. C. *Who* is a relative pronoun. **See Lesson: Pronouns.**

11. D. *Ashley's determined to learn.* Ashley's stands for Ashley is and is the only correct use of an apostrophe in the examples. **See Lesson: Punctuation.**

12. D. With a word ending in -f, you drop the -f and add -ves. **See Lesson: Spelling.**

13. C. *Pronunciation* is the only correct spelling. **See Lesson: Spelling.**

14. B. This sentence has a predicate within a predicate. The "inside" predicate is *who I have visited for years*, and the "outside" predicate is *my dentist has suddenly disappeared*. **See Lesson: Subject and Verb Agreement.**

15. B. He ate a lot on vacation, but he did not gain any weight. These two clauses are of equal grammatical rank and can be connected with a coordinating conjunction. "But" is the conjunction that makes the most sense. **See Lesson: Types of Clauses.**

16. C. This is a compound sentence joining two independent clauses with a comma and the conjunction *but*. **See Lesson: Types of Sentences.**

17. B. *Publishing his own book* would be parallel in structure to the other items since they are longer phrases and use the gerund form of the verb. **See Lesson: Types of Sentences.**

18. D. *Are* is not the correct helping verb to form a question with *take*. *Do* is the correct helping verb, and *will* and *can* can also be used because they are modals. **See Lesson: Verbs and Verb Tenses.**